Breakdown, Breakup, Breakthrough

POLICIES AND INSTITUTIONS
Germany, Europe, and Transatlantic Relations

Published in Association with the American Institute for Contemporary German Studies (AICGS), Washington, D.C.
General Editor: **Carl Lankowski**, Research Director of the AICGS

BREAKDOWN, BREAKUP, BREAKTHROUGH

Germany's Difficult Passage to Modernity

Edited by
Carl Lankowski

Berghahn Books
New York • Oxford

Published in 1999 by

Berghahn Books

© 1999 AICGS

Library of Congress Cataloging-in-Publication Data

Breakdown, breakup, breakthrough : Germany's difficult passage to
modernity / edited by Carl Lankowski
    p.   cm. — (Policies and institutions ; v. 4)
A festschrift for Andrei Markovits.
Includes bibliographical references and index.
ISBN 1-57181-211-3 (alk. paper)
    1. Democracy—Germany. 2. Political culture—Germany.
3. Germany—History—Unification, 1990. 4. Germany—Politics and
government—1990- .   I. Lankowski, Carl F., 1949- .   II. Markovits,
Andrei S.   III. Series.
  JN3971.A91 B72 1999   99-28045
  320.943'09'04—dc21   CIP

British Library Cataloguing in Publication Data

A catalogue record for this book is available from the British Library.

Printed in the United States on acid-free paper.

Contents

A Festschrift for Andrei Markovits

INTRODUCTION

Carl Lankowski

Written specifically for this volume, these essays offer an integrated assessment of the historical antecedents and functioning of German democracy fifty years after two postwar German states were launched as part of the architecture of the cold war. At the same time, the book also celebrates a teacher, mentor, colleague, collaborator, and friend of the authors, whose work has inspired a stream of scholarship only partially represented here. Andrei S. Markovits's influence has been important in sustaining the highest standards of scholarship and teaching in comparative politics, and especially in advancing the understanding of German politics and society in the United States, his adopted homeland.

Professor Markovits has established a formidable presence in academic circles as well as in public forums. His influence in academia comes from more than twenty years of dedicated service since he was awarded the doctorate in political science by Columbia University in 1976, where he also earned a B.A. (1969), the M.B.A. (1971), and an M. Phil. (1974), after crossing the Atlantic with the *Matura*, the Gymnasium certificate conferred by the Theresianische Akademie in Vienna. Markovits's scholarly output is prodigious by the usual standard: the publication of twelve books, over ten dozen scholarly articles, several dozen reviews, the bulk of this oeuvre in leading scholarly presses and refereed journals. Criticism of America's unperfected democracy was a major theme of the 68 generation, but Markovits's experience with America in 1968 was one of liberation of his Jewish identity as well as freedom to develop intellectually. His first trip to Germany and Berlin came in 1974. There he developed an immediate and abiding interest in the prospects for German democracy and reform. A project on organized labor was his first sustained effort, and produced the international study (co-authored with Christopher Allen), *Unions and Economic Crisis: Britain, West Germany, and Sweden* (George Allen & Unwin, 1984) and also his *Politics of the West German Trade Unions: Strategies of Class and Interest Representation in Growth and Crisis* (Cambridge University Press, 1986), whose major contribution lay in its trenchant and nuanced characterization of the reflexes of these major actors in Germany's highly organized polity. Markovits's analysis developed out of keen sensitivity for the relationship between the incentives provided by Germany's institutional framework and the meaning attached to it by actors with a reform agenda explicitly connected to the memory of Germany's moral tragedy in this century – i.e., his work is most deeply about political culture. Later, when the reform project received new impetus from the Green Party, Markovits (with Philip Gorski) offered the first full length American analysis of the party, *The German Left: Red, Green, and Beyond* (Oxford University Press, 1993; also published in German in 1997). His (with Simon Reich) *German Predicament: Memory and Power in the New Europe* (Cornell University Press, 1997) has in its German edition elicited favorable commentary from public figures such as Green Party leader and current German Foreign Minister Joschka Fischer (who contributed the foreword) and Hans-Dietrich Genscher, the Federal Republic's longest serving foreign minister.

However, his influence on the outlook of a generation of scholars is underestimated by the quantity of his publications. As important as the analyses themselves is the teamwork he fostered on joint projects over many years, mainly in and around Harvard University's Center for European Studies, Markovits's intellectual *Heimat*, which he thought "embodied historically oriented political sociology at its best." At Harvard, Markovits teamed up with budding academic talents who went on to establish their own careers and further parts of the overall research program that preoccupied Markovits in the same spirit of generous scholarly collaboration. This volume is a product of that activity.

Markovits's 68-generation pedigree is demonstrated in developing analyses that have immediate relevance for public affairs. One has the sense that he was led to Germany because the German experience in the twentieth century teaches us more about what to make of our citizenship in a liberal democratic setting than any other study. It is this public side of Markovits's scholarship that helps us understand the urgency, acuity, and compassion that animate his texts. It also makes explicit the links between scholarly analysis and politics. Witness the printed commentary and speaking engagements on both sides of the Atlantic on topics as various as the student movement, the strategy of organized labor, popular music, the organization of sports, German foreign policy, political parties, German unification, and the Holocaust.

This book takes up the key issues of democracy in the Bonn and Berlin republics. Philip Gorski opens the volume with a neo-Weberian reworking of Barrington Moore's question about the antidemocratic denouement in 1933 Germany.[1] His question: what could resist the encroachments of absolutism at work all over Europe in the early modern period? Gorski finds the answer in neighboring Netherlands. Absorbing the social movement literature that began to appear a full decade after the publication of *Social Origins*, he argues that the Calvinist movement gave powerful impetus to republican virtues that did not persist in Lutheran Germany, despite quite similar starting points on the eve of the Reformation.

Thomas Ertman adds an additional layer to the redefinition of the analytical premise of "German exceptionalism" by focusing on nineteenth-century constitutional arrangements, and by expanding the scope of cross-national comparison beyond Britain and France to encompass the other European late industrializers: Switzerland, Belgium, Denmark, Norway, and Sweden. Once again, Moore provides the basic orientation, but fails the ultimate test, for

---

1. Barrington Moore, *Social Origins of Dictatorship and Democracy. Lord and Peasant in the Making of the Modern World* (Boston: Beacon Press, 1967).

constitutional dualism was a common starting point, unaffected by late industrialization, social mobilization (bourgeois revolution), reactionary bureaucrats, or institutional barriers. Germany's "exceptionalism" consisted instead in the stability of this constitutional dualism, quite unlike the evolution towards parliamentarism in all the other cases. Consequently, Germany's real breakthrough to democracy came with the adoption of full parliamentarism in 1949.

A natural question to emerge from these two historical chapters concerns the relationship between Germany's postwar democratic institutional "container" and the legacy of predemocratic attitudes. Though studies have suggested a dramatic evolution of attitudes in Germany supportive of democracy by the 1970s at the latest, the chapters in this volume suggest a nuanced view of the infrastructure of postwar republican German democracy. They suggest that part of Germany's democratic experience consists in a collective and consensual approach to issues of public policy. It is notoriously hard to define an attitudinal constellation of the ideal or typical "democrat." Whatever that may be, individual attitudes may matter less in producing a functioning democracy to the degree that the groups populating Germany's highly organized public sphere are licensed to develop, contest, and implement public policy. One important theme running through these chapters is the promises and limitations of the neocorporatist mechanisms associated with the notion of Modell Deutschland – in their starkest form, trade unions and trade associations bargaining over work and economic issues, but also including a welter of parapublic institutions supervising many other dimensions of public life.

Institutions and attitudes both play a central role in Christopher Allen's account of the challenges to be negotiated by Germany's social market economy at the edge of the twenty-first century. Starting from the premise that the social market economy has served Germany exceptionally well both economically and politically, Allen frets about an "unintentional departure" from this institutional matrix under the siren songs of neo-Liberalism. For it is not so much the "external" shocks of German unification, European integration, and globalization that threaten Germany's unique brand of organized capitalism, but an almost Platonic forgetfulness of the handsome anatomy and virtues of Modell

Deutschland by a new generation of bankers, industrialists, and politicians, as opportunities provided by the new international context make it easier for them to bail out of the German institutional matrix.

Sluggish job creation in reunified Germany is frequently cited as prima facie evidence for the superiority of British-American style labor markets. In grappling with this aspect of Germany's economic policy challenges Michael Huelshoff attempts to demonstrate that policy innovation not only can, but in fact does continue to be defined without abandoning Modell Deutschland. The author argues that Germany's ideology of social consensus, a key cultural trait, is a precondition of institutional arrangements and provides a uniquely German method to generate responses to the so-called Standort problem (attracting industrial investment) that other models – the Anglo, the Dutch or the European – cannot. In particular, in contrast to the others, despite significant decentralization of decision making in the labor market, the German approach leaves trade union power intact.

Whatever the role of ideology in producing social consensus, Germany's political institutions virtually require it. In recent years the complaint has been aired that the urgency of policy reform makes these institutions a luxury Germany can no longer afford. The central target of this thinking has been the Bundesrat. Stephen Silvia's analysis of Bundesrat involvement in Germany's episodes of legislative gridlock presents a periodic pattern caused mainly by shifting majorities in the Federal Republic's two legislative houses. He notes that policy gridlock has become more acute of late, lending credence to the theory that increasing complexity of policy is driving a corresponding intensification of intergovernmental relations. If true, then governability could be enhanced in either of two ways: greater decisional efficiency or greater social consensus.

At this point, some commentary about the relevance of the European Union is required. Already in the 1930s, the Ordo-Liberals were impressed with the contribution of both competition and the state in producing economic success that worked for society as a whole, hence, the social market economy. Increasingly, the EU is becoming an important locus of state-like market regulatory functions, be it by way of market definition (product standards) or surveillance of the behavior of market agents. As this role has developed, another layer of government has been superimposed on the already complex system of intergovernmental relations. It is probable that "Brussels" is part of the pattern of even greater grid-lock in German legislative affairs. In this sense, the "Bundesrat issue" is actually one about the evolving constitution of Europe. New information technologies comprise only one important field in which EU internal market concerns have constitutional rever-berations for the member states. Beth Noveck's analysis of Ger-many's 1997 media law in this volume portrays the Länder-Bund contest over competence in this area as the defining feature of the legislative process and raises the question of whether the democ-ratizing impulse behind the Federal Republic's media-relevant Grundgesetz articles are being inadvertently sacrificed in the unseemly struggle.

It is of course still too early to judge the impact of EMU – eco-nomic and monetary union – on the content and structure of social policy and more broadly the Ordnungspolitik of the member states, Germany included. However, it is at least possible that the passing of the Deutsche Mark and its substitution by the euro, along with the new powers assigned to the European Parliament by the Treaty of Amsterdam, will provide significant new opportuni-ties for identification of the EU as a – if not the – legitimate frame-work for major policy decisions. As important, Germany's "third sector" – the social movements and movement organizations, especially in the environmental area – is reflecting major changes in Germany's social structure that have already challenged the centrality of the Modell Deutschland institutional complex. The increasing importance of the service sector is creating the condi-tions for a Euro-level recalibration of Germany's institutions, a process that is likely to take a generation to consolidate, but whose leading indicators – European works councils, increasingly Euro-peanized regulatory standards, and movement toward a new bal-ance between public regulatory and redistributive measures (bluntly: more environment, less entitlement) – are already at hand, even if responsibility for job creation measures continues to be decentralized. Europeanization will also create a new political context for affiliation and identification, including greater attention to supranationality on the one hand and local regionalism on the other, affecting Länder governments in particular. Whether Germans embrace this situation as "European domestic politics" or react defensively will depend on EU policies, general economic conditions, and cues from German elites.

In addition to issues of political economy, the futures of Germany and the EU are mutually contingent to a high degree with respect to attitudes about Brussels and the world beyond German and European borders. Karen Donfried's analysis of German foreign policy after 1990 confirms Markovits and Reich's thesis about Germany's "culture of reticence."[2] She shows that while Russia's present efforts to reconcile great power status and democracy mirror those of Imperial Germany, in the context of imperial decline overlaid with anarchic developments – terror bombings carried out by self-styled holy warriors – disguised as clashes of cultures, present day parliamentary Germany now has to be coaxed into playing its role in upholding international order. The centrality of Germany's role under its new "red-green" government in managing the Kosovo crisis constitutes a major breakthrough in this regard.

The psychological infrastructure of this reticence is the real subject of Carolyn Höfig's reflection on the relationship of the Germans to the automobile. If the triumph of consumerism has given the lie to pretensions to the Kulturstaat hoped for by some after the War, it has also taken the German particularism out of attitudes toward the rest of the world. Indeed, what was perhaps most surprising about unification is the relative absence of nationalist sentiment. Recent opinion polls give Germans nearly the highest scores on European, as opposed to national, orientation. To some extent, the operation of the EU internal market may be a powerful stimulus to the creation of a multicultural, if not cosmopolitan, reality. In the case of automobiles, models from all EU producers freely circulate in Germany, subject to heavy EU involvement in the ongoing evolution of automobile technology, inter alia, via environmental and safety standards. One has only to recall "le Waldsterben," that 1980s addition to the French lexicon, to appreciate the Europeanization of critical elements in Germany's consumer culture. Equally worth noting is the critical support of Bündnis 90/Die Grünen, Germany's new third political force with special strength in the younger age cohorts, for the project of European integration.

Despite these developments, EU consumerism, even its critical variety, has not resolved serious contradictions in the functioning of Modell Deutschland that challenge us to contemplate afresh the meaning of democracy and reassess the degree of its attainment in the Federal Republic. At core, the problem is that the inclusiveness that has facilitated the functioning of German democracy is not complete. Systematic exclusion of various groups from putative citizenship rights point to serious flaws in the design of Modell Deutschland. Any egalitarian pretensions Germans may harbor are challenged by the deteriorating situation of women, even as the workforce becomes increasingly feminine. In their analysis of the structure of Germany's welfare institutions, Patricia Davis and Simon Reich identify a troubling pattern in Germany's gendered system of workforce participation. Despite increasing financial outlays in the 1990s, access to social resources by women has actually decreased. The authors argue that this regressive outcome is an artifact of the male, full-time, skilled worker archetype, which defines the structure of the system and the entitlements it dispenses. More darkly, they argue that this result is the more or less foreseeable outcome of a bipartisan strategy of protecting the core Facharbeiter constituency, a strategy that antedates unification and the globalization debate. It is also notable that, according to the authors, this strategy encompassed resistance to EU-mandated standards for equality between men and women.

If Modell Deutschland has not achieved a proper balance between collective rights and (social) citizenship, it is similarly burdened by the external boundaries citizenship imposes. To address foreigner-bashing is to return to the issues raised by Gorski's analysis of republican virtues, a leading one of which is tolerance of cultural difference, a major step beyond the taming of nationalistic atavism via consumer complacency or even a functioning welfare

---

2. See *The German Predicament: Memory and Power in the New Europe* (Ithaca: Cornell University Press, 1997). Long-serving German foreign minister, Hans-Dietrich Genscher confirms the basic thrust of the authors' analysis in his August 1998 review, *Berliner Morgenpost*, 16 August 1998.

system for those fortunate enough to be entitled to its fruits. At one level, treatment of Ausländer has been a sad and ironic correlate of Europe's faltering labor markets and the corresponding decline of welfare institutions. The mix of public and consumer goods defining the German welfare state has been a central element of the social contract – viewed as emancipatory act by some or bread and circuses by others. Economic restructuring, post-cold war opening to the East and the disintegration of the Soviet empire all conspire, by increasing the number of Ausländer in Germany, to make the Germans confront their political culture like nothing else since the creation of the German empire in 1871. Some steps have been taken towards incorporating Ausländer, but citizenship, the ultimate sign of membership, continues to be decided predominantly on ethnic grounds, even after the legislation that came into force in 1999 extending citizenship to a larger number of immigrants. It remains to be seen whether "free movement" of EU nationals will serve as a bridgehead to a more expansive understanding of inclusion for "third country nationals." For now, indecision is troubling. It permits authorities to adopt strategies of physical and social separation that create targets and stereotypes for elements spouting nationalist and xenophobic slogans, and who all too frequently give vent to rage and cynicism in acts of brutality.

Our fascination with Germany comes in large part from the mixture of impatience and humility with which we seek to understand the conditions under which democracy emerges and thrives and to evaluate democracy's ever unfinished agenda in America and elsewhere. Germany's catastrophic course in the first half of this century continues to transfix us. And of various aspects of Germany's tragedy, none is more compelling than the Holocaust. It is eminently appropriate that this volume presents Jeremiah Riemer's essay about the reception of Daniel Goldhagen's controversial book, *Hitler's Willing Executioners* as its concluding chapter. Though it is absent as an explicit element of every other chapter of this volume, this nightmare necessarily haunts them all. In a book whose contributions labor to present the specific character of German politics against the many elements that provide the basis of comparison with other countries, the Holocaust is the experience which imparts to everything else its specific place in the summing up. It is the meeting place of the subject and object of inquiry, a crucial feature of Germany's collective consciousness, as well as the limiting case for our time in the study of comparative politics.

Riemer explains the oddity of hostile reactions to the book among liberal scholars as an effect of some fundamental misunderstanding of Goldhagen's central point. "Eliminationist anti-semitism" proved too dissonant to the cognitive maps of this postwar generation, more experienced with large historical ideas rather than the simpler doctrines of state-sponsored hatred. In the end, the Holocaust was a matter of political culture, a culture that could be and was successfully transformed after the War, not only by American efforts but also in part by the results of painful discussions over many dinner tables between generations. The strikingly positive reception of Goldhagen during his German lecture tour and the bestseller status of his book stand in odd juxtaposition to the reaction of many critics. On the other hand, according to this view, that very reception provided vindication for Goldhagen's position that, like any other people, the Germans were educable, that there was choice, and that consequently there is deliverance from the German nightmare. It only remains to be said that, in effect, Goldhagen's analysis challenged these historians by contributing to a much more nuanced interpretation of Germany's historical Sonderweg than that which held sway thirty years ago, a theme that runs through the contributions in this book as well.

In the end, our preoccupation with Germany is an artifact of our concern for each and every issue raised in this volume. Germany has played and will continue to play a central role in the drama of defining modernity. At one level, the issues are enduring. At another level, they are new: how can a humane, civil, and democratic order be fashioned in the postnational era? Both institutions and attitudes matter. Since the 1970s, first in the academic arena and more recently in broader citizens forums, through a compassion born of personal experience and memory, through his sharp-witted analyses, through his engagement in the public sphere, Andrei Markovits has not only been a continual source of insight into European politics; he has been the conscience of a generation. With these essays we celebrate his ongoing contributions.

Even a labor of love is still labor. For excellent manuscript management I wish to offer heartfelt thanks to Jodi Smith, Research Program Assistant at the American Institute for Contemporary German Studies. Even if this book is a celebration, it is fundamentally a statement about Germany, its past and future. For its support of the gathering at which the chapters of this volume were first presented, AICGS gratefully acknowledges the German Marshall Fund of the United States.

6 August 1999

Chapter 1

CALVINISM AND DEMOCRACY
The Case of the Dutch Republic (1555-1787)

⌾

Philip S. Gorski

We may have learnt from sacred History, and times of Reformation, that the Kings of this World have both ever hated, and instinctively fear'd the Church of God. Whether it be for that thir Doctrin seems much to favour two things to them so dreadful, Liberty and Equality, or because they are the Children of that Kingdom, which, as ancient Prophesies have foretold, shall in the end break to peeces and dissolve all thir great Power and Dominion (John Milton).[1]

If one had taken a riverboat trip from, say, Frankfurt to Amsterdam in the year 1500 or thereabouts, it would have been difficult to say where "Germany" ended and the "Netherlands" began – and not only because there were no nations or national borders in the modern-day sense. For fifteenth century Frankfurt and Amsterdam were remarkably similar in many ways.[2] Both were major

---

1. John Milton, "Of the differences in point of Church-Government," in *Complete Prose Works* Vol. 3: 1648-49 (New Haven: Yale University Press, 1962), p. 509.
2. For a general discussion of this point, see Olaf Mörke, "The political culture of Germany and the Dutch Republic: similar roots, different results" in Karel Davids

centers of trade and commerce. Both had strong traditions of municipal autonomy and self-government. Both, finally, were part of the Holy Roman Empire. And much the same could have been said of the various ports of call which lay between the two cities – Bonn, Cologne, Düsseldorf, Leiden, and so on. Moreover, if one had continued the journey, sailing out through the Ijsel into the North Sea, down the Elbe, and overland to the Baltic, stopping along the way in Bremerhaven, Hamburg, Lübeck, and Kiel, the similarities would have been more striking still. For these cities resembled Amsterdam not only in terms of their economic, social, and political structures, but in terms of their language, their culture, and even their architecture. Even today the sights and sounds of Hamburg and Bremen are more reminiscent of Amsterdam and Leiden than of Munich or Berlin.

But for all their similarities, these two regions – northwest Germany and the northern Netherlands – followed remarkably different political trajectories. In the one case, the influence of the bourgeoisie and the burghers ultimately declined, while that of the nobles and the princes gradually increased. In the other case, the reverse was true: the influence of the bourgeoisie and the burgher steadily increased, while that of the nobles and princes ultimately declined. Northwest Germany was dragged down an absolutist path, which culminated in authoritarian – and totalitarian – rule, while the northern Netherlands plunged down a republican path, which culminated in parliamentary – and democratic – rule.

Why? For the most part, the answers given by German historians have focused on social and political factors – on the weakness of municipal government and the middle-classes, and the strength of the territorial princes and the landed nobility. No doubt, there is a good deal to this interpretation, especially where southern and eastern Germany are concerned. The social and political circumstances of these areas were quite conducive to the establishment of princely absolutism, and it was the dominant states of these two areas (Austria and Prussia) which ultimately vied for hegemony over Germany as a whole. Still, there is much which is left unex-

and Jan Lucassen eds., *A miracle mirrored. The Dutch Republic in European Perspective* (Cambridge: Cambridge University Press, 1995), pp. 135-72.

plained by these factors. In particular, one wonders why northwest Germany did not give rise to a republican state that might have served as a counterweight to the expansionary aims of the southern and eastern powers, particularly since its social and political structures were so much like those of its Netherlandish neighbor.

One way of approaching this question – and the one which I intend to follow here – is to ask why the northern Netherlands *did* give rise to a republican state which served as a counterweight to the expansionary aims of nearby monarchies – in this case, Spain and France. One possible answer to this question – the one which I will explore in this essay – has to do with religious factors, and, in particular, with the impact of Calvinism. In what follows, then, I will focus on the political development of the northern Netherlands during the centuries leading up to the French Revolution, and on the role which Calvinism and Calvinists played in this development, in order to shed light on why the Netherlands' path to modern democracy was so smooth, and why that of Germany was so tortuous.

This argument is not altogether original. Indeed, there is a long and venerable tradition which sees a direct and inexorable link between Calvinism and democracy. Advocates of this position have generally pointed to the prominent role which Calvinists played in prosecuting the Dutch Revolt against Spain (1559-1611), developing theories of resistance to unjust authority, and in propagating a more individualistic ethos.[3] Calvinism, it is argued, helped to block the rise of monarchical absolutism, defend the power of representative institutions and lay the foundations for a democratic political culture. Indeed, up until around 1970, the connection between Calvinism and democracy was a widely, if not universally, accepted tenet of early modern historiography and one which still enjoys a great deal of currency among social scientists.

Among historians, by contrast, it has gradually fallen into disrepute. The link between Calvinism and democracy, it is generally argued, was neither inherent nor inevitable. In particular, it is claimed that the arguments which Calvinists employed to justify

---

3. The role of Calvinists in the Revolt is emphasized in Pieter Geyl, *The Revolt of the Netherlands, 1555-1609* (London: Cassel, 1988 [1932]). The role of the Calvinists in the development of resistance theory is underlined by A.C.J. Vrankrijker, *De motiveering van onzen opstand* (Utrecht: HES, 1979).

antimonarchical resistance were first forged by Medieval scholastics, later sharpened by German Lutherans and thus not distinctively Calvinist;[4] that Calvin and his followers were relatively indifferent to political questions and generally opted for whatever form of government appeared the most expedient, whether absolute monarchy or civic republicanism; and that the political outlook of the Calvinists was deeply inegalitarian or even authoritarian.

The interpretation presented here charts a middle course between these two positions. It is argued that there *was* a link between Calvinism and democracy, albeit an indirect and contingent one, and, more specifically that Calvinism tended to create circumstances favorable to democratization, though only under certain social and political conditions. These circumstances included the preservation of representative institutions, the mobilization of egalitarian sentiments, and the creation of an orderly society. The key preconditions which were necessary for these effects to take hold included a relatively high level of urbanization, the conversion of the common people to Calvinism, and the establishment of a congregational system of religious discipline. Just why these preconditions were necessary, and how these circumstances favored democracy will become clearer in the historical discussion which follows.

Fully appreciating the significance which Calvinism had for the development of modern democracy will thus require us to (1) focus on Calvinism as a *movement*, with a certain social base and organizational form, and not just as a body of ideas; (2) measure the significance of an idea in terms of its influence rather than its originality; and (3) understand democracy as a form of governance, and not just as a type of regime. Finally, it will require us to adopt a longer-term perspective, one which extends beyond the tumultuous events of the Dutch Revolt and the English Revolution.

The argument which will be advanced here will focus on the connection between Calvinism and democracy in the Dutch Republic. The central thesis is that Calvinism tended to promote

4. For a particularly cogent and forceful statement of this argument, see Quentin Skinner, *Foundations of Modern Political Thought* (Cambridge: Cambridge University Press, 1978), vol. 2, Ch. 7.

the three principal elements of modern democracy – liberty, equality and fraternity. In particular, it will be argued (1) that the Calvinists and republicans in the Netherlands were initially linked together by a shared notion of liberty, and that the outbreak and success of the Dutch Revolt owed much to the militancy and organization of the Calvinists; (2) that the Calvinist vision of the Dutch Republic as a covenanted nation or "New Israel" was fundamentally incompatible with the system of aristocratic republicanism which emerged after the Revolt, and that orthodox Calvinists were the most powerful and effective proponents of political equality and popular sovereignty during most of the seventeenth and eighteenth centuries; and (3) that the Calvinist program of religious and social discipline rested on a notion of spiritual and communal "fraternity," and that the imposition of discipline was a critical precondition for the growth of democracy.

Before defending these theses in greater detail, however, it will first be necessary to provide a brief sketch of the key historical developments in the Dutch Republic during the period in question, and in particular of the way in which the interaction between religion and politics helped to shape them.

Religion and Politics in the Netherlands from 1555 to 1789

The history of the Dutch Republic begins with the Dutch Revolt against Spain, 1566-1589, and ends with the Patriots' Revolution of 1783-89. It is punctuated at fairly regular intervals by constitutional crises and popular rebellions of various kinds: the "religious quarrels" of 1617-1618, the Orangist coup of 1650, the Orangist uprisings of 1672, and the Orangist revolution of 1747. The issues and cleavages which underlay these different episodes of collective action were all fundamentally similar, and they all had their origins in the Revolt.

The Revolt itself was the product of a potent combination of political and religious discontent. Politically speaking, its causes lay in the protoabsolutist policies of the Habsburg emperor, Philip II – in his attempts to impose taxes without the consent of the

States General and fill the main governmental councils in Brussels with members of the Spanish court. Religiously speaking, its causes lay in Philip's efforts to restore confessional unity by suppressing Dutch Protestantism and to revitalize Dutch Catholicism by reforming the church hierarchy.

These streams of discontent were never entirely separate – politics and religion being of a piece in this era – and they were rapidly channeled together during the late 1550s and early 1560s by two events. The first was the intensified persecution of Protestant heretics by the recently reestablished courts of the Spanish Inquisition, which violated the judicial autonomy of the towns, the so-called *ius de non evocando*. The second was the abrupt shift of power from the Council of State in Brussels, in which many of the Netherlands' great noble families were represented, to a narrow circle of advisors, the so-called Spanish Council, which was dominated by Antoine de Perrenot, the Spanish clergyman who had spearheaded the drive to restore Catholic unity. Perrenot and the Inquisition both became foci of intense religio-political opposition.

The event which triggered the Revolt – or, rather, the first of the three revolts which are known as the Revolt – was the "petition of the league," a formal request for religious toleration which was drafted by a group of middling nobles in early 1565 and presented to the Spanish governess, Margaret of Parma, in person, by over three hundred men. Hoping to buy time and pacify the unrest, Margaret issued a religious "moderation" temporarily suspending the anti-Protestant edicts.

The moderation was widely (and perhaps willfully) misinterpreted by Dutch Protestants as a declaration of religious freedom. During the spring and summer of 1566, enormous open-air church services were held in many parts of the Netherlands, and in the late summer and fall, the Low Countries were swept by a wave of Calvinist-led image-breaking (the so-called iconoclastic fury) followed by a noble-led rebellion in the late fall and winter. Furious, Philip II dispatched the Duke of Alba, one of his most trusted generals, to put down the upstarts. Numerous Protestants were burned at the stake, several prominent nobles were arrested and executed, and many thousands more were forced to flee. By 1568, the first Revolt was clearly over.

The second revolt did not begin until four years later, in 1572. But its preparation began almost immediately. Its leader was William of Orange, a prominent Dutch nobleman, who had narrowly escaped arrest and execution. And its most devoted partisans were the Protestants, who quickly reassembled in various safe havens, such as London, Emden, Frankfurt, and Wesel. While Orange patiently assembled an international alliance against the Spanish, the Protestants were busily organizing a network of refugee churches within the Netherlands proper. Orange planned a three-pronged assault: he would invade with a band of German mercenaries from the East, his brother would lead a rebel fleet from the North, and Louis de Coligny would attack with a force of French Huguenots from the South. In the event, however, he was upstaged, when the coastal city of Brill was invaded by a small band of Calvinists known as the Sea Beggars. After capturing Brill, the Sea Beggars stormed town after town and soon had much of Holland and Zeeland under their control. Orange had little choice but to follow their lead, and by the summer of 1572, he had occupied most of the southern Netherlands. But his troops were thin on the ground and the massacre of thousands of French Protestants on St. Bartholomew's Day meant that the expected Huguenot reinforcements would not be forthcoming, so he was forced to retreat behind the Rhine and the Maas. Peace negotiations were begun in the city of Breda, but soon stalled over the religious question. In the meantime, Orange worked to establish a Calvinist republic in the north, and Alba restored Spanish control over the south.

The third revolt began in 1577, and once again it was radical Calvinists who took the lead. Fierce as it was, Alba's campaign of persecution only succeeded in driving the Calvinists underground. Thus, when the leaders of the northern and southern provinces proclaimed a truce in 1576 – the Pacification of Ghent – the Calvinists quickly came out into the light again. When the new Spanish governor attempted to restore his authority in 1577, radical Calvinists in the southern cities ousted the local leadership and proclaimed popular republics. Orange reached out to the radicals, but events soon slipped beyond his control. By 1578, the rebellion had spread through most of Flanders and Brabant, much to the alarm of moderate Catholics, many of whom had supported the more limited aims of the Pacification. As the center-left alliance between Catholics and Calvinists came unglued, so, too, did the Low Countries as a whole. Attempts to restore peace once again foundered on the religious question, and in early 1579, the southern provinces of Artois, Hainault, and Douai signed a treaty committing themselves to "the maintenance of the Roman-Catholic religion, the obedience due to the king, and the privileges of the land." They were soon followed by the northern provinces of Holland, Zeeland, Utrecht, and Groningen, who committed themselves to a "closer union" for the defense of reformed Protestantism, the rule of the states, and the privileges of their land. The Dutch Revolt had become a civil war.

The fighting continued for over thirty years and was not officially ended until 1648. During the late 1570s and most of the 1580s, it was the Spanish who had the upper hand. The south was reconquered as was much of the north; only the provinces of Holland and Utrecht remained unscathed. Beginning in the late 1580s, however, Dutch forces under Maurice of Orange gradually liberated the seven Northern provinces and parts of the border provinces as well. Wearied by the fighting, the two sides finally signed a truce in 1609.

But peace without was followed by turmoil within. In Holland and Utrecht, where liberation came earliest, trouble had been brewing since the late 1580s. In Holland, the source of the trouble was a dispute between two theologians regarding the doctrine of predestination. The first, Jacobus Arminius, argued that salvation was achieved through the voluntary acceptance of divine grace. The second, Franciscus Gomarus, contended that salvation was given to some and denied to others, and that the individual's fate was independent of his or her actions. In Utrecht, the source of the trouble was a dispute between two congregations regarding the proper form of church government. The first congregation, the Jakobskerk, rejected the Calvinist system of consistorial discipline and was effectively governed by the local magistrate. The second congregation, known as the "consistorians," rejected the oversight of the town council and defended the autonomy of the consistory. The two battles were both similar, in that they pitted orthodox

Calvinists against their less orthodox coreligionists, and it was not long before they became fused together by a series of disputes over pastoral appointments. At issue in these disputes were both the theology of the candidates (Arminian or Gomarian?) and the right to appoint them (did it belong to the consistories or to the magistrates?) and, at a deeper level, the meaning of the Revolt (was it about religious freedom or about political liberty?) and the character of the Republic (popular or aristocratic?). As the religious quarrels intensified, they also took on a regional flavor as well, for while the libertine position (i.e., Arminian, Erasmian, antidisciplinarian, and oligarchic) was the dominant one among the regents of Holland and Utrecht, it was the precisionist (i.e., Gomarian, consistorian, disciplinarian, and populist) which generally won out in peripheral provinces, such as Zeeland and Friesland. Or, to put it differently, it was the animosity of the peripheral elites towards the core provinces which disposed them to ally with precisionist clergymen and parishioners. The dispute was a bitter one, and by 1617, the fledgling Republic once again found itself poised on the brink of civil war. In the end, the dispute was settled in favor of the precisionist/periphery alliance by the Dutch stadholder, Maurice of Orange, who disarmed the States of Holland and convened a National Synod. Libertine magistrates were then purged from the town councils, and Arminian pastors were dismissed from their posts. For the remainder of Maurice's term and beyond, the precisionists retained the upper hand in church and state. It was the beginning of two alliances, one between Calvinist orthodoxy and the House of Orange, the other between libertinism and the States of Holland – alliances which defined the fault lines of political contention in the Dutch Republic for the better part of two centuries.

Under Maurice's successor, Frederick Henry, the domestic politics of the Republic became more peaceful again. This was not because the tensions had subsided – they had not – but because the new stadholder managed to establish an equilibrium between them. A pragmatist by nature, Frederick Henry steered a middle course between the two alliances, playing them off against one another whenever he could. By clipping the wings of the Arminian regents and checking the States of Holland, he maintained the support of the precisionists and peripheral provinces, and by tolerating religious dissent and protecting maritime interests, he won the allegiance of the Arminians and the towns of Holland. Meanwhile, the presence of an external threat – in the shape of the Thirty Years' War – helped to quell elite opposition, while Frederick Henry's success in countering this threat – he retook much of Flanders and Brabant – helped to rally popular support. Frederick Henry's strategy was thus one of divide and conquer – in every sense.

During the second half of Frederick Henry's term, however, this dual balance of forces, internal and external, became increasingly difficult to maintain. The first sign of trouble came during his peace negotiations with Spain during 1632. Having recently captured the cities of 's Hertogenbosch and Maastricht, thereby gaining control over much of Brabant, the stadholder was in a strong position, and he sought to extract major concessions from the Spanish crown. The Arminian block had initially backed the peace negotiations, but when the Spaniards balked at the Dutch demands, and Frederick Henry announced his intention to withdraw from the negotiations, they continued to press for peace. After several months of anguished deliberation, Frederick Henry made an abrupt about-face, pronouncing his willingness to proceed with the war and canvassing the precisionist alliance for support. The old fault line was thus reopened, with Frederick Henry perched perilously atop it. Having alienated the Arminians, he had no choice but to rely on the precisionists. But the precisionists had misgivings of their own. With no solid base of support, the stadholder soon found himself floundering, with funds and victories both increasingly elusive. Political equilibrium thus gave way to political paralysis.

During the brief tenure of William II (1647-1650) as stadholder, the fault line between Arminians and precisionists became active once again. As in the 1610s, it was the return of peace which unleashed the pressures. The death of Frederick Henry in 1647, and the divisions within his family which followed, had allowed the States of Holland to take the lead in the peace negotiations at Münster and to force through a treaty which was not much to the liking of Zeeland and Utrecht, who feared it would compromise their mercantile interests, or of the precisionists, who felt it made too many concessions to Spain and to Catholicism.

The return of peace also prompted Holland and the other "peace provinces" to release many of the soldiers in their hire, much to the chagrin of the new stadholder, who felt that the troop reductions were too rapid and too deep. A confrontation ensued. Seeking to rally support, the stadholder appealed to the precisionists and peripheral provinces by means of a carefully orchestrated campaign of propaganda and misinformation, which portrayed the Arminians as enemies of the people and traitors to the Republic. He then attempted to force Holland's hand, by placing The Hague under military occupation and arresting several of his most prominent opponents. From there, he marched north to Amsterdam, hoping to take the city by surprise. Finding the gates closed, he promptly laid siege, forcing the city council to purge its Arminian leaders and cancel its planned troop reductions. Letters were dispatched to the Precisionist provinces and towns, and initial reactions were favorable. But the promising life of the new regime was cut short by the accidental death of the young stadholder in 1650.

The political pendulum now swung back in an Arminian direction. Following the death of William II, the States of Holland and four other provincial assemblies declined to appoint a new stadholder. They then summoned a Great Assembly (Groote Vergadering) of the States General, a sort of constitutional convention which deliberated over many of the basic questions that had remained unresolved since the inception of the Republic – the distribution of sovereignty, relations between church and state, control over the army, and the status of Drenthe and the states of Brabant, captured provinces desiring admission to the States General. While the resulting agreement contained a few concessions to the precisionists (e.g., a confirmation of the Acts of the Synod of Dort), it accorded, on the whole, with the wishes of the Arminians and the States of Holland: the individual provinces were free to fill the position of Stadholder or leave it vacant, as they saw fit; precisionist demands for a stricter enforcement of the religious decrees were denied; control over the army was given to the States General and Council of State, not the stadholder; and Brabant and Drenthe, both solidly precisionist, were refused admission to the States General. The result was a weakly centralized system of governance, which was dominated by its strongest member: the States of Holland.

For the next twenty years, the de facto leader of the Dutch Republic was the Grand Pensionary of Holland, John De Witt, a skillful politician and diplomat, who managed to keep the precisionists and peripheral provinces in check, and fight the English navy to a standstill on two separate occasions. Under De Witt, the Netherlands evolved into an aristocratic republic in which political power was concentrated in the hands of the urban patricians, and the House of Orange and the common people were excluded from any meaningful role in the political process. Defenders and apologists for the De Witt regime compared it to the classical republics and held it up as an example of "True Freedom" (Waere Vryheid).

The era of the True Freedom came to an end in 1672. In this year, still known as the "Year of Tragedy" (Rampjaar), the Netherlands were invaded by a powerful international coalition led by Louis XIV. Precisionists regarded the defeat as a form of divine punishment for the moral and spiritual laxity which had overtaken the Republic during the years of republican rule, and the Orangists were quick to mobilize this popular resentment to their own advantage, a task made easier by the fact that the heir apparent to the stadholderate, William III, had recently reached his majority. De Witt was lynched by an Orangist mob in The Hague, and Arminian magistrates were purged from the city governments of Holland and Zeeland. William III was appointed stadholder, and the French attack was miraculously repelled.

The new regime was to last for thirty years. Initially, William III tried to rule in the same way that his father and grandfather had: by means of noble cliques and bourgeois clients. But as the popular enthusiasm of the war years began to wane, and the power and confidence of the Arminian regents started to return, he was forced to adopt a more pragmatic policy of compromise and conciliation beginning during the late 1670s. Realizing that he could not govern effectively without at least some support from Arminians and republicans, he encouraged the sharing of power among the different religio-political factions by means of formalized "contracts of correspondence," which portioned out political and ecclesiastical offices amongst the local factions in each city.

The international stock of the House of Orange rose dramatically in 1689, when William III was proclaimed King of England.

His claim on the office was grounded upon his blood relationship with Charles II and his marriage to Princess Mary, the eldest daughter of James II, who was next in line for the throne. But William was a Catholic and an authoritarian, and his succession was thus anathema to many in England. The States General, for their part, were fearful of the increased power and prestige which the English throne would confer on the Dutch stadholder, but they were even more afraid of the threat which a renewed Anglo-French alliance posed to their commercial and imperial interests. So it was that they financed the massive invasion of England which swept William and Mary into power in 1689.

Following William's death in 1702, five of the seven provinces declined to appoint a new stadholder. Once again, the Republic was dominated by the Arminians and the States of Holland. The transition was not an entirely smooth one. Indeed, it was marked by considerable unrest in Utrecht, Overijssel, and Gelderland, where Orangist militias and guilds demanded the appointment of a new stadholder and a greater say in political affairs. But the ongoing turbulence in the periphery made it all the easier for Holland to assert its dominance.

The second period without a stadholder lasted until 1747. Like the first, it was brought to an end by a French invasion of the southern Netherlands. The invasion was, in fact, a rather small one, but the historical precedent set off a popular panic. Faced with rising unrest, the States of Holland hastily appointed William IV as stadholder. Meanwhile, Orangist leaders sought to shore up support for the new regime with a massive propaganda campaign proclaiming the "sovereignty of the people" and their right to unseat undeserving magistrates. Despite its many similarities to the Year of Tragedy, the Revolution of 1747 was different in several respects: a small but vocal group of radical democrats emerged from the ranks of the Orangist camp and eventually split off from it; and popular violence was directed not only at Catholics and Arminians, as in the past, but also at tax collectors and rich burghers.

Over the next three decades, the old religious and political cleavages underwent a gradual metamorphosis. While they did not explicitly renounce their support for the principle of popular sovereignty, the Orangists now began to articulate a more regal and absolutist interpretation of the stadholdership. The radical republicans, for their part, now started to align themselves more openly with the Arminians and the States of Holland, claiming their heroes and traditions as their own. Tensions between Orangists and republicans were further intensified by the outbreak of the American Revolution, for the Orangists tended to sympathize with the King of England, while the republicans were more inclined to favor the colonial upstarts. Indeed, it was the American militias which provided the key model for the radical republicans, who set about organizing local "Free Corps," armed burgher groups whose goal was to topple the Orangist regime and open the town councils.

The result of this agitation was the Patriots' Revolution of 1780-87. The first anti-Orangist purges occurred in 1784, and by 1786, republican "Patriots" had seized control of town councils throughout the Republic. Only the Orangist strongholds of Zeeland and Friesland remained beyond their grasp. The Free Corps now began to press for a greater role in local government, a demand which was firmly resisted by the republican regents they had helped hoist into power. The republican coalition now broke apart, with the radicals seizing the upper hand.

The Calvinist Contribution to the Revolt

To appreciate fully the significance of these events, one must see them within their larger context. For the Dutch development was atypical for the period. In most parts of Europe – in Spain, France, Germany, Italy, Scandinavia, and so on – liberty was on the wane, and absolutism on the rise, as traditions of urban autonomy and representative government fell victim to the centralizing policies and fiscal demands of territorial princes. Only through force of arms and only in a handful of countries – Scotland, England, the Netherlands and Poland, to name the most important – were the territorial "estates" able to short-circuit this trend and preserve their role in government.

To understand the contribution that the Dutch Calvinists made to the preservation of political liberty in the Netherlands, then, one must first grasp the contribution which they made to the success of the revolt against Spain. It was considerable. It consisted, firstly, in what can only be called their "fighting spirit" – their willingness to use force and their unwillingness to compromise. If we look at the three stages of the Dutch Revolt – the rebellion of the nobles, the Orangist invasion, and the revolution in the South – we see that it was the Calvinists, in each instance, who were the first to use force. Thus, the first stage of the Revolt began with the Calvinist-led "league of nobles" at Brussels; was continued by the Calvinist-led image-breakers in the cities; and culminated with the Calvinist-led "rebellion of nobles" under Brederode. Similarly, the second stage of the Revolt was planned in cooperation with the Calvinist refugee churches, precipitated by the landing of the Calvinist Sea Beggars at Brill, and carried out with the help of Huguenot soldiers. The third stage of the Revolt, finally, was triggered by Calvinist-led coups in Flanders and Brabant.

With this willingness to use force went an unwillingness to compromise, which was also evident in each stage of the Revolt. The individual decisions of thousands of Dutch Calvinists to face exile or martyrdom rather than submit to Spanish rule after 1566, the refusal of the returning exiles and their allies to share power with Catholics or "neutrals" after 1572, the reckless violations of the Pacification of Ghent which they committed after 1576, and their unwillingness to cut a deal with the Spanish after 1579 are all examples. The Calvinists, in short, were the first to disturb the peace and also the first to break it. Had it not been for their militancy and determination, it seems highly unlikely that the political discontent of the 1550s would have escalated into a full-fledged rebellion, and highly likely that the Revolt would have been ended through some sort of political settlement with the Spanish. Without the Calvinists, in other words, the Revolt would probably never have occurred, and would almost certainly have been settled.

If the outbreak and escalation of the Revolt owed much to the fighting spirit of the Dutch Calvinists, its consolidation and success owed much to the flexibility and strength of their organization. What made the Calvinist system of ecclesiastical organization so flexible was its decentralization and lack of hierarchy. Under this system, each congregation was, in essence, a church unto itself, which could function without external ties or clerical supervision. Indeed, many of the early congregations, the so-called churches under the cross, were founded by laymen and functioned for years without benefit of clergy. The advantage of this system is clear: since it is acephalous, it cannot be decapitated; thus, a blow struck at one congregation, even an important one, does not compromise the viability of another. This lack of a head does not imply the lack of a center. Once the Calvinist movement had established a significant and lasting presence in an area, the individual congregations were aggregated into local "classes" and regional and national "synods." Thus, when circumstances permitted, the Dutch Calvinists were quickly able to combine their various congregations into a cohesive, national body. The strength of this system, in turn, derived from its representative and non-hierarchical character. For the leadership of the church was entrusted not to the pastor but to the consistory, a collegial body composed of the pastor together with prominent laymen chosen by and from the members of the church. The consistory itself was organized so as to represent the various districts or quarters of the parish or city. Because each congregation was governed primarily by laymen, and because these laymen represented particular constituencies, it served as a mechanism for mobilizing the local populace and for shaping public opinion. The ecclesiastical system of the Reformed Church was thus a many-headed hydra which was ideally suited to the task of political resistance.

The contribution of the Calvinists to the Revolt was not just practical and organizational, however; it was intellectual as well. It was a Calvinist who first argued that the right of resistance extended to the common people as well. Agge Albada, a Frisian Calvinist, contended that "God created men free," and that this implied a natural right of resistance to tyranny.[5]

Calvinist authors were not only the earliest defenders of the Revolt, but some of the loudest as well. The most influential spokesman for the rebels, for instance, was undoubtedly Marnix van St. Aldegonde, a Calvinist nobleman who became William of Orange's spokesman and chief propagandist. In this capacity,

---

5. See E. H. Kossmann and A. F. Mellink, *Texts Concerning the Revolt of the Netherlands* (Cambridge: Cambridge University Press, 1974), Doc. 44, p. 197.

Marnix authored many of Orange's political broadsheets, including the Edict of Abjuration (1581), in which the States General officially renounced the authority of the King of Spain – without question the best known and most influential document of the Revolt. Marnix also wrote many other pamphlets and treatises, both anonymously and under his own name, some of which went through many editions, and he played a critical role in the formulation and transmission of a Reformed theory of resistance inspired by the writings of Calvin and the French Monarchomachs. In a tract written shortly after the Pacification of Ghent and the appearance of Beza's *Vindiciae*, Marnix argued that the States General "have been called by God and men to be protectors of the privileges, rights and freedoms of the common people, whom they represent in the three estates of clergy nobles and towns."[6]

The Dutch Calvinists did not limit themselves to defending religious freedom; they were ardent supporters of political liberty as well. Indeed, for many of them, religious and political liberty were inextricably bound up with one another. The association between Calvinism and republicanism was particularly strong in the cities of Flanders and Brabant. In Ghent, for example, where guild leaders and civic militiamen had ousted the ruling oligarchy and established the rule of a new Committee of Eighteen Men – a sort of Calvinist Committee of Public Safety – one of the local ministers, Peter Dathenus, urged his coreligionists to stand fast, arguing that the French Huguenots "were almost entirely ruined when they wanted to maneuver, to dissimulate and to adapt themselves to circumstances."[7] In his view, Calvinism and liberty were inherently linked: to defend the one was to defend the other. This point was made even more explicitly by Peter Beutterich, a Calvinist military officer from the Palatinate who was sent to Ghent by Queen Elizabeth. In his view "maintaining the one and only Roman Catholic

6. From Marnix's "Cort verhael van de rechte oorsaecken ende redenen, die de Generale Staten der nederlanden ghedwonghen hebben hen ti versiene tot hunder beschermenise teghen den heere Don Jehan van Oostenrijck", 1577. Here I quote from the excerpted translation in Kossmann and Mellink, Texts, Doc. 27, p. 139.
7. From Dathenus "Wachtgheschrey" of 1578. Here I cite the excerpted translation in Kossmann and Mellink, Texts, Doc. 34, p. 158.

religion in this country and maintaining tyranny there, comes to the same thing."[8]

While the more moderate and less zealous currents within the anti-Spanish coalition openly rejected the protodemocratic and quasitheocratic vision of the Flemish radicals, they did not hesitate to borrow the rhetoric and arguments of the religious left. Thus, the anonymous author of a plea for peace published in 1576 cites the text of I Samuel 9: 11-19 in support of the claim that "the community is not created and ordained for the King's sake, but the Kings for the sake of the community"[9] – the same passage and the same argument advanced by Calvin in his Bible commentary! Another anonymous pamphlet published at Malines in 1582 invokes the sacred covenant established between God and the ancient Jews to support the argument that "Kings are bound by oath in two respects, first to God and then to the People."[10]

Thus, whether or not one regards their political thought as original and innovative, it is clear that the Dutch Calvinists were key promulgators of the various theories of political resistance and liberty that were introduced into the Netherlands. This is not to say that all Calvinists advocated resistance or espoused republicanism; nor is it to say that those who did agreed about who could resist or who should hold power. On the contrary, there were significant divisions and disagreements within the Calvinist camp, especially between the noble and patrician leaders of the movement, who tended to advocate a more restricted and less democratic understanding of resistance and liberty, and the lower and middle-class members of the rank and file, who supported a more expansive and less oligarchic view of these subjects. As always, persons from different strata gave different inflections to the theory. There were also purely intellectual disagreements, especially

8. From Beutterich's "Le vray aux bons patriots." Here I cite the excerpted translation in Kossmann and Mellink, Texts, Doc. 35, p. 160.

9. From the "Address and Opening to Make a Good, Blessed and General Peace in the Netherlands, 1576. Here I cite from the English translation in Martin van Gelderen, *The Dutch Revolt,* (Cambridge: Cambridge University Press, 1993), p. 104.

10. From "Political Education," 1582. Here I cite the English translation in Van Gelderen, *Dutch Revolt,* p. 193.

within the clergy, regarding the legitimacy of resistance and the role of the church. Nonetheless, it seems clear that there was a kind of elective affinity between Calvinism and resistance, a certain attraction or compatibility between the ethos and institutions of Reformed Protestantism and those of urban republicanism.

Still, it has been objected that the kind of liberty for which the Calvinists were fighting was quite different from the kind of liberty which their republican allies had in mind. And, indeed, the idea of liberty did begin to take on a more restricted and less political meaning within Calvinist circles during the 1580s, and had been transformed into an epithet ("libertine") and term of opprobrium ("libertinism") by the early seventeenth century.[11] Still it would be misleading and anachronistic to project these divisions too far back into the past or to ignore the context out of which they arose. Embodied and symbolized by men such as William of Orange and Marnix van St. Aldegonde, the Calvinist-republican synthesis was the linchpin of the anti-Spanish coalition and remained a vital force within Dutch politics until at least 1610. What broke it apart was not some inherent or putative incompatibility between Calvinism and republicanism, but the conflicts which arose during the late sixteenth and early seventeenth centuries over two interrelated questions: the church-state question – the question of who was to control appointments to church office, the town magistrates or the church consistories, and the toleration question – the question of just how much freedom was to be granted to Catholics and other religious dissenters.

Given the divergence between Calvinists and republicans during the decades after the Revolt, one might conclude that the focus of the story should now shift to the republicans, for it was they, after all, who went furthest towards developing a secular and truly political theory of representative government. That is indeed the conclusion which most Dutch historians have drawn, but it is not the conclusion which will be drawn here. For as important as the development of representative institutions is to the history of democratic

---

11. Benjamin Kaplan, *Calvinists and Libertines: confession and community in Utrecht, 1578-1620* (Oxford and New York: Clarendon Press and Oxford University Press, 1995).

governance, there is another story which is equally important: the story of equality. It is in this story that the Calvinists figure.

Calvinism and Popular Sovereignty

The exercise of liberty was quite restricted under the Republic, and became more so during the seventeenth century. At the municipal level, the town councils evolved into closed oligarchies. New magistrates were generally appointed, and in many cases special "contracts of correspondence" were drawn up, specifying how the various offices and their spoils were to be divided up between the various families and factions in each town.[12] A similar process of "aristocratization" occurred within the church consistories as well.[13] Like the town magistrates, church elders were increasingly chosen from the local patriciate. These local processes of social and political closure rippled upward to the national level, since it was the city councils of the leading towns which chose most of the delegates to the provincial estates, and the provincial estates which chose most of the delegates to the States General. The only real checks on the power of the urban patriciate were the provincial stadholders, who supervised elections in many of the towns and often served as supreme commanders of the military forces, and the nobles *(ridders)*, who often sat as ex officio delegates in the provincial estates and sometimes presided over their deliberations. For obvious reasons, this arrangement was not entirely to the satisfaction of the *ridders* or stadholders, both of whom longed for more substantial roles in government; nor was it amenable to those members of the population who were excluded from government altogether. Resentment was particularly keen among the guilds and militias, which had previously played a much greater role in the government of some towns, such as Utrecht and Deventer, and among those regent families or factions who had been written out

12. On this, see Julia P. Adams, *The Family State* (Ithaca: Cornell University Press, forthcoming).

13. On this, see especially A. Th. van Deursen, *Bavianen en Slijkgeuzen: kerk en kerkvolk ten tijde van Maurits en Oldebarnevelt* (Assen: Van Gorcum, 1974), Ch. 5.

of the contracts of correspondence for one reason or another. To this must be added the jealousy which the provincial elites felt towards Amsterdam, which dominated the States of Holland, and towards the States of Holland, which dominated the States General. Managing these manifold sources of discontent was a formidable task, and consumed much of the political energy of the Amsterdam regents and the grand pensionaries of Holland.

Unfair as it may have appeared, this system was not without its apologists. Indeed, beginning in 1609, right around the time when the battle between Gomarians and Arminians first exploded into a national crisis, a number of prominent humanist intellectuals, including Peter Scriverius and Hugo Grotius, set forth a mythical account of the Republic's origins, which seemed to legitimate the existing system and the preeminent role which the States of Holland played in it. Drawing on Tacitus's description of the Netherlands in *Germania*, Scriverius and Grotius argued that the putative predecessors of present-day Hollanders, the ancient Batavians, had never been conquered by the Romans, had never paid tribute to them, and had never known the dominion of an absolute sovereign. In addition, they contended that the Batavians had always been great lovers of liberty, had always been careful householders and had always been ruled by the States. They suggested, in short, that the Batavians had always been free, while their neighbors – Belgians, Frisians, Gauls – had not. It was a questionable interpretation, which strained (and indeed distorted) the sources in various ways (e.g. by ignoring the role played by Claudius Civilus, the noble leader of the Batavian Uprising), but it was a useful interpretation, which helped legitimate the Republic, and Holland's place in it. It was an influential interpretation, as well, which was elaborated by subsequent generations and deployed in official representations of the Republic.

It was not, however, the only interpretation of the Republic, nor even the oldest. This honor belongs to a second myth of origins, whose roots go back to the early days of the Revolt. In this myth, the Netherlanders are compared not to the ancient Batavians but to the ancient Israelites. One of the first places where this comparison appears – perhaps *the* first place – is in the popular ballads known as the "Beggars' Songs" (*Geuzenliederen*), which spoke of the Dutch people as God's chosen people, William of Orange as their Moses or David, and the king of Spain as a new pharaoh. Of course, the Beggars were not the first to use Old Testament imagery for political purposes; early modern rulers were often celebrated as "new Davids" or "new Solomons." What was unusual about the Beggar mythology was that it focused not on the Temple period and the glories of the Jewish kings, but on the Exodus story and God's liberation of the Jewish people from the dominion of the Egyptians. During the late sixteenth and early seventeenth centuries, Hebraic imagery appeared in many different media and many different contexts. It appeared on coins minted by city councils to memorialize their liberation from Spain, in civic processions organized to honor the heroes of the Revolt, in political tracts written to celebrate Dutch victories over the Spanish, and even in the plays of Joost van den Vondel, the gray eminence of Dutch letters – and a Catholic.

There was nothing inherently incompatible about the Batavian and Hebraic mythologies. Both depicted the Republic in constitutional terms, and both suggested that republicanism was the best form of government. In fact, it was not entirely unusual for the two mythologies to be combined, at least during the early seventeenth century, just as Biblical and constitutional arguments were often juxtaposed in writings on resistance during the 1570s and 1580s.

But beginning around 1620, in the years following the (Pyrrhic) victory of the Gomarians at the Synod of Dort, the Batavian and Hebraic mythologies were gradually transformed into opposing political ideologies. Supporters of the Arminian or States position used the Batavian analogy to argue for a more secular and federalist vision of the Republic. In particular, they attempted to justify Holland's special place in this system, by drawing the boundaries of Batavia more narrowly, so as to exclude Zeeland, Friesland, and Flanders, which could also claim at least some degree of Batavian ancestry. Supporters of the Gomarist or Orangist position, on the other hand, used the Hebraic analogy to press for a more theocratic and monarchical vision of the Republic. In particular, they demanded greater authority for the stadholders, by emphasizing the role of David and his successors in the development of the Jewish state.

The Batavian and Hebraic myths thus came to stand for two competing visions of the Republic, and it was around these poles that the political upheavals of the next 150 years generally tended to coalesce.[14] On the one side stood Holland and the Arminians; on the other, Friesland, Zeeland, and the orthodox Calvinists; between them, a large and diverse group of political pragmatists and religious moderates; and above them, the stadholders and the house of Orange. So long as the stadholders were personally or politically weak, or unwilling to ally themselves with the Calvinists, as in the two stadholderless periods, the periphery remained fragmented, and Holland ruled the Republic. In those periods where there was a strong and dynamic stadholder, such as Maurice or William III, who was willing to reach out to the Calvinists, the periphery was united, and Holland was held in check. Indeed, the entire political history of the Republic can basically be seen as oscillating between these two poles – an aristocratic republic led by Holland and a populist (if not popular) republic led by the stadholder. The oscillations toward aristocracy tended to be slow and peaceful. They began when the stadholders discovered that they could not rule without Holland, and reached their apogees when the estates realized that they could rule without a stadholder. The oscillations toward populism, on the other hand, were quick and often violent. They occurred when ambitious stadholders allied with disgruntled Calvinists and restive elites. Of course, it would be wrong to suggest that the opposition between Batavians and Hebraicists was the only political cleavage in the Republic. Familial rivalries often played a significant role at the local level, and the split between landlocked and maritime provinces was sometimes critical at the national level. But insofar as local disputes escalated into national ones, and insofar as these national disputes were ide-

14. On these upheavals and the role of religion in them see S. Groenveld, *Evidente factiën in den staet* (Hilversum: Verloren, 1990); Wayne Ph. te Brake, *Regents and Rebels. The Revolutionary World of an Eighteenth-Century Dutch City* (Oxford: Basil Blackwell, 1989); M. Van der Bijl, *Idee en interest. Voorgeschiedenis, verloop en achtergronden van de politieke twisten in Zeeland en vooral in Middelburg tussen 1702 en 1715* (Groningen: Wolters-Noordhoff, 1981); and D. J. Roorda, *Partij en factie. De oproeren van 1672 in de steden van Holland en Zeeland, een krachtmeting tussen partijen en facties* (Groningen: J.B. Wolters, 1961).

ological, rather than commercial, they tended to crystallize around the Batavian and Hebraic poles.

On one level, the level of practical politics, the debate between the Batavians and Hebraicists revolved around three main issues: the constitutional character of the Republic (an alliance of seven sovereign states, or a sovereign state made up of seven provinces?), the rightful role of the stadholders (agents of the provincial states, or leaders of the States General?), and the proper place of the Reformed Church (not just first among equals, but a chief without rivals?). At a second and deeper level, the level of political theory, the debate raised a more fundamental set of issues concerning sovereignty – its ultimate source (historical tradition or natural law), rightful bearers (estates or people), and effective location (provincial states or States General). The Batavian myth clearly implied that sovereignty was rooted in historical tradition (the traditions of the ancient Batavians), borne by the estates (as representatives of the people) and located in the provincial states (the building blocks of the Republic). By contrast, the Hebraic myth seemed to suggest that sovereignty was rooted in natural law (since God made men free), borne by the Dutch people (who had made a sacred covenant with God), and located in the States General (to which the people had collectively transferred it). Implicit within the debate between Batavians (Arminians) and Hebraicists (Orangists), then, was a debate over who was the ultimate source of sovereignty – the states or the people.

Of course, it would be wrong to draw too sharp a line between these two positions. There were Arminians, such as Van Slingelandt, who believed that the Republic needed a stronger stadholderate, and there were Orangists, including the stadholder William IV himself, who rejected a stronger stadholderate. These underlying assumptions were not always fully articulated. Few Batavians would have gone so far as to argue that sovereignty did not reside in the people in some limited sense. And few Hebraicists would have argued.

Thus far, I have focused on the contribution which Calvinism made to the institutional and ideological foundations of modern democracy, that is, to ideas of liberty and equality. I now turn to a third and less recognized contribution – the role which Calvinism played in creating a disciplined and pacified population, susceptible to democratic forms of rule.

Calvinism and the Micro-Political Foundations of Democratic Governance

In contemporary discussions of democracy, fraternity is rarely afforded the same pride of place as liberty and equality. It is, so to speak, the forgotten step-child of the revolutionary triad. And yet, for the revolutionaries themselves, it was an indispensable element of the revolutionary vision. Without fraternity, they believed, liberty would deteriorate into license, and equality into passivity. Only through the mutual watchfulness and admonition which prevails between brothers (and perhaps sisters) could revolutionary virtue be sustained.

This position was anything but revolutionary. Political theorists had long emphasized the role which communal discipline plays in sustaining republican virtue, and the dangers which arise when it breaks down. Cicero had warned the Roman elites that "freedom itself punishes with slavery a people whose freedom knows no bounds."[15] Machiavelli had advised lovers of liberty that "where good discipline prevails there also will good order prevail …"[16] Rousseau suggested that liberty consists, not in casting off one's chains, but in learning to walk in them. When the revolutionaries pointed to the connection between discipline and liberty, they were standing squarely in the republican tradition.[17]

A similar point has been made by Michel Foucault, in his discussions of modern classical liberalism.[18] While contemporary lib-

15. Cicero, *On the Commonwealth*, transl. George Holland Sabine and Stanley Barney Smith (New York and London: Macmillian and Collier Macmillan, 1976), p. 150.

16. Machiavelli, *The Prince and the Discourses*, transl. Max Lerner (New York: Modern Library, 1950), p. 119 (*Discourses*, Ch. 4).

17. Recall the famous opening line of *The Social Contract:* "Men are born free, but everywhere they are in chains." Jean-Jacques Rousseau, *On the social contract*, translated and edited by Donald A. Cress (Indianapolis: Hackett), p. 3.

18. See especially Foucault's widely-discussed essay on "Governmentality" in Graham Burchell, Colin Gordon, and Peter Miller, eds., *The Foucault Effect. Studies in Governmentality* (Chicago: University of Chicago Press, 1991), pp. 87-104.

erals (which is to say, *economic*, not social liberals), tend to think of liberalism in negative terms, as an absence of government, Foucault urges us to think of it in positive terms, as a *mode* of government. Liberalism, he contends, is simply a mode of rule in which power is exercised indirectly, by private elites and institutions, such as psychiatrists and hospitals, rather than directly by the state or other public bodies.

But there is a theoretical gap between these two arguments – and a historical gap between classical republicanism and modern liberalism. For while the republican theorists emphasize the importance of virtue, they do not explain how it was instilled in modern populations. And while Foucault suggests the answer to this question with his focus on disciplinary infrastructure, he does not explain where this infrastructure comes from. The answer to both these questions, I will suggest, can be found in the rise of Calvinism, and, more specifically, in the process of social disciplining which it unleashed, a process which I have elsewhere referred to as the "Calvinist disciplinary revolution."[19] This revolution occurred in three distinct but overlapping stages. It began within the church proper, spread to society as a whole, and then reverted upon itself. The timing of these stages varied somewhat from one context to the other.

In the Dutch Republic, the disciplinary revolution began in the 1560s and continued well into the seventeenth century. In the first and predominantly religious stage, which was coterminous with the establishment of the Dutch Reformed Church, parishioners were placed under the supervision of local consistories, collegial bodies consisting of the minister and several lay elders. They were responsible for watching over the congregation and punishing public sinners, that is, those whose offenses had become widely known within the community and thus threatened to bring opprobrium upon the

---

19. See Philip S. Gorski, "The Protestant Ethic Revisited: Disciplinary Revolution in Holland and Prussia", *American Journal of Sociology*, 99 (1993), pp. 255-316; "The Disciplinary Revolution: Calvinism and State Formation in Early Modern Europe", (Ph.D. Dissertation: University of California, Berkeley, 1996); and "The Disciplinary Revolution: Confessionalization and State Formation in Early modern Europe", in George Steinmetz, ed., *State/Culture* (Ithaca: Cornell University Press, 1999), pp. 147-81.

Reformed Church – and vengeance from God. The most commonly punished offenses were of a sexual nature (fornication, adultery, sodomy), followed by various forms of social misconduct (fighting, drunkenness, swearing), with crimes in the modern sense (theft, assault, murder) making up only a relatively small percentage of the total. For the most part, then, the consistories were simply enforcing moral principles which had long been in existence. The severity of discipline varied from time to time and place to place. Where there was an energetic pastor and an active congregation, as in Utrecht during the mid-seventeenth century, discipline was severe. Where clerical leadership was weaker or where the congregation was disaffected, discipline tended to be more lax. The speed with which discipline was imposed also varied. In the larger cities of Holland and Zeeland, the imposition of ecclesiastical discipline was more or less complete by the late 1570s. In the small towns and the peripheral provinces, where trained clergymen were sparse and Spanish invasion was a recurrent threat, things proceeded more slowly. Nonetheless, it would probably be safe to say that "disciplined churches" were present in most of the northern Netherlands by the time of the Synod of Dort. Of course, there were many Netherlanders who were not subject to Calvinist discipline because they did not belong to the Reformed Church, but this does not mean that they escaped discipline altogether. The Baptist sects practiced an even stricter form of discipline, in which offenders were shunned by the entire congregation, including their own families. The Catholic Church was also compelled to keep a strict eye over its parishioners, since excesses of one kind or another sometimes prompted the local authorities to enforce the anti-Catholic decrees. Communal surveillance of this sort was facilitated by the growth of confessionally-based social services of various kinds – elementary schools, old-age homes, poor-houses and so on. By the mid-seventeenth Century, then – the height of the Dutch "Golden Age" – the population of the northern Netherlands was enmeshed in an encompassing network of religious discipline and control.

The second and more properly social wave of disciplining was stimulated by the first and followed closely on its heels. It involved the rationalization of various social practices and institutions, most notably in the arena of poor relief. The irrationality of traditional forms of poor relief – their inefficiency, redundancy, and indiscriminate nature – had long been criticized by humanistically-oriented reformers, but in most parts of Europe, including the Netherlands, attempts at reform had been squelched or undermined by conservative Catholics, led by the mendicant orders. Beginning in the 1570s, however, the northern Netherlands were swept by a more powerful – and more radical – wave of reform. In many ways, the Dutch reforms were similar to those which had been carried out in Lutheran Germany beginning in the 1520s, and to those implemented in a number of Italian city-states during the late fifteenth century: poor-relief funds were centralized, placed under lay oversight, and distributed only to the "deserving" (i.e., the young, the old, and the infirm). What distinguished the Dutch reforms, and those carried out in other Calvinist polities, was their focus on transforming the "able-bodied poor" into "productive citizens" and their use of incarceration as a means to this end. Forced labor and enclosure had been tried before; but the Dutch – and the English – were the first to combine the two. The result of this synthesis was the House of Discipline (Tuchthuis), more commonly (if less accurately) known as the workhouse, a sort of secular monastery in which unwilling "novices" were subjected to an unremitting and carefully-regulated regime of religious exercises and physical work designed to free them from the dominion of their fallen natures. The first Tuchthuis was established in Amsterdam during the 1580s. It was wildly popular (if not demonstrably successful) and was soon imitated. By the 1620s, there were dozens of workhouses throughout the Netherlands. The significance of the Tuchthuizen lay not so much in the impact which they had on their inmates, who were small in number and, by all indications, fairly intractable. Rather, their significance lay in the impact which they had on their administrators, who used these new-found laboratories to accumulate a new and objective knowledge of the poor, and in the impact which they had on the general population, for whom the Tuchthuizen provided an object lesson on the consequences of undisciplined behavior.

In the third stage of the disciplining process, which began around 1620 and picked up steam through the 1650s, the focus shifted from society towards the self. Alarmed by a perceived decline in public morality, Reformed theologians such as Willem Teelink and Gisbertus Voetius began calling for a second or "further reformation" *(nadere reformatie)*, a reformation, not merely of the church, but of life. Inspired by Puritan authors such as Richard Baxter, they also began elaborating a theory of the "signs" or "seals" of "divine election." Their followers, meanwhile, were encouraged to foster the workings of grace and monitor their spiritual progress through a variety of means including regular exercises (e.g., Bible-reading and prayer), personal journals (with a careful accounting of sins), and weekly conventicles (i.e., small, devotional circles). Precisionist clergymen and parishioners were not content to reform themselves, however; they also wished to impose the new self-discipline on others. To this end, they agitated for harsher sumptuary and police legislation, including stricter enforcement of the Sabbath, tighter regulation of pubs and saloons, and even a ban on periwigs! Naturally, the Dutch regents were generally (if not uniformly) resistant to such reforms, particularly insofar as they were personally affected by them (as in the "periwig debate"). But it would be wrong to conclude that they were resistant to self-discipline per se. Indeed, the growth of Dutch precisionism among the middle and lower classes was paralleled by the spread of neostoicism among the upper classes and the nobility. Of course, precisionists and neostoics practiced self-discipline for very different reasons: for the precisionists, self-discipline was good because it was pleasing to God (and helped deflect his wrath); for the neostoics, self-discipline was good because it promoted personal happiness (by holding dangerous and disruptive passions in check). But they practiced many of the same techniques of self-control (rigorous exercises, strict schedules, written journals, etc.), and they agreed (if only implicitly) about the connection between self-governance and political stability. This connection was more than theoretical: foreign observers often commented on the orderliness and self-control of the Dutch, not only in their day-to-day lives, but in periods of social and political conflict as well.

There is no reason to believe that the discipline of the Dutch – religious, social, and individual – actually hastened the process of democratization: indeed, modern parliamentary democracy was not introduced into the Netherlands until the 1860s, following a long period of monarchical rule. It does, however, seem likely that the discipline of the Dutch made the process of democratization considerably easier, not only because the various confessions provided a natural basis upon which to construct the party system, but also because they provided an invisible source of social order which obviated the need for authoritarian forms of political domination. In short, discipline created a strong political body which could be governed by a weak political head.

The Religious Roots of Liberal Democracy

The contribution of the Calvinist movement to the process of democratization in the Netherlands would appear to have been three-fold: 1) through its role in the Dutch Revolt against Spain, the Calvinist movement helped to defend and strengthen the representative organs of the *Ständestaat* (polity of the estates), thus preserving the institutional foundations on which parliamentary democracy would later be erected; 2) through its ideology of the sacred covenant, it helped to popularize the theory of popular sovereignty and disseminate a belief in political equality; and 3) through its program of religious and social discipline, it helped to forge an infrastructure of moral regulation and a culture of self control – a strong political body which could be more easily ruled by a weak political head. In sum, the Calvinist movement helped to preserve and create a set of institutions, ideologies, and practices which were favorable to the emergence and growth of "liberty, equality, and fraternity."

This raises an important question: given the religious and political similarities between the Low Countries and northwest Germany, why did the Netherlands develop in a democratic direction, while Germany developed in an authoritarian one? The answer, I believe, lies in two subtle differences between the two regions, one political, the other religious.

As we have seen, the cities of northern and western Germany were far more autonomous than their Dutch counterparts. The imperial cities of the Rhineland, for example, were subject only to the authority of the emperor himself, which is to say that they were essentially independent city-states, since the oversight of the emperor was usually quite lax. Because they were not integrated into a system of territorial estates, the imperial cities found themselves without allies and without recourse, when the tide began to turn against urban autonomy and towards princely absolutism. The free cities of northern Germany found themselves in a somewhat more favorable position: as members of the Hanseatic League, they were not entirely without allies, but they were no match for the great powers which surrounded them on all sides, particularly given the fact that they lacked the sorts of natural geographical defenses which England and the Netherlands possessed. Thus, on the political and geo-political planes, the initial conditions were actually less similar than they may have seemed at first glance.

There were also subtle but significant differences on the religious plane. For while Reformed Protestantism found a great many followers in the free cities of northwestern Germany, particularly among the merchant classes, it faced much stiffer competition there than it did in the Low Countries. By the time Calvinism began to penetrate into Germany (c. 1570), Lutheranism had already made considerable inroads into the population, and had become the official faith in many cases. The German Calvinists thus had to reckon not only with the Catholic Church, but with orthodox Lutherans as well, and could not count on special protection or assistance from the local magistrates. The result was that Reformed Protestantism became a minority faith in most areas, the faith of foreigners and the well-to-do, and therefore lacked a strong, indigenous base of the sort which it possessed in Switzerland, Scotland, England, the Netherlands, and even France. Under these circumstances, it was highly unlikely that the Calvinist movement would become a vehicle of political resistance, and more unlikely still that it would become a bearer of protodemocratic ideals. Thus, the situation in northwestern Germany, already somewhat less favorable to democratization in 1500, had grown hostile by 1600.

Of course, it would be facile to suggest that there was a direct or necessary connection between Calvinism and democracy, on the one hand, or between Lutheranism and authoritarianism on the other. In some cases, Calvinism was associated with absolutism, as in the Palatinate or Brandenburg. In others, Lutheranism was associated with antimonarchical resistance, as in the County of Lemgo or the Duchy of East Prussia. Nonetheless, it still seems fair to argue that there was a certain affinity between Calvinism and democracy – and between Lutheranism and authoritarianism. Virtually all of the early democratizers had a Calvinist past – even France.[20] Virtually all the Lutheran principalities developed in an absolutist direction, Sweden being the sole exception – and only a partial one at that. Hence, even if there was not a direct or necessary connection, then there does seem to have been an indirect and probabilistic one.

But what was the character of this connection? Why did Calvinism tend to be associated with republicanism and Lutheranism with absolutism? Three differences seem to have been key. The first had to do with Luther's and Calvin's understandings of the worldly and spiritual kingdoms, and the relation between them. Luther viewed the two kingdoms as distinct: the worldly kingdom is *weltlich*, which is to say "corrupt," and the spiritual kingdom is *geistlich*, which is to say "invisible." And because he viewed the kingdoms as distinct, he had a low opinion of political authority, and of its potential to transform the world. Lutheran doctrine thus had a deep (if not irresistible) affinity with (royal) conservatism and (popular) passivity. Calvin, by contrast, viewed the two kingdoms as inseparable: the worldly kingdom is the site of the spiritual battle between the forces of good and evil. Because he viewed the kingdoms as inseparable, he had a high opinion of worldly government, and of its capacity to change society. Indeed, he regarded politics as the highest of all worldly callings. Calvinist doctrine thus bore a profound (if not invariable) affinity towards (elite) activism and (popular) resistance. The second key difference had to do with Luther's and Calvin's understandings of the church. For Luther, the church was a sanctuary from the corruption of the world, a place where individual faith could be restored and renewed. If the church no longer dispensed grace, as it had under Roman dominion, it could at least

20. See Dale K. van Kley, *Religious Origins of the French Revolution* (New Haven: Yale University Press, 1996).

provide solace. For Calvin, by contrast, the church was a weapon for fighting the corruption of the world, the primary means through which God worked in the world. Its purpose was not to provide solace or grace, but rather to subjugate the community to the will of God. The Lutheran Church, to put it pointedly, served primarily as a vehicle for fleeing the world, while the Reformed Church effectively functioned as an instrument for transforming it – whence its much greater emphasis on discipline. Lutheranism and Calvinism thus tended to create different kinds of "personalities" and different kinds of societies, the one more susceptible to authoritarian rule, the other more suited to democratic governance. The third and final difference had to do with their attitudes towards the old and new covenants, and the relationship between them. For Luther, the disjunction between the two was complete: the new covenant abrogated the old. For Calvin, by contrast, the new covenant was a continuation of the old: grace was simply transferred from one chosen people to another. This made it possible for Calvin's followers to conceive of the new covenant in a collective and historical manner – that is, in quasi-nationalistic terms – which would have been unthinkable from a Lutheran standpoint.

The differences between Lutheran and Calvinist theology were actually smaller than the preceding paragraph might seem to suggest – smaller, for example, than those between Protestant and Catholic theology. But small differences sometimes have large consequences, particularly when they are allowed to work themselves out over long periods of time. This is perhaps why two paths, so close together in 1550, had diverged so widely by 1933.

Chapter 2

LIBERALIZATION AND DEMOCRATIZATION IN NINETEENTH AND TWENTIETH CENTURY GERMANY IN COMPARATIVE PERSPECTIVE

*Thomas Ertman**

Like the second wave before it, the third wave of democratization, which began in southern Europe and Latin America in the 1970s and finally arrived in the Soviet Bloc in the late 1980s, has sparked a renewed interest in that earlier process of liberalization and democratization that changed the political face of western Europe between the French Revolution and the end of the First World War and which suffered so many reverses during the interwar years. In reexamining this antecedent historical transformation, social scientists from a variety of disciplines have sought to derive general insights which might be relevant to today's democratizers. At the same time, recent developments have often cast

* An earlier version of this paper was presented at the annual meeting of the American Political Science Association in 1995. Generous financial assistance from the Humboldt-Stiftung during the revision process is gratefully acknowledged. Above all I would like to thank Andy Markovits for all the support, encouragement, and intellectual stimulation with which he has provided me over many, many years.

events prior to 1945 in a new light. Above all, they have once again raised the old question as to why Germany, in sharp contrast to its western neighbors, experienced such great difficulties in becoming a stable, democratic nation-state.

The German case has always occupied a central place within studies of nineteenth- and twentieth-century European political development. The primary reason for this is, of course, the world-historical significance of the collapse of democracy in Weimar and the triumph of Nazism in this culturally and economically advanced country. But for many observers, German exceptionalism did not begin in 1918 or 1933. Even before 1914, commentators both within Germany and abroad pointed to the ways in which the German state and its system of government differed from those of its western neighbors, France and Britain. Since 1933, prominent analysts with backgrounds as varied as those of Barrington Moore, Alexander Gerschenkron and Hans-Ulrich Wehler have posited a causal connection between pre-1914 German exceptionalism and the Nazi catastrophe which followed.

More recently, this idea of a German Sonderweg (special or aberrant path of development) has come under attack from a variety of quarters.[1] As the two most perceptive critics of the Sonderweg literature have stressed, its methodological underpinnings are weak, for it constructs an image of German exceptionalism before 1914 based on an idealized picture of British, French, and American conditions, rather than on a detailed comparison of the political system of imperial Germany and those of all other relevant western states.[2]

In this chapter, I seek to reevaluate the process of liberalization and democratization as it occurred (or failed to occur) under the Kaiserreich by correcting this methodological deficiency of the Sonderweg literature. By comparing Germany not just to France and Britain, but also to the other six economically advanced western European states of the pre-World War I period (Switzerland, Belgium, the Netherlands, Denmark, Norway, and Sweden), I hope to

1. For an overview of these recent attacks, see Stefan Berger, "Historians and Nation-Building in Germany after Unification," *Past and Present,* no. 148 (August 1995), pp. 187-222, especially pp. 188-200.

2. David Blackbourn and Geoff Eley, *The Peculiarities of German History* (Oxford: Oxford University Press, 1984), pp. 10-11.

distinguish in a more convincing way those features of Germany's political development prior to 1914 which were, in fact, unique. This broadly-based comparison will permit me, using Mill's "method of difference," to reject many of the reasons most often cited for this German exceptionalism. I will then employ the "method of agreement" by introducing new cases (Austria-Hungary, Russia) which share a common outcome but little else with the Kaiserreich in order to generate possible explanations for Germany's special fate and then test them against the historical evidence.[3] Finally, I will examine the broader consequences of imperial Germany's failure to make substantial progress towards parliamentarism before 1914 for the future course of that country's development and draw some broader implications from the German experience.

Re-examining German Exceptionalism before 1914

Despite differences in other areas, adherents of the Sonderweg thesis are generally in agreement on how one should characterize the imperial German state in the political realm. In contrast to Britain and France, which possessed stable parliamentary governments, wide suffrage, and a full range of well-protected civil liberties by the 1880's at the very latest, in the Kaiserreich executive power lay firmly in the hands of the hereditary monarch and his chosen chancellor. The Reichstag, by contrast, was a largely powerless body, at best an annoyance to the government and at worst a talking shop that enjoyed little public respect. True, that body was elected by universal manhood suffrage as early as 1871, but this "advanced" feature of the imperial constitution was more than offset by the fact that in the state of Prussia, which covered two thirds of the Reich's territory, the peculiar three-class voting system was still in use. Hence the common categorizations of the Kaiserreich as embodying "monarchical de-facto absolutism" (Bracher) or "autocratic, half-absolutist, pseudo-constitutionalism" (Wehler).[4]

3. On the use of the "method of difference" for macro-historical comparisons, see Theda Skocpol and Margaret Somers, "The Uses of Comparative History in Macrosocial Inquiry," in Theda Skocpol, *Social Revolutions in the Modern World* (Cambridge: Cambridge University Press, 1994), pp. 72-95, here at pp. 78-82.

As stated above, this characterization, which focuses on institutional differences between the liberal British and French polities on the one hand and the supposedly peculiar features of Wilhelmine government on the other, is in fact built upon a quite narrow basis for comparison. How can this basis for comparison be extended? If we assume that there is indeed something about the German outcome which is distinctive, then the method of difference dictates that other cases for comparison should be chosen which share as much in common with imperial Germany in other spheres of life, but which differ from that country in the area of political outcomes. In this way it may be possible to identify in a more controlled manner those factors which might have accounted for German exceptionalism. Since it is widely recognized that many other features of life, such as workforce distribution, degree of urbanization, and extent of literacy, vary directly with the level of economic development, it seems advisable first to identify those countries closest to Germany from an economic perspective.

Thanks to the exhaustive work of Paul Bairoch, we now possess reliable data on levels of per capita gross national product in nearly all European states from the early nineteenth century through World War I. If we examine these statistics for 1913, we find that the countries of Europe can be divided into two very distinct groups, the first consisting of ten advanced industrial states enjoying per capita GNP's of $680 or more in constant 1960 U.S. dollars, and a second group of ten less developed countries with a GNP per capita below $520. This first group, to which Germany belongs, contains nine states. In descending order of GNP per capita they are: Britain ($965), Switzerland ($964), Belgium ($894), Denmark ($862), the Netherlands ($754), Norway ($749), Germany ($743), France ($689), and Sweden ($680).[5]

What generalizations can one make about the nature of the political systems and the process of liberalization and democratiza-

4. Karl Dietrich Bracher, *Die Auflösung der Weimarer Republik* (Düsseldorf: Droste, 1984), p. 7; Hans-Ulrich Wehler, *Das Deutsche* Kaiserreich *1871-1918*, 5th edition (Göttingen: Vandenhoeck & Ruprecht, 1983), p. 63.

5. Paul Bairoch, "Europe's Gross National Product: 1800-1975," *Journal of European Economic History*, vol. 5, no. 2 (Fall 1975), pp. 273-340, here at p. 286. The ten less developed states are: Finland ($520), Austria-Hungary ($498), Italy

tion more generally in these nine highly developed western European states? In answering this question, I focus primarily on the time and the manner in which parliamentary government was introduced, since a necessary (though not sufficient) condition for the establishment of such a political regime is that the state in question also have institutionalized equality before the law and effectively protect a range of civil liberties. On the other hand, since parliamentary government does not presuppose any minimum level of enfranchisement, variations in the pattern of suffrage extension will also be noted.

Of the nine countries under consideration, three achieved full parliamentary government (or, in the case of Switzerland, its functional equivalent) by 1848: Britain, Belgium, and Switzerland. In Britain, the process of parliamentarization took place over the course of more than a century, beginning with the Glorious Revolution of 1688 (or perhaps even with the Civil War) and reaching completion by the 1780's at the latest, though it was not until 1834 that a British monarch last exercised his prerogative right to dismiss a government because of his disapproval of it.[6] The starting point for the eventual emergence in Britain of this full and exclusive responsibility of the executive to the legislature (the essence of parliamentary government) was a situation, in existence practically since the birth of Parliament in the thirteenth century, in which the executive power was taken to be the exclusive domain of the sovereign and his chosen advisors and officials. Legislative power, on the other hand, was to be shared by the representative body and the ruler, since the approval of the king, the lords and the commons was necessary in order to create any new law.

This combination of a separation of powers (independence of king from Parliament and vice versa) and power-sharing in the sphere of legislation is an example of a more general pattern of government known both at the time and in the current constitutional literature as "dualism."[7] It should be stressed here that exclusive

---

($441), Spain ($367), Romania ($336), Russia ($326), Greece ($322), Portugal ($292), Serbia ($284), and Bulgaria ($263). Bairoch estimates that the average European GNP per capita in 1913 was $534.

6. Klaus von Beyme, *Die parlamentarischen Regierungssysteme in Europa* (Munich: Piper, 1970), pp. 727-731.

control of the executive by the legislature did not emerge in England or indeed anywhere else in nineteenth century Europe as the result of programmatic demands by political progressives backed by widespread political mobilization. Indeed, "parliamentary government" as a theoretical construct did not even appear in the political philosophy literature until the mid-nineteenth century, when it was invented to account for the new balance of political forces, which had manifested itself at least half a century earlier in England.

Rather, parliamentarism emerged as the unintended consequence of the complex political struggles both within Parliament and between the monarch and the legislative body as a whole.[8] Because the king required support in Parliament to pass legislation, he was forced repeatedly to turn for assistance to those men who could provide such support. Similarly, parliamentarism always made more rapid advances during periods when party identities were stronger and discipline firmer as a result of the existence of strong cleavage lines, such as during the late 1670s (the Exclusion Crisis), the 1690s (in the aftermath of Glorious Revolution), the 1720s (in the aftermath of the Hanoverian Succession), and the 1790s (as a reaction to the French Revolution).

In Belgium as well, parliamentary government emerged between 1833 and 1847 out of a dualist order that, unlike the British case, was set down in a formal constitution adopted after the separation from the Netherlands in 1830.[9] Only in Switzerland was the pattern different, with the election of the collegial executive emerging in 1848 following a civil war (the Sonderbundkrieg) that swept away

7. Ibid., p. 30; Thomas Nipperdey, *Deutsche Geschichte 1800-1866: Bürgerwelt und starker Staat* (Munich: Beck, 1993), pp. 295-296. The English traditionally captured this dualism with the claim that sovereignty in the kingdom rested neither exclusively with the king nor Parliament, but rather with the king *in* Parliament.

8. Dankart Rustow makes a similar point based in part on a comparison of the British and Swedish cases in his article, "Transitions to Democracy: Toward a Dynamic Model," *Comparative Politics*, vol. 2, no. 2 (April 1970), pp. 337-363, here at pp. 352-363.

9. For the earlier date see von Beyme, *Parlamentarische Regierungssysteme*, pp. 124-128. For the later date see Aristide Zolberg, "Belgium," in: Raymond Grew (ed.), *Crises of Political Development in Europe and the United States* (Princeton: Princeton University Press, 1978), pp. 99-138, here at p. 111.

the old confederal structure which had been restored in 1815 in the wake of the demise of the Helvetic Republic.[10]

The pattern of parliamentarization found in France exhibits certain parallels to the British and Belgian cases, but in a much more complicated and drawn-out form. The Restoration introduced a dualistic constitutional monarchy into the country, and by the 1820s something approaching parliamentary government had emerged out of the complicated interplay of daily politics. Indeed, it was a royal attempt to reverse this development which led to the Revolution of 1830 and the advent of the July Monarchy. The constitution of this new regime was once again formally dualistic, but de facto parliamentarism quickly reappeared.

While this parliamentarism was finally recognized formally in the constitution of the Second Republic, inaugurated in 1848, that regime preserved a remnant of the dualist principle in the person of a directly elected president with broad executive powers, thereby setting the stage for the reappearance of a new kind of dualism in the imperial polity of Napoleon III. Here again, strong tendencies towards parliamentarism reemerged in the late 1860s as Napoleon, reeling from several foreign policy defeats, sought increasingly to buttress his position with the help of majorities in the National Assembly. It was only after the collapse of the Second Empire in the wake of the Franco-Prussian War and after the executive pretensions of Marshal MacMahon were defeated, that legislative control of the executive combined with the universal manhood suffrage which had survived since 1848 to produce the parliamentary democracy of the Third Republic.

The pattern of parliamentarization found in four of the other states under consideration (the Netherlands, Norway, Denmark, and Sweden) is much closer to that of Britain and Belgium than that of France, although, as in France, parliamentary government did not make an irreversible breakthrough in any of these countries until well after 1848. As in Britain and Belgium, the starting point for a gradual process of parliamentarization was in all of these cases a dualistic constitutional monarchy, established (as in Belgium)

---

10. William Martin, *Histoire de la Suisse* (Lausanne: Librairie Payot, 1943), pp. 257-271.

through a written constitution introduced in two instances in connection with the upheavals of the Napoleonic period (1809 in Sweden and 1814 in Norway) and in two others with the events of 1848 (1848 in the Netherlands and 1849 in Denmark).

As in Britain and Belgium, the transition from dualist to parliamentary government occurred gradually, and often with reverses, out of the complex interplay of everyday politics and without either substantial popular agitation or formal changes in the constitution. As a result, parliamentary government was firmly established in the Netherlands in 1868, Norway in 1884, and Denmark in 1901. While the definitive triumph of parliamentarism in Sweden can only be dated to 1917, an early experiment with parliamentary government had already taken place between 1880 and 1883, and after 1905 governments headed by party leaders were the norm, even though the king was not yet willing to abandon his prerogatives for all time. In the Netherlands and Norway, as in Britain and Belgium, universal manhood suffrage was introduced after full parliamentarization, whereas it arrived before full parliamentarization in Denmark and Sweden.[11]

How does the German case fit in with those discussed above? While political development in nineteenth century Germany may indeed have diverged strongly from the patterns found in either contemporaneous Britain or France outlined above, in fact it had very much in common with the experience of the four "late parliamentarizers" just mentioned. As in these polities, dualistic systems of government based on written constitutions often directly inspired by similar French documents of 1791 or 1814 were introduced into the various German territories in waves following the upheavals of 1815, 1830, and 1848.[12] Following unification in 1871,

11. Stein Rokkan, "Nation-Building, Cleavage Formation, and the Structuring of Mass Politics," in Rookan, *Citizens, Elections, Parties* (New York: David McKay, 1970), pp. 72-144, here at pp. 84-85. In the Netherlands, suffrage extensions were granted in 1887 and 1896, and universal manhood suffrage took effect in 1917. In Norway, suffrage was extended in 1885 and universal manhood suffrage arrived in 1898. In Denmark, on the other hand, universal manhood suffrage took effect in 1849, and in Sweden, the extension of suffrage occurred in 1866, and universal manhood suffrage was granted in 1909.

12. Dieter Grimm, *Deutsche Verfassungsgeschichte 1776-1866* (Frankfurt: Suhrkamp, 1988), pp. 74-75, 161, 215-216, 229. Bavaria and Baden introduced

those German states not annexed by Prussia remained in existence, but above them now stood an imperial government also organized as a dualistic constitutional monarchy, but with a lower house (the Reichstag) elected by universal manhood suffrage rather than the property-based franchises found in the territorial states.

The constitutional dualism of the German principalities – including Prussia – and of the Reich differed in no fundamental way from the political regimes found in the Netherlands, Norway, Denmark, and Sweden and, earlier, in Britain and Belgium before the triumph of full parliamentarism. In Germany as in these states, the government was appointed by and directly responsible to the ruler, whose prerogative it was to exercise full executive powers. At the same time, however, it was incumbent upon the government to find majorities in the legislature in order to pass new laws and, more importantly still, the budget, which, in the case of the Reich, financed the armed forces.

There is little evidence that governments in Germany engaged in electoral manipulation or fraud like their counterparts in Spain, France, or England. This meant that German legislatures – including the Prussian Landtag – proved no more amenable to direct royal control than did the Dutch States General, the Norwegian Storting, the Danish Folketing or the Swedish Riksdag. Indeed, even Bismarck spent a good portion of his time as chancellor painstakingly constructing working parliamentary majorities.

Furthermore, in Germany as in both the early and late parliamentarizers, ideological support for the dualist model of constitutional monarchy ran deep not only among conservatives but also among many progressives. In England, even Whigs remained attached to the idea of the sovereignty of the "king in Parliament" and of "mixed government" until well into the nineteenth century, and no fully-fledged theory of "parliamentary government" emerged there until Bagehot's famous work appeared in 1867. The strong attachment in the Kaiserreich even among liberals to dualism, or "German constitutionalism" as it was called, was common among

---

their constitutions in 1818, Württemberg in 1819, Hessen-Darmstadt in 1821, Hessen-Kassel and Saxony in 1831, Braunschweig in 1832, Hannover in 1833, Prussia in 1850, and Austria in 1848 and 1861.

the late parlamentarizers during the second half of the nineteenth century.[13] Thus J. R. Thorbecke (1798-1872), the great Dutch liberal leader and father of parliamentary government in practice, remained a supporter of dualism in his theoretical writings, including in a commentary on the 1848 constitution for which he was largely responsible.[14] The Norwegians long retained a special attachment to the dualist constitution of 1814, and the Swedes developed during the last quarter of the nineteenth century a theory of nonparliamentary "Swedish constitutionalism," which mirrored almost exactly its German counterpart. In none of these countries was the introduction of parliamentary government the result of broad popular mobilization. As in Germany, such mobilization as there was surrounding constitutional issues was directed at suffrage reform (in the German case, elimination of three-class voting in Prussia and later Saxony). Finally, it is also worth noting that tax-weighted voting of the kind found in the infamous three-class system was by no means unique to Germany, but was used in Scandinavia as well, at least at the local level.

So if political theory and practice in imperial Germany was similar throughout much of the second half of the nineteenth century to that of its neighbors, was the Kaiserreich in any way exceptional in the political sphere? The answer is most certainly yes. What was different about imperial Germany was *not* its constitutional dualism and its institutions of government more generally, as is often alleged, but rather the failure of that dualist system to show any sign of movement in a parliamentary direction. In all the other cases we have mentioned, dualist systems proved to be unstable over the long term, with the dynamics of daily politics pushing them uniformly and inexorably toward parliamentarism. Even in Sweden, the country most resembling imperial Germany in its domestic politics, tangible signs of a transition to parliamentarism were clearly visible as early as the 1880s, and government was already semiparliamentary after 1905. One looks in vain for any comparable developments within the Kaiserreich.

13. von Beyme, *Parlamentarische Regierungssysteme*, pp. 238-242; Nipperdey, *Deutsche Geschichte*, pp. 295-296.
14. von Beyme, *Parlamentarische Regierungssysteme*, p. 282.

In summary, a broader comparative analysis indicates that examining imperial Germany only from a British or French (or American) perspective is highly misleading, because this implies that there was something peculiar about the Kaiserreich's institutional arrangements or dominant political ideology. A brief glance at smaller, wealthy late industrializers like the Netherlands and the Scandinavian kingdoms quickly undermines this component of the Sonderweg argument. At the same time, these additional cases underscore the fact that what was truly different about late nineteenth and early twentieth century Germany was the failure of its dualist government to evolve into parliamentarism. It is thus the "blocked" character of imperial Germany's dualism, rather than its existence per se, that requires explanation.

Accounting for Germany's Absent Transition to Parliamentarism

While a comparison with nineteenth and early twentieth century Europe's eight other most economically advanced states may not by itself provide us with a definitive answer as to why the Kaiserreich failed to continue down the path followed by its neighbors, it can help us to eliminate explanations often generated by looking only to the British and French cases as points of reference. Thus late, rapid industrialization cannot provide the key to Germany's political exceptionalism, for all four late parliamentarizers also share this characteristic. Likewise the argument, presented by Barrington Moore and many subsequent commentators, that it was Germany's lack of a successful bourgeois revolution which determined its subsequent course of development looks at first glance convincing when the triumphs of the English, French, and Belgian uprisings are contrasted with the failure of the Paulskirche in 1848. However, none of the late parlamentarizers experienced bourgeois revolutions either, and yet this did not prevent them arriving at the same end point as Britain, France, and Belgium, although it may have taken longer to do so.[15]

---

15. Robert Dahl also criticizes Barrington Moore's stress on the significance of bourgeois revolutions in the process of democratization in his *Polyarchy* (New

Finally, Max Weber first suggested that certain institutional features of the German constitution of 1871 – most notably a clause (article 9) which for all practical purposes barred the imperial chancellor and the secretaries of state (ministers) from membership in the Reichstag – might have prevented the Kaiserreich from advancing towards parliamentarism. Yet such "incompatibility clauses," the aim of which was to uphold the separation of powers within a dualist system, were also present in both the Dutch and Norwegian constitutions. In neither instance did this practical obstacle prove fatal to the cause of parliamentarism.[16]

A closer comparison of the Kaiserreich with Denmark and Sweden also makes it possible to discard a number of common explanations for German political exceptionalism. For example, it is often claimed that the early appearance in Germany, as compared to Britain or France, of a radical, explicitly Marxist workers' movement organized around a powerful social democratic party rendered any further parliamentarization of the Reich impossible, since it would have opened the door of government to the much-feared Social Democrats (SPD). By the 1890s, Denmark and Sweden also possessed strong social democratic movements, both directly inspired by and modeled upon the German SPD. Indeed, fourteen social democrats already sat in the Danish Folketing in 1901, and their Swedish counterparts had already come to form the largest single group in the second chamber of the Riksdag by 1914. Yet in neither case did the presence of a radical workers movement prevent a breakthrough to parliamentary government.[17]

Similarly, the presence in Germany of a conservative bureaucracy and an influential class of large landowners (the Junkers),

---

Haven: Yale University Press, 1971), p. 45. Timothy Tilton has made a similar point in relation to Sweden alone in his article "The Social Origins of Liberal Democracy: The Swedish Case," *American Political Science Review*, vol. 68, no. 2 (June 1974), pp. 561-571, here at p. 569.

16. Max Weber, "Parlament und Regierung im neugeordneten Deutschland," in Weber, *Gesammelte Politische Schriften* (Tübingen: J.C.B. Mohr, 1980), pp. 306-443, here at pp. 342-344; von Beyme, *Parlamentarische Regierungssysteme*, pp. 233-234, 283, 571-572.

17. T. K. Derry, *A History of Scandinavia* (Minneapolis: University of Minnesota Press, 1979), p. 266; Michael Metcalf (ed.), *The Riksdag: A History of the Swedish Parliament* (New York: St. Martin's, 1987), p. 217.

both strongly opposed to further democratization, has been cited by all adherents of the Sonderweg thesis as a major reason for the Kaiserreich's political exceptionalism. Once again the examples of Denmark and Sweden cast doubt upon this argument. During the seventeenth and eighteenth centuries, both polities built up non-proprietary, professional administrations modeled closely on those of the German principalities, and by the late 1800s there were no state apparatuses that more resembled those of Prussia and of the German Reich in terms of recruitment patterns, training, internal organization, and ethos than those of Denmark and, to an even greater extent, Sweden. As in Germany, the Danish and Swedish sovereigns often chose professional administrators as ministers prior to the advent of full parliamentarization, and in both cases state officials were largely opposed to the latter development, but in the end proved powerless to prevent it.

The case of the Junkers looks more promising, for it is taken as an article of faith by most authors on the subject – most recently, for example, by Dietrich Rueschemeyer, Evelyne Huber Stephens, and John Stephens – that agriculture in the Nordic countries was dominated by small and medium-sized peasant proprietors, whereas in Germany the dominance of the Junkers continued unbroken through World War I and beyond. This key difference in the structure of agriculture, it is alleged, is ultimately what propelled the Scandinavian kingdoms down a separate, more democratic path of development despite the great cultural influence long exercised by Germany upon the statebuilding process in those countries.[18]

While this claim may be true for Norway, it is not supported by the evidence as far as Denmark and Sweden are concerned. In the first decades of this century, large estates (greater than 50-60 hectares or 125-150 acres) covered 33 percent of the arable land in Denmark, 30 percent in Germany and 20 percent in Sweden, whereas medium-sized peasant holdings (5-50 hectares or 12.5-125 acres) accounted for a clear majority of farmland in all three

---

18. Dietrich Rueschemeyer, Evelyne Huber Stephens, and John Stephens, *Capitalist Development and Democracy* (Cambridge: Polity Press, 1992), pp. 80, 83-84, 91-92. These authors explicitly acknowledge their debt to Barrington Moore for this argument.

countries (Denmark: 62 percent, Germany: 54.1 percent, Sweden: c. 50 percent).[19] Even in their heartland of eastern Prussia, Junker estates covered only 40.5 percent of all arable land.[20] In fact, as these numbers indicate, agricultural structure was largely similar in all three cases, especially when compared to countries like Austria and Hungary, where 48 percent of all land was grouped in large estates, or the United Kingdom, where the corresponding figure was 70 percent.[21] Hence despite all of the opprobrium directed at the Junkers in both the contemporary and the subsequent academic literature, it remains to be demonstrated that they played a significant role in preventing the advent of parliamentary government in their country before 1918, something their counterparts in Denmark and Sweden proved unable to do.

If a more broadly-based macro-comparative analysis indicates that neither late industrialization, nor the absence of a bourgeois revolution, nor institutional barriers, nor the social democratic threat, nor reactionary bureaucrats and Junkers can account for imperial Germany's absent transition to parliamentary government, then what can? While the comparative method may not provide a definitive answer, it can perhaps generate some plausible candidates. After having cast doubt upon the causes enumerated above, several factors still remain which do seem to have been relatively unique to the Kaiserreich and hence might explain its divergent outcome. The first of these is late and incomplete unification (12 million Germans remained outside the Reich) and the problems associated with national identity and national integration which resulted from this. A second factor that set Germany apart from the other late parliamentarizers with which it had most in common (though not from Britain and France) was its position as a great power and the intense geo-political pressures associated with this,

19. Jerome Blum, *The End of the Old Order in Rural Europe* (Princeton: Princeton University Press, 1978), p. 437; Friedrich-Wilhelm Henning, *Landwirtschaft und ländliche Gesellschaft in Deutschland. Band 2: 1750 bis 1976* (Paderborn: Ferdinand Schöningh, 1978), p. 150; G. Westin Silverstolpe, *Svenskt Näringsliv i Tjugonde Seklet* (Stockholm: Kooperativa Förbundets Bokförlag, 1938), p. 33.

20. Alan Milward and S. B. Saul, *The Development of the Economies of Continental Europe 1850-1914* (Cambridge: Harvard University Press, 1977), p. 57.

21. Clive Trebilcock, *The Industrialization of the Continental Powers 1780-1914* (London: Longman, 1981), pp. 86, 328.

pressures that were subsequently exacerbated by the country's desire to become a global, as opposed to a merely European, force.

Momentarily widening the range of cases considered to include the continent's less economically developed states provides some initial support for the hypothesis that it was a combination of insufficient national integration and great power aspirations which played a decisive role in determining Germany's subsequent domestic political trajectory. It is striking that the only two other European countries that made no progress towards parliamentarization before World War I – Austria-Hungary and Russia – were precisely the states which, despite many other differences, shared these two factors with imperial Germany.

But what was the precise mechanism which permitted these factors to block the arrival of parliamentary government in the Kaiserreich? In none of the cases mentioned above did parliamentarization come about because the sovereign willingly relinquished his executive prerogatives or because he was forced to do so by broadly-based popular mobilization aimed at eliminating the dualist system. Rather, it was the need to find working majorities with their respective legislatures which eventually drove monarchs into the arms of opposition politicians who could command those majorities. At the most superficial level, this never happened in imperial Germany because the Kaiser and his chancellors were always able to find a majority, usually consisting of some combination of conservatives, liberals, and Catholics, to pass the only item of legislation which really mattered: the federal budget which financed much of the armed forces. In practical terms, it was the support provided after 1890 by the entire non-socialist political spectrum – from conservatives through right- and left-liberals to Catholics – for the government's policy of Weltpolitik which permitted the constitutional status quo to continue until nearly the end of World War I.

Furthermore, the majority of Reichstag deputies did more than simply support the government on matters of finance and defense. They, along with the much of the rest of the German intelligentsia on both the right and even the moderate left, actually believed that the introduction of parliamentarism – from which they would personally benefit – would threaten Germany's newly won position on the international stage.[22] Thus in an argument repeated by many others, the far from reactionary Otto Hintze maintained that constitutional dualism was a more suitable system for Germany than parliamentarism because if the executive were directly responsible to the people (through their chosen representatives), the fractious and poorly integrated nature of German society, itself a consequence of late unification, would soon result in weak government which would prove incapable of defending the country's foreign policy interests.[23]

Thus it appears to have been a combination of the pressures associated with intense geo-political competition on first a continental and then a global scale – competition which was in part at least inevitable given Germany's size and geographic position – and perceived internal divisions resulting from late and incomplete national integration which seems to have led the majority of German political society before 1914 to reject parliamentary government for the country's special situation. The consequences of this rejection for Germany's future development would be far-reaching.

Historical and Theoretical Implications

This result, however, begs two final questions. First, why did imperial Germany's failure to introduce parliamentary government before World War I matter? And what is the broader theoretical significance of the explanation for German political exceptionalism outlined above?

As to the first question, the persistence of dualism until late 1917 or 1918 meant that when military pressures finally did force a political opening, with the concomitant arrival of parliamentarism, that parliamentarism quickly became identified with defeat and humiliation. The fathers of the Weimar constitution reacted to this unfortunate association by reintroducing the dualism linked in the public mind with happier times into the new state in the form of a mixed parliamentary-presidential system of rule. This failure to intro-

22. von Beyme, *Parlamentarische Regierungssysteme*, pp. 238-246.

23. Otto Hintze, "Das Verfassungsleben der heutigen Kulturstaaten," in Hintze, *Staat und Verfassung*, ed. Gerhard Oestreich (Göttingen: Vandenhoeck & Ruprecht, 1970), pp. 390-423, here at pp. 399-400.

duce full parliamentary government even after the upheaval of World War I had especially grave consequences for Germany because of the presence there, as in the other wealthy late industrializers – the Netherlands, Norway, Denmark, and Sweden – of powerful, relatively centralized organized interest groups. As the experiences of those four countries during the interwar years show, such groups can be made to work together, even under the conditions of extreme economic upheaval prevalent at that time, provided they are operating within a pure parliamentary political system that forces mutual accommodation upon leading political and social actors by eliminating all other sources of executive power (monarch, president) not based upon alliance building and compromise within the legislature.

This point can be underlined by considering the divergent fates of the Reich and Prussian governments during Weimar. Whereas the former with its dualism remained weak and unstable right down until 1933, the Prussian government, based as it was upon pure parliamentarism but otherwise representing a perfect microcosm of the Reich as a whole, remained a model of stability until von Papen destroyed it from above in 1932. Furthermore, it could also be argued that the key institutional difference between the contentious, unstable Weimar Republic and the prosperous Bonn Republic (or indeed the compromise-oriented Scandinavian democracies) lies not so much in either attitudes or organizational forms found within civil society, both of which have changed less across the various twentieth century German regimes than one might think, but rather in the introduction for the first time ever of pure parliamentarism into West Germany after 1949.

As to the second question, the results of this comparison seem to indicate that, contrary to a widely held assumption, it may be possible to industrialize rapidly and democratize at the same time as long as one lays aside grandiose geopolitical ambitions (the experience of all of the four late parliamentarizers and Belgium and Switzerland as well). However, it is far less likely that economic modernization, political liberalization and great power aspirations can all be combined successfully, especially if national identity or national integration are fragile. This hypothesis casts the contemporary experience and future choices of rising powers like China, India, Indonesia, and Brazil in a new and interesting light.

Chapter 3

GERMANY ON THE GLOBAL STAGE
The U.S.-German Relationship after Unification

∽⌇∽

*Karen Donfried**

Unified Germany is in a position to take a more assertive role in world affairs than was possible in the Cold War era, when foreign policy in a divided Germany was largely consumed by the contest of political and security issues that two competing alliance systems played out on its soil. After the Second World War, West Germany anchored its economy in the European Community and depended on NATO for military security. Leaders of the united Germany assert that the state's external policies will continue to be expressed through international institutions, a move in part meant to reassure those concerned about a Germany of increasing power and influence. At the same time Germany's restored sovereignty, strong economy, and geographic position provide it with a greater voice in shaping the course of those institutions. Some observers criticize Germany for not playing a greater international role, particularly in the area of peacekeeping and peacemaking, while others express uneasiness over what they see as increased German assertiveness in the international arena.

*   This paper was last updated in January 1998.

Thus, questions remain about the substance and style of German foreign policy. The answers to these questions are critical for defining the future course of German-American relations. In addressing these issues, I will explore three areas. First, I review the participation of the Bundeswehr in international military missions – arguably, the area of German foreign policy in the 1990s in which change has been most striking. My conclusion in this section is that, while Germany has undergone a dramatic transformation in terms of the use of the military, policy in this area remains tempered by a desire to participate only in multilateral missions sanctioned by the United Nations. Military force is thus a viable option for Germany only in this restricted context. Second, I examine the implications of greater German global activism for U.S. policy, looking at the examples of German participation in the NATO-led force in Bosnia and German policy toward Iran. In the case of Iran, Germany has been willing to pursue a policy distinct from that of Washington. Finally, I suggest how transatlantic cooperation after the Cold War might be enhanced. One concrete example of how links are already being strengthened is the training of German troops in the United States.

German Participation in International Military Missions

The primary focus of united Germany's foreign policy is on its immediate European environment. West Germany played a crucial role in constructing the European Community (EC) and reaching out to eastern Europe through *Ostpolitik*, while limiting its role on the international stage. In the post-war years, a "culture of reticence" took root in West Germany. Germany's dark past, including Hitler, militarism, and the Holocaust, led policy-makers to avoid unilateralism and seek to embed West Germany in multilateral institutions, such as the EC, the North Atlantic Treaty Organization (NATO), and the United Nations. West Germans labored to gain the trust of their neighbors, to demonstrate that the days of German power politics and aggressive ambitions were over. The resulting reticence was most evident in the area of military operations abroad. The

West German constitution was understood to forbid an "out-of-area" military role for its armed forces. West Germans proved to be generous contributors to the budget of the United Nations and in the area of development assistance, but when international political leadership or military contributions were called for, Germans kept a low profile. The allies of West Germany, including the United States, appeared to support this division of labor.

The international system changed fundamentally with the end of the Cold War, the revolutions throughout eastern Europe, and the disintegration of the Soviet Union. With German unification, the United States came to expect that Germany would play a larger global role. The Bush administration spoke of "partners in leadership" and appeared to envision increased sharing of responsibility with the Germans. When the Germans proved unwilling or unable to contribute forces and instead offered substantial financial support, such as during the Gulf War, critics complained about German "checkbook diplomacy." Many felt that Germany could no longer absolve itself of military responsibilities in the international arena.

Following unification, the issue of what role German troops should play abroad became a central topic of political debate in Germany. Since 1991, under the tutelage of Chancellor Kohl, Germany has been playing a larger global role. However, the deeply rooted "culture of reticence" reflected in German public opinion has meant that the changes in foreign policy have been evolutionary, rather than revolutionary. Many Germans interpreted their constitution as strictly limiting military involvement outside of the NATO area. Chancellor Kohl did not believe the constitution imposed such limits, but, in order to build a societal consensus around a broader understanding of the role of the German military, he committed himself to revising the constitution in a way that would clearly permit German forces under U.N. or other multilateral auspices to operate in and outside of Europe. The opposition Social Democrats (SPD), whose support was necessary in parliament to bring about constitutional change, believed that German forces should participate only in U.N. peacekeeping, not combat, missions. Thus, agreement on a suitable constitutional amendment appeared unattainable. Instead, the Social Democrats and, at one point, the Free Democrats (Kohl's coalition partner) brought cases before the Constitutional Court on the correct interpretation of the constitution.

While the political and legal debate continued, the Kohl government took steps to widen the role of the German military. In 1992 and 1993, German military personnel participated in multilateral operations in Cambodia, the former Yugoslavia, and Somalia. In mid-May 1992, 140 German army medics left for Cambodia to take part in a United Nations peacekeeping force. The U.N. mission there ended officially on 31 August 1993; one German soldier was killed.

The war in the former Yugoslavia posed the next military challenge. On 15 July 1992, Germany announced plans to join the joint sea and air patrol assembled by the Western European Union (WEU) and NATO to enforce United Nations sanctions against Serbia and Montenegro. The SPD greeted that decision by bringing a charge before the Constitutional Court on 9 August, claiming the government had overstepped its powers because it did not consult the parliament before sending soldiers abroad. Despite this SPD opposition, Chancellor Kohl proceeded to commit more German resources to efforts to stop the fighting in the former Yugoslavia. On 22 November 1992, NATO and WEU established a naval blockade of Serbia and Montenegro in the Adriatic, in which a German destroyer participated with some restrictions. In late March 1993, the German air force joined U.S. and French military aircraft to air-drop emergency supplies to eastern Bosnia. German crews also comprised 30 percent of NATO's AWACS aircraft fleet engaged in monitoring Bosnian airspace. Kohl's Christian Democratic Party endorsed the use of these crews in enforcing a U.N.-sanctioned no-fly zone, but the foreign minister's Free Democratic Party (FDP) argued that, if the U.N. were to request NATO to use force against aircraft in Bosnia's airspace, Germany could not participate without violating the German constitution. In early April 1993, the Free Democrats, joined by the opposition Social Democrats, petitioned the Constitutional Court for an injunction to ban German involvement in enforcing the no-fly zone. The FDP wanted to establish a clear legal basis for German involvement in enforcing the no-fly zone, whereas the SPD wanted that involvement to end. The court cleared the way for

German participation in the no-fly operation, maintaining that Germany's credibility as a reliable NATO partner and its international standing would suffer if the German crews withdrew.

German participation in the U.N. operation in Somalia represented the first time armed German forces had been deployed outside the NATO area since the creation of the Bundeswehr in 1955. The Kohl government announced on April 20, 1993 that it would send roughly 1,700 soldiers to help in the reconstruction of Somalia under U.N. operational control, in response to a direct request from the U.N. secretary-general. The first contingent of German troops arrived in Somalia in May 1993. The soldiers, the last of whom returned to Germany in March 1994, were deployed in areas where there was no fighting among Somali clans and were allowed to use weapons only in self-defense. Bundeswehr troops killed one Somali intruder on January 21, 1994. The SPD petitioned the Constitutional Court on the Somalia mission as well.

Together with the military activities outlined above, a German defense white paper released in early April 1994 seemed to confirm a fundamental shift in German defense policy. The white paper stated that Germany would create a rapid reaction force for foreign deployment in peacekeeping and international crisis management missions. German defense planners appeared to assume that the Constitutional Court would rule in favor of the international deployment of German forces.

On July 12, 1994, the Constitutional Court ruled that German troops could take part in both U.N. peacekeeping and peacemaking missions, as long as the Bundestag approved each operation by a simple majority. The 142-page decision specified that Germany can assign forces to NATO and WEU operations directed at implementing resolutions of the U.N. Security Council. The court thus rejected the objections raised about German participation in the NATO/WEU naval blockade in the Adriatic, in the AWACS monitoring over Bosnia-Herzegovina, and in the U.N. mission in Somalia.[1] The SPD's efforts to undermine the chancellor's decision to widen the role of the German military had failed.

---

1. Press Release issued by Federal Constitutional Court, Karlsruhe, No. 29/94, 12 July 1994.

The Court's ruling gave the constitutional green light for German participation in U.N. military operations (in other words, the Germans would not march off to a foreign battlefield on their own), but it shed no light on which political criteria the German government would use in choosing when and where to get involved. However, German officials have stated that they will exercise extreme caution in deciding which U.N. missions German soldiers will participate in. In the words of Defense Minister Rühe, the Court's decision "is not a marching order for worldwide deployment, as is constantly claimed, but a responsible decision will be made in each and every case. Our main responsibility lies in Europe and in the areas near to it."[2] Foreign Minister Kinkel pointed out that Germany will continue its "policy of restraint," saying "no more often than yes" when asked to participate militarily.[3]

The immediate case facing the German government was the war in the former Yugoslavia. No German soldiers participated in the United Nations Protection Force (UNPROFOR), and Germany had stated that it would not put ground troops in Bosnia because of Germany's controversial history in the region. On 30 November 1994, NATO military command requested six to eight Tornado fighter-bombers with special electronic capabilities to use against Serbian surface-to-air missile batteries and to protect NATO air patrols over Bosnia. Reportedly, Chancellor Kohl leaned toward approving the request, but he was unsure that he could muster the parliamentary majority necessary to approve such an action and thus chose not to pursue it.[4] Kohl apparently did not want to set a negative precedent following the Constitutional Court ruling in July. Early in December, NATO then asked Bonn how it might be willing to assist the withdrawal of UNPROFOR from Bosnia, should that be necessary. The German government

2. Speech by Defense Minister Volker Rühe in Bonn at a special Bundestag session, N-TV, 22 July 1994, in *Federal Broadcast Information Service – West Europe-94-142*, 25 July 1994, p. 28.

3. Interview with Foreign Minister Klaus Kinkel by Heribert Prantl, *Süddeutsche Zeitung*, 16 July 1994, p. 12, as translated in *FBIS-WEU-94-137*, 18 July 1994, p. 15.

4. Rick Atkinson, "Germany Debates Whether to Join NATO Air Mission Over Bosnia," *Washington Post*, 3 December 1994, p. A26; Craig Whitney, "Germany Ignores a NATO Request for Planes," *New York Times*, 8 December 1994, p. A8.

responded on 21 December, saying that it would provide logistical assistance and combat air cover. In terms of actual equipment, Bonn would offer NATO the use of six to eight Tornado jets for missions against Serb anti-aircraft emplacements, another six Tornado jets for reconnaissance missions, up to 12 Transall transport aircraft, a squadron of minesweepers, a patrol boat unit, and a field hospital. These plans called for the deployment of over 1,000 German soldiers in the former Yugoslavia. Consensus prevailed in Bonn in favor of showing solidarity with its closest allies in the event of a withdrawal.

In early June 1995, the Kohl government announced that it would participate in NATO military support for a redeployment of UNPROFOR to more defensible locations in Bosnia, and that it was considering whether to provide Tornado jets as part of this. On 30 June, the Bundestag approved a government motion to assign roughly 1,500 German troops to protect and support the U.N. Rapid Reaction Force (RRF) in the former Yugoslavia. The German contingent could assist with a withdrawal of UNPROFOR if that became necessary.

The forces assigned to the RRF included eight ECR-Tornados (capable of detecting and destroying surface-to-air missile sites), six Tornados for reconnaissance to be stationed in Italy, two Breguet Atlantic aircraft for electronic reconnaissance to be stationed in Italy, up to 12 Transall transport aircraft based in Germany for logistical support of U.N. forces outside Bosnia, a military hospital to be operated with French troops in Croatia, and German liaison personnel to NATO and U.N. headquarters. In the event of a U.N. troop withdrawal, Germany would also make a minesweeper flotilla and a speedboat flotilla available. For 1995, the costs estimated for this deployment totaled roughly $241 million.[5]

This deployment marked the first time that Germany has assigned combat units to a U.N. mission. Opposition politicians criticized the deployment, arguing that the use of the German military would escalate the conflict in light of the atrocities Nazi troops had committed during World War II. The government maintained that

5. "Germany Commits Troops to UN Rapid Reaction Force," *Spotlight on ...*, Washington: German Embassy, 30 June 1995.

Germany had to show solidarity with its NATO allies and signal its willingness to shoulder international burdens. On 1 September 1995, German Air Force planes flew reconnaissance missions over Bosnia, risking combat for the first time since World War II.

On 28 November 1995, Chancellor Kohl's cabinet decided to commit 4,000 troops for 12 months to the NATO-led Implementation Force (IFOR) to safeguard the peace in Bosnia. German soldiers primarily have supported logistics, transport, medical, and engineering units; most of them were stationed in Croatia. Germany's difficult history in the region and sensitivity there to a German military presence explains why the government chose to play largely a support role in IFOR with its troops based in a neighboring state. The contribution to IFOR represents the largest military mission deployed by Germany outside the NATO area since 1945. The Bundestag approved this plan by a wide majority on 6 December, with most of the opposition Social Democrats and many Greens voting with the government. Opinion polls suggest that most Germans approve of German participation in the Bosnia mission. The government's decision to contribute to the NATO force has been widely interpreted as further evidence of Chancellor Kohl's desire for Germany to accept greater responsibility for European security.[6]

The clarification and widening of the role German troops can play in international military missions following unification has been striking. Germany's allies, including the United States, have welcomed Germany's greater willingness to share military responsibilities on a global scale.

German-American Relations after Unification

When Helmut Kohl visited Washington in February 1995, the President declared: "America has no better friend than Chancellor

6. Also, on 7 February 1996, Chancellor Kohl's cabinet and on 9 February, the German Parliament approved the deployment of Tornado fighter-bombers to support the U.N. peace mission in the Serb-occupied Croatian region of Eastern Slavonia. "Auf Grundzuge eines deutschen Beitrags für Bosnien geeinigt," *Frankfurter Allgemeine Zeitung*, 12 October 1995, pp. 1, 2; Robert Birnbaum, "Bonn to offer troops to keep peace in Bosnia," *Reuters*, 11 October 1995; "Most Germans back sending troops on Bosnia mission," *Reuters*, 14 October 1995.

Kohl."[7] The Clinton administration views Germany as a critical ally and has repeatedly called on it to assume greater international responsibilities.[8] Interestingly, Clinton's July 1994 visit to Germany coincided with the Constitutional Court's decision on a global role for the Bundeswehr. In responding to a journalist's question about the decision, President Clinton said that he was "completely comfortable" with it:

> [O]f course, I can envision German forces being involved in something like the United Nations' effort in the Gulf. Why: because of the leadership of Germany; because of the conduct of Germany; because of the role Germany has played in developing the European Union; because of the values Germany has demonstrated in taking hundreds of thousands of refugees from Bosnia. Germany, now united is – yes, it's the largest country in Europe in terms of population and its economic strength. But Germany has been the leader in pushing for the integration of Europe, for the sharing of power among the European nations and for setting a standard for humane conduct and support for democracy and diversity.[9]

Clinton had answered the question with such enthusiasm that Chancellor Kohl immediately stepped in to temper the President's remarks, saying that the Germans would not be "rushing to the front."[10]

Shortly after Clinton's visit, the last Russian troops were withdrawn from eastern Germany and the Allied presence in Berlin officially ended. Germany had regained full sovereignty and thus complete freedom over its foreign policy. One journalist captured Germany's dilemma as follows: "We are needed. But to what

7. Press Conference of the President and Chancellor Helmut Kohl, The White House, 9 February 1995. Commentary on the visit in German newspapers was positive, see Martin Lambeck, "When a Friend Brings His Friend Closer to Another Friend," *Die Welt*, 11-12 February 1995, p. 6 and Martin Sueskind, "Splendid State Visit with Precarious Outcome," *Süddeutsche Zeitung*, 11-12 February 1995, p. 1, as cited in *FBIS- WEU-95-030*, 14 February 1995, pp. 11-12.

8. Justin Burke, "Clinton Calls For Tolerance, Unity in Europe," *Christian Science Monitor*, 13 July 1994, p. 1; Rick Atkinson, "'All Things Are Possible; Berlin is Free,' Says Clinton," *Washington Post*, 13 July 1994, p. A19.

9. Remarks by President Clinton, Chancellor Kohl, and President Delors, Berlin, Germany, 12 July 1994.

10. Ibid.

end?"[11] The answer to this question is critical to the future of U.S.-German relations.

Change or Continuity

Germany's evolution on the use of the Bundeswehr has been a public one, easy for all to follow. Changes in the way Germany conducts its foreign policy have been more subtle, and the subject of some debate. Some point to an increased German assertiveness on foreign policy, citing its early recognition of Croatia and Slovenia, and its policy on Iran. Others argue that – even with these two examples – what is striking about both cases is Germany's desire to pursue its policy objectives through multilateral means, namely by getting the European Union's imprimatur on what began essentially as German policy. These analysts argue that West Germany pursued its foreign policy aims in a similar way and they see little difference in style or substance. Which assessment is correct carries implications for U.S. interests, and two case studies – on policy toward the former Yugoslavia and toward Iran – follow to help provide an answer.

Policy Toward the Former Yugoslavia

The United States and its European allies have had difficulty formulating a coherent policy in trying to halt the war in the former Yugoslavia. At times, the Clinton administration has singled out Germany for criticism, for instance, on the issue of Germany's successful drive for European Community recognition of Slovenia and Croatia in late 1991. In mid-June 1993, Secretary of State Warren Christopher contended that Bonn "bears a particular responsibility" for the breakup of Yugoslavia and the escalation of war, because of its premature recognition of Croatia and Slovenia. The Kohl government has rebuffed this critique as unjustified. Whether Germany's recognition policy was premature or constructive, all

---

11. Nina Grunenberg, "Wir Werden Gebraucht. Aber Wozu?," *Die Zeit*, 19 May 1995, p. 3. See also Jochen Thies, "End of the Pause for Reflection," *Die Welt*, 9 July 1994, p. 4, as quoted in *FBIS-WEU-94-132*, 11 July 1994, p. 25.

observers agreed that Germany was playing an unfamiliar role in being the leading backer of a controversial policy. However, this new assertiveness was tempered by the traditional desire for multilateralism; Germany brought its diplomatic weight to bear in the effort to gain European Community acceptance of early recognition.

SFOR

The NATO-led Stabilization Force (SFOR) replaced IFOR on 20 December 1996.[12] Germany is contributing 2,000 soldiers to SFOR's ground forces, and an additional 1,000 air force and navy personnel in support of SFOR.

Based on its support for the Dayton peace accords, the German government felt it important to contribute to the NATO-led force for two major reasons. First, it believes that the conditions for lasting stability in the former Yugoslavia can only be guaranteed if the military safeguards for the peace agreement are provided. Germany has a particular interest in creating stable conditions in Bosnia to allow for the return of over 300,000 refugees from the region who are currently living in Germany. Second, the Germans wanted to show solidarity with their NATO allies.

Germany's decision to contribute troops to SFOR is a landmark for two reasons. First, the 2,000 troops are deployed *in Bosnia*. (Recall that during Germany's participation in IFOR most German soldiers were stationed in Croatia.) Second, roughly 600 of those soldiers are infantry and reconnaissance elements, marking the first time German combat troops are participating fully in a ground mission with their NATO allies. These steps, in light of previous inhibitions, indicate the success with which Germany viewed its participation in IFOR and its desire to share the same responsibilities as its allies. On 13 December 1996, the Bundestag overwhelmingly approved the deployment with a 499-to-93 vote. German officials saw the appointment of a German two-star general as chief of staff for SFOR, serving under the U.S. mission commander, as another sign of the significance of the German role in Bosnia.

12. For a detailed discussion of German military engagement in the former Yugoslavia prior to its participation in SFOR, see previous section on "international military missions."

In December 1997, German Foreign Minister Kinkel stressed that the international military presence in Bosnia should be extended beyond the SFOR mandate of 30 June 1998 in order to prevent "a relapse into war, chaos, and bloodshed." However, he stated that any new mandate should be limited to eighteen months "because it should not give the impression that we can ensure Bosnia's stability in the long run with soldiers from the outside." The Kohl government appears willing to have German soldiers participate in a follow-on force, as long as there is U.S. participation as well. A broad political majority in support of an extension of the current Bundeswehr mission in Bosnia appears to be forming in the Bundestag.

Refugees

Since 1992, Germany has taken in almost one-half of the roughly 700,000 Bosnians who fled to other European countries as fighting spread. Germany spends about $2.5 billion annually to care for these 320,000 refugees. In August 1996, the sixteen federal states and the Interior Ministry agreed on a three-phase program to return the refugees – either voluntarily or by force – beginning with criminals, single people, and childless couples. The agreement went into effect on 1 October 1996. Bavaria and Berlin have the largest concentrations of Bosnian refugees and both states began to deport refugees. As of August 1997, roughly 65,000 refugees had left Germany and about 400 had been deported. More than half of the refugees in Germany are believed to be Muslims from areas controlled by Serbs who drove them away and some have questioned whether it is safe for these refugees to return. Some politicians have expressed concern that the deportations will damage the image of Germany, reduce its influence in Bosnia, and conceivably introduce greater tensions there.[13]

Policy Toward Iran

Germany's diplomacy on Iran has been singled out as an example of the country's readiness to conduct a foreign policy distinct from

---

13. William Drozdiak, "Germany Escalates Drive to Repatriate Bosnians," *Washington Post*, 3 April 1997, p. A28.

that of Washington. In an attempt to dissuade Iran from sponsoring international terrorism, developing nuclear weapons, and working to sabotage the Middle East peace process, the Clinton administration has sought to isolate Iran by banning all U.S. trade and investment. Most west European countries and Japan share U.S. concerns over Iranian intentions, but they do not agree on the appropriate response. The Kohl government has pursued the EU's policy of "critical dialogue," believing that limited political and economic engagement are the best means to moderate Iranian behavior. This policy is driven in part by economic motives and in part by political motives, namely the desire to retain at least some influence in Iran. Iran owes Germany several billion dollars from previous commercial deals and makes annual debt servicing payments. On the trade front, German exports to Iran have dropped to 2.3 billion marks in 1995 from 8 billion marks in 1992 while imports from Iran have stagnated at 1.1 billion marks. Of the 200 countries with whom Germany trades, Iran ranks forty-fifth in terms of exports and forty-ninth in terms of imports.[14]

On 15 March 1996, Germany's Federal Court of Justice ordered the arrest of Iran's intelligence minister Ali Fallahiyan, who was suspected of ordering the 1992 killing of exiled Iranian Kurdish leaders in Berlin. At the time of Fallahiyan's arrest, that murder trial (the "Mykonos trial") was underway in Berlin. Officials in Bonn said that Fallahiyan's extradition from Iran was practically impossible, but that the warrant was a "diplomatic gesture" which the Kohl government had hoped would never be issued. Fallahiyan had made an official visit to Germany in October 1993 which reportedly irritated U.S. officials, who were highly critical of any links between German and Iranian intelligence. In July 1996, Germany brokered a prisoner exchange between Israel and Iranian-backed Hezbollah guerrillas, a breakthrough German officials

14. For a fuller discussion of this policy divergence, see Peter Rudolf, "Critical Engagement: The European Union and Iran," Prepared for a conference on "Transatlantic Tensions: The Challenge of Difficult Countries," The Brookings Institution, 9-10 March 1998; and Peter Rudolf and Geoffrey Kemp, "The Iranian Dilemma: Challenges for German and American Foreign Policy," *Conference Report*, American Institute for Contemporary German Studies, Washington, D.C., 21 April 1997.

felt was only achievable because of the relationship they had culti-
vated with Iran.

The Mykonos trial created considerable ill will between Bonn
and Teheran. The judge ruled on April 10, 1997 that the killings
were orchestrated by a secretive "Committee for Special Operations" in Teheran whose members included the country's spiritual
leader, president, minister of intelligence, and other senior security
officials. Within hours of the ruling, the German Foreign Ministry
announced that it was recalling its ambassador to Iran and that
four Iranian diplomats would be expelled. Iran then withdrew its
ambassador in Bonn and expelled four German diplomats in retal-
iation. The European Union suspended its policy of "critical dialogue" with Iran, and EU countries, with the exception of Greece,
recalled their ambassadors from Teheran. The U.S. State Department said that the verdict "corroborates our long-held view that
Iran's sponsorship of terrorism is authorized at senior levels of the
Iranian Government."[15]

EU foreign ministers reassessed Europe's policy toward Iran at
a meeting on 29 April 1997, and agreed to continue to suspend the
policy of critical dialogue, halt bilateral ministerial visits with Iran,
deny visas to Iranians with intelligence and security posts, expel
Iranian intelligence personnel already in EU states, and maintain
the ban on arms sales to Iran.[16] EU countries agreed to send
ambassadors back to Iran, but Teheran would not accept the German and Danish envoys, leading EU members to decide that no
ambassadors would return until Iran would allow all fifteen back.
The election of a relative moderate, Mohammad Khatemi, as
Iran's president in May 1997 led some in the EU to urge a revival
of the critical dialogue. In September, Iran stated that EU ambassadors could return any time, but Germany's ambassador would

15. See Kenneth Katzman, "Iran: Implications of Germany's Terrorism Trial,"
CRS Report for Congress, 17 April 1997; Alan Cowell, "Berlin Court Says Top Iran
Leaders Ordered Killings," *New York Times*, 11 April 1997, pp. A1, A10; Frederick
Stüdemann and Lionel Barber, "EU adopts tougher attitude over Iran," *Financial
Times*, 11 April 1997, p. 1.

16. Lionel Barber, "Brussels fires shot across Iran's bows," *Financial Times*, 30
April 1997, p. 8; William Drozdiak, "EU Nations' Envoys Going Back to Iran,"
Washington Post, 30 April 1997, p. A15.

have to be the last to return. The EU deemed this condition unacceptable. The EU and Iran reached a compromise on 13 November, under which twelve of the fifteen EU ambassadors returned to Tehran on 14 November, followed by the German and French representatives on 21 November.[17]

On 23 February 1998, the EU agreed to lift its ban on high-level contacts with Iran in order to buttress moderate political forces led by President Khatemi. Reportedly, the decision represented a compromise between pressure by the French and Italians for a speedy normalization of relations and concerns of Britain and Germany to move ahead cautiously.[18] This move underscores the fact that the EU continues to reject the U.S. approach of isolating Iran.

Germany, together with its EU partners, has strongly objected to the extraterritorial application of U.S. law through the Iran-Libya Sanctions Act (ILSA), signed by President Clinton in August 1996, imposing sanctions on foreign companies that make substantial investments in energy projects in Iran or Libya. U.S. Undersecretary of State Thomas Pickering arrived in Paris on 7 January 1998, in search of an agreement with France that would allow it to waive possible sanctions against Total of France, Gazprom of Russia, and Malaysia's Petronas, which have signed a $2 billion gas deal with Iran seemingly in violation of ILSA.[19] In February 1998, U.S. policy on sanctions against Total and Gazprom has been complicated by the possibility of military action against Iraq, for which the administration continues to seek support from France and Russia. Washington also does not want to alienate Britain and Germany, countries that support U.S. policy on Iraq, but would denounce any decision to move forward with sanctions.[20]

17. "EU and Iran End Diplomatic Standoff," *The Week in Germany*, 21 November 1997, p. 2.

18. Lionel Barber, "EU to allow Iran contacts," *Financial Times*, 24 February 1998, p. 2.

19. Nancy Dunne, "US seeks fresh approach on Iran," *Financial Times*, 7 January 1998, p. 5.

20. Bruce Clark, "Crisis forces US rethink on Iran sanctions," *Financial Times*, 9 February 1998, p. 4.

Policy Divergence

The two cases analyzed above yield different conclusions about the extent of divergence in U.S. and German policies. In the case of the former Yugoslavia, Germany's pressure for the early recognition of Croatia and Slovenia appears to have been an aberration in terms of German support overall for commonly held western positions. Other than the spat over early recognition, Germany has been an exemplary ally from the U.S. perspective, as detailed in the account of German participation above. The European – and thus German – role in the likely follow-on force to SFOR will increase, further demonstrating Germany's willingness to accept greater responsibility in the post-Cold War era.

The case of policy toward Iran is a much more problematic one for German-American relations. The divergence described above has been discussed through official channels both bilaterally and multilaterally, in the context of the U.S.-EU dialogue. Some have even suggested the issue be raised within NATO. However, the underlying problem is not that an appropriate forum for discussion is lacking. The dilemma is so complex because the Europeans, including the Germans, see the issue of Iran through an entirely different prism than do the Americans. The question of how to respond to problematic Iranian behavior – through engagement or isolation – is fundamental. U.S. officials argue it is critical to isolate a "rogue state," while the Europeans believe it is necessary to engage an "important regional player." The European position appears immutable. U.S. policy would likely shift only in light of a concrete change in Iranian behavior. Europeans point to the election of Khatemi as evidence of such a transition, but Americans want to see his election result in explicit policy changes. It seems unlikely that this dilemma can be resolved in the near term. In fact, if the Clinton administration were to declare that the Total deal violates U.S. law, triggering sanctions, the divergence over Iran policy could have a deeply corrosive effect on the U.S.-European relationship as a whole. The Germans would certainly join their European partners in categorically rejecting any such extraterritorial application of U.S. sanctions law.

Germany was the principal author of the EU policy of critical dialogue toward Iran, pursuing its preferred policy through European channels, rather than unilaterally. Particularly in light of U.S. opposition to the policy, the Germans sought to coordinate policy with their European allies. In discussions with U.S. officials, German government representatives consistently repeat that they are pursuing a European, rather than a strictly German, policy toward Iran. In this case, rather than openly stating German policy preferences, German officials opt for the comfortable cover of the European Union. Some observers see this tactic in a negative light, claiming it leads to a Germany which never accepts responsibility or blame for controversial policies, but rather diffuses accountability among EU member states. Others applaud this tactic, viewing the resulting subjection of German policy to EU vetting as evidence of Germany's commitment to creating a European Germany, rather than a German Europe.

Enhancing Transatlantic Ties

The basic harmony between U.S. and German policy approaches has not quieted concerns about the possibility of estrangement following the end of the Cold War.[21] As the ultimate guarantor of its security, the United States was West Germany's most important ally during the Cold War. West Germany's strategic position, bordering the Iron Curtain, gave it unique significance to Washington too. Some worry that with the common enemy gone and the concomitant weakening of the security link, Germany and the United States will drift apart as common interests and pursuits gradually disappear. Further, U.S. policy-makers appear preoccupied by a pressing domestic agenda, and many Europeans perceive a "Pacific tilt" in U.S. foreign policy, which accords priority to Asia and Latin

21. Much of this concern has been voiced on the European side, see Stanley R. Sloan, "European Proposals for a New Atlantic Community," Congressional Research Service Report 95-374S. 10 March 1995; and Wolfgang Reinicke, "Transatlantic Economic Relations in a Changing Global Environment," prepared for the project on The Future of the Transatlantic Relationship sponsored by the Bertelsmann-Stiftung and the Council on Foreign Relations, Munich, June 1995. However, some U.S. observers, such as Jacob Heilbrunn, argue that "united Germany and the United States are being driven inexorably apart by new geopolitical realities," see Heilbrunn, "Springtime," *The New Republic*, 16 October 1995, pp. 21-25.

America and seems to lack direction when it comes to Europe. Many Europeans also express concern over what they see as a political trend in the United States toward neoisolationism and unilateralism. Nonetheless, on issues of central importance to Germany, such as policy toward Russia or NATO expansion, U.S. and German positions converge.[22]

In recognition of the changing times, the Clinton administration's first ambassador to Germany, Richard Holbrooke, sought to revivify the German-American relationship. Ambassador Holbrooke launched a program of "New Traditions" through which he sought to redirect the alliance with Germany from its primary focus on security to one with parallel and equal tracks emphasizing commercial, cultural, and even crime-fighting links. In keeping with administration priorities, the ambassador particularly emphasized the promotion of U.S. business interests.[23] Chancellor Kohl wholeheartedly supported this approach in a June 1994 interview:

> In the past, during the time of the East-West conflict, the transatlantic link binding us firmly to the United States of America and Canada was primarily geared toward matters of security policy. Today, we are duty-bound to broaden this link to take in other sectors and, in particular, to intensify cooperation in the areas of the economy, culture, and science. It is also important to reinforce exchanges of young people, thus consolidating ties of friendship between young people on both sides of the Atlantic.[24]

The stated desire on both sides to deepen the bilateral relationship across a wide range of issue areas is significant. However, security policy is likely to remain a key dimension of the German-American relationship. The current base figure for U.S. troops stationed in Germany is 65,000, as compared to 207,600 in 1990. However, that 65,000 represents the bulk of the 100,000 U.S.

22. The clearest example of divergent perspectives relates to policy toward Iran. See discussion in preceding section.

23. Thom Shanker, "America's Evolving Policy," *Chicago Tribune*, 3 July 1994, sec. 4, p. 5; Martin Sieff, "U.S. Ambassador to Germany to Don State's European Hat," *Washington Times*, 15 June 1994, p. A13.

24. "Kohl and Mitterrand: a Shared European Belief to Guarantee Peace," *Liberation*, 6 June 1994, pp. 4-5, as quoted in *FBIS-WEU-94-109*, 7 June 1994, p. 3.

troops remaining in Europe. While some Germans question the U.S. commitment to keeping forces deployed in Europe, some Americans wonder whether Germans will continue to want foreign forces stationed on their territory in peacetime, particularly since the withdrawal of the 338,000 troops of the former USSR from the eastern German states, completed on 31 August 1994. The Kohl government has made clear its desire for a continued U.S. presence, because Germany is bordered by economic, social, and political turmoil to its east.

On the security side, one innovative development in the 1990s to enhance U.S.-German military cooperation has been the initiation of a German Air Force flight training program at a U.S. base. This program, at Holloman Air Force Base in New Mexico, has been pointed to by most as a model. However, some U.S. critics were alarmed by the prospect of what they see as a permanent foreign military base on American soil.

German Troops in the United States

The United States has a long history of training with its allies, both at home and abroad. Germany first began training its pilots in the United States in 1955.[25] The scope of these training programs has grown ever since.

The German Military Presence at Holloman AFB

In the fall of 1990, the U.S. Secretary of Defense and the German Defense Minister agreed to deepen military cooperation. In this context, the United States offered the German Air Force the opportunity to expand training at Holloman AFB. Holloman, in Alamogordo, New Mexico, is the home base of the U.S. Air Force 49th Fighter Wing and its stealth fighters (the F-117).[26]

In addition to the F-4 Phantom jets that had been transferred to Holloman from George AFB, the United States agreed that the

25. "Germany begins pilot training at U.S. base," Reuters, 1 May 1996.
26. Information for this section was taken from: Transcript, News Briefing by Ken Bacon, Defense Department Spokesperson, Washington, D.C., 2 May 1996; and "Holloman I and II," Press Section, German Embassy Washington, 30 April 1996.

Germans could station German Tornado jets there. In May 1994, a memorandum of understanding was signed which covered construction of the German Air Force Tactical Training Element and the stationing of 12 Tornado and roughly 300 military and civilian employees, along with their families. Known as Holloman I, these planes and personnel are part of a weapons instructor and flight training program; the Germans invested about 62 million German marks ($40 million) for constructing the necessary infrastructure, including hangars and maintenance facilities. On 1 May 1996, U.S. Defense Secretary Perry and German Defense Minister Rühe activated the German Tactical Training Center (TTC) at Holloman AFB.

Starting in October 1999, the German Air Force will send an additional 30 Tornado jets and 600 military and civilian employees to Holloman to further expand training. This will allow the Germans to perform all basic and weapons systems training for Tornados at Holloman AFB and thus ensure "comprehensive training." According to the German embassy in Washington, D.C., this program, called Holloman II, "will considerably improve the efficiency and quality of flight training of Tornado crews, because the training duration can be shortened and the structure of the training can be designed uniformly."[27] The Germans will invest another 175 million German marks (about $114 million) to construct hangars, a noise suppression facility for engine test runs, a flight simulator, and housing for the permanent and training staff. Upon completion of Holloman II in the fall of 1999, 24 F-4 Phantoms, 42 Tornados, and approximately 900 German Air Force staff members will be stationed at the TTC at Holloman AFB.

There are several important reasons for Germany's decision to invest in the TTC. To begin, Holloman is situated in the state of New Mexico which is about the same size as Germany; however, New Mexico has a population of 1.5 million as compared to Germany's 80 million. The training opportunities permitted by the vast air space are simply not available to German pilots at home. Given New Mexico's sparse population and the existing special

27. "Holloman I and II," Press Section, German Embassy Washington, 30 April 1996, p. 2.

use air space, German pilots have a greater opportunity to conduct flying training at low altitudes and high speeds. They can use the full array of radar jamming equipment and conduct live bombing exercises. Second, the weather is much better in New Mexico than in Germany which ensures training continuity because a pilot can fly a much greater number of hours per month or year than he can in Germany. In New Mexico, pilots can train all year long. Finally, Holloman AFB is relatively close to Fort Bliss, Texas, the headquarters for German Air Force operations in North America.

Since the Germans have been training in the United States for decades, some may wonder what is special about the operation at Holloman. For the first time, the German Air Force has assumed responsibility for a flying training program on U.S. soil. Previously, the German military was essentially buying training courses from the United States, complete with U.S. instructors and U.S. aircraft. In those cases where the Germans actually owned planes being used in the training courses, those planes were maintained and serviced by the U.S. Air Force or by civilian contractor companies. This will continue to be the case with the F-4 Training Component used for German flight training at Holloman. With the TTC now activated, the Germans both own and maintain the Tornado jets, and German instructors will teach the courses. The TTC thus may represent a new model under which allies can train beside their U.S. counterparts.

U.S. Interests and the German Presence at Holloman

The official response in the United States to the activation of the German Training Center at Holloman Air Force Base has been overwhelmingly positive. Supporters of German operations at Holloman have stressed the importance of German training in the United States for the strength of the Atlantic Alliance. Others, however, have raised concerns about the command structure at the base and the financing of the project.

COMMAND ISSUES: A PERMANENT GERMAN MILITARY BASE IN NEW MEXICO?

On 1 May 1996, CNN broadcast a report entitled "German Air Force Invades Holloman in New Mexico." CNN's military affairs correspondent, Jamie McIntyre, described the situation: "As German fighter planes streaked across the New Mexico sky, on the ground a German flag was hoisted higher than the American flag, signifying the first time the U.S. has allowed another country to establish a permanent military base on U.S. soil."[28] Other press reports also suggested that Holloman AFB had been, in essence, taken over by the Germans.[29] The facts, however, suggest that these reports reflect certain misconceptions.

At a press briefing on May 2, Ken Bacon, the Pentagon spokesperson, said that it was "not quite accurate" to say that the Germans had established a permanent military base on U.S. soil. Rather, he said, "they are tenants at an American military base … I think that we should not look at this, this should not be portrayed by anybody as a German invasion or occupation of U.S. space. It's not that. This is an opportunity for two allies to train together."[30] During the briefing, Bacon was asked again and again about the precise status of the German Air Force at Holloman. The briefing card he used stated: "Holloman is a U.S. Air Force Base, has been in existence since 1942 and will remain a U.S. Air Force installation … The U.S. Air Force 49th Fighter Wing Commander shall exercise overall responsibility and will have command and control of all base operations. The Germans are a tenant unit under his operational control."[31]

As for the permanence of the German presence, the year 2004 is the end date of the memorandum of understanding covering the two German programs, Holloman I and II. Thus, if for whatever reason either side grew unhappy with the arrangement, it could be terminated or altered in 2004. Both U.S. and German officials view

28. Quoted from Transcript #1347-7, Cable News Network, 1 May 1996. According to the Pentagon, both the U.S. and German flags were displayed at the TTC activation ceremony on May 1; the U.S. flag was properly displayed, on the proper side, and higher than the German flag. The U.S. flag is the only flag flown on the base.

29. See, for instance, John Roper, "Perry, German counterpart christen base," UPI, 1 May 1996; "German defence for talks in Washington – opens air base," Deutsche Presse-Agentur, 26 April 1996.

30. News Briefing by Ken Bacon.

31. "Tactical Training Center for German Air Force," Briefing Card, Office of the Assistant Secretary of Defense (Public Affairs), 2 May 1996.

the TTC as a longterm commitment and expect the memorandum of understanding to be extended. Whenever the Germans do decide to stop training at Holloman, the facilities they have built will become part of the U.S. infrastructure at the base.

THE COST OF GERMAN OPERATIONS AT HOLLOMAN: WHO PAYS?

News reports about the German Training Center at Holloman triggered some questions about which government was bearing the cost for the expansion of German operations. Two points are important here.

First, the Germans are bearing the entire cost for expanding their training programs at Holloman, including about $40 million for construction of new buildings for Holloman I and an anticipated $114 million for additional facilities for Holloman II. The Germans must pay for all supplies used (from fuel to pencils), and for a proportionate share of the operating costs of the base.[32]

Second, many argue that the increasing German presence offers direct financial benefits to the community around the base. The Pentagon maintains that the "expansion of mission and facilities at Holloman is an economic windfall to the city of Alamogordo and the state of New Mexico."[33] Currently, German air crews and their families are living in the community of Alamogordo, not on the base. A reporter from the *Wall Street Journal* went to Alamogordo last summer to cover the story of the growing German presence, which he interpreted as a financial boon:

> With base closings threatening other military towns, this desert outpost is thrilled about the buildup planned for nearby Holloman Air Force Base ... They [the 300 German personnel] are expected to bring a $12 million payroll and as many as 800 dependents to the area, where most will live off-base ... For a struggling military town that hasn't built so much as a new apartment complex in 20 years, this German invasion means boom times.[34]

32. News Briefing by Ken Bacon; and "German military are 'tenants' at U.S. base, Pentagon says," Deutsche Presse-Agentur, 2 May 1996.

33. "Tactical Training Center for German Air Force," Pentagon Briefing Card, 2 May 1996.

34. Robert Tomsho, "Alamogordo Braces Itself for an Invasion By the Luftwaffe," *Wall Street Journal*, 29 June 1995, p. 1.

The one point of tension the article mentioned may be competition for good housing – which is in short supply – between German military personnel and their American counterparts, who receive smaller housing allowances.

Bolstering the Atlantic Alliance

While the German presence at Holloman may bring tangible financial gains for Alamogordo and New Mexico as a whole, the benefit highlighted by both U.S. and German officials relates to the much broader aim of strengthening the Atlantic Alliance. First, the type of joint training which is taking place at Holloman is seen as directly improving the readiness of NATO. In the words of the Pentagon spokesman, "by training in the United States, they are increasing the capability of their Air Force and therefore increasing the capability of the alliance, and this alliance remains an extremely important alliance as we are demonstrating in Bosnia today … We are always looking for ways to operate more closely with our allies so that should a combat situation ever come we can operate as a seamless unit."[35]

Second, the importance of deepening transatlantic military cooperation and increasing joint training in the United States was felt keenly with the end of the Cold War as the United States dramatically reduced its troop presence in Europe. Both the Bush and Clinton administrations deemed it valuable to increase contacts with the closest allies of the United States as this military drawdown was occurring.

Third, officials cite a direct benefit for U.S.-German relations. The German facility at Holloman represents a step forward for bilateral friendship and cooperation. It also underscores a growing reciprocity in the relationship. The United States stations about 100,000 troops in Europe (down from over 300,000 at the height of the Cold War), and the lion's share of those troops have always been based in Germany. Over 100 U.S. Air Force planes are stationed in Germany. A Pentagon spokesman described the German training facility as "an opportunity for us to actually return 40 years

---

35. News Briefing by Ken Bacon.

of training that we have performed on German soil. This is not a complicated operation. We train extensively around the world on other people's soil without much controversy. I would expect the Germans to be able to train on our soil with no controversy whatsoever as allies, friends and neighbors."[36]

This example of the German Air Force's training program at Holloman demonstrates that even in traditional areas of cooperation, such as security policy, there is room for creative approaches and deepening ties. Time will tell whether the Germans – or other NATO allies – use the Holloman experience as a model for the transfer of additional training programs to the United States.

Prospects for the Future

A question vital to the future shape of the German-American relationship is whether the unified Germany will remain largely a regional power, focusing its foreign policy efforts on European affairs, or instead will develop into a truly global power, deploying its foreign policy resources more broadly to troubled spots around the world. Germany still conceives of itself, first and foremost, as a regional power, and the regional role Germany plays in Europe is generally perceived positively in the United States. Like any country, Germany has limited resources and some observers see those resources as most effectively used if concentrated in Europe. One U.S. policymaker argues that Germany, in its regional role, serves as the U.S. "branch manager" for Europe.

In the near term, Germany's influence will be felt primarily in Europe. As the economic and political burdens connected with bringing the eastern part of the country up to the western level lessens, the Germans may well assume greater global responsibilities. This development is already underway in the role of the German military. While these changes may appear incremental, rather than dramatic, they do reflect an evolution in German foreign policy. Much of this greater international engagement, particularly in the

---

36. Ibid.; see also Remarks by Defense Secretary Perry at TTC Activation Ceremony, Holloman AFB, 1 May 1996.

political and security areas, is likely to be pursued through multi-lateral organizations, including the United Nations. The Clinton administration, unquestionably, is encouraging this development.

With the common enemy gone and the concomitant weakening of the security link, some have asked if the United States and Germany will drift apart or if common interests and pursuits will hold them together. Most analysts believe the latter outcome to be more likely, but they point out that as Germany assumes a greater global role, it may not always share U.S. policy objectives. It will be a challenge for policy makers on both sides of the Atlantic to manage a long-standing alliance in a time of unclear threats and national interests which at times diverge.

Chapter 4

THE POLITICS OF ADAPTING
ORGANIZED CAPITALISM

United Germany, the New Europe,
and Globalization

*Christopher S. Allen**

While Germany is an advanced industrialized country with a democratic-parliamentary system, it has developed and retained many distinctive institutional forms that differentiate it from other countries in the Organization for Economic Cooperation and Development (OECD). Among the most remarkable are its organizational structure, regulatory framework, and labor movement. These structures are not random idiosyncrasies, but institutional patterns that have evolved for a specific set of reasons. Moreover many of these patterns are interconnected in ways that are not immediately apparent. These characteristics have proved durable and salutary for much of the Federal Republic's history.

* This article was first presented as a paper at Johns Hopkins University's American Institute for Contemporary German Studies in Washington, D.C., October 17, 1997. I would like to thank the conference participants for their comments, especially Phil Gorski, Steve Silvia, Carolyn Höfig, Beth Noveck, Manik Hinchey, Jeremiah Riemer, Karen Donfried, Tom Ertman, and Andy Markovits.

However, the mid- and late-1990s have witnessed much criticism of the health of the German economy, only part of which can be attributed to the extraordinary costs of unification.[1] Of course, even during the years of Modell Deutschland's successes, some observers continued to offer critiques of institutional arrangements of the German political economy.[2] While many adherents of the "German Model" might have been able to discount such criticism through the 1980s and into the early 1990s, the triple challenge of unification, Europeanization, and globalization prompt a new critical look at the efficacy and structure of the German political economy. The enviable strength of the German economy has been based on powerful organized capitalist institutions during the last half-century. Among these are the symbiotic relationship between finance and manufacturing sectors, the powerful role of industry and employer organizations, and worker participation features such as Mitbestimmung (codetermination) and Betriebsräte (works councils). Yet these pillars of the economic structure are now coming under scrutiny since some observers believe that they are no longer able to handle adequately the formidable challenges facing the Federal Republic's political economy.

The basic question this article addresses is: How will the distinctive forms of German business, specifically banking and labor, address these challenges? More theoretically, these questions embody a fundamental – and contemporary – debate that lies at the heart of both comparative politics and international relations, namely the tension between globalization and domestic political structures.[3] This is, of course, not a new issue. Eminent scholars have addressed these tensions in their work for over twenty years.[4]

1. Peter Neckermann, "What Went Wrong in Germany after the Unification?" *East European Quarterly*, 26 (4), 1992, pp. 447-470.

2. Mancur Olson, *The Rise and Decline of Nations: Economic Growth, Stagflation, and Social Rigidities* (New Haven: Yale University Press, 1982).

3. Helen Milner and Robert Keohane, eds., *Internationalization and Domestic Politics* (Cambridge: Cambridge University Press, 1996); Suzanne Berger and Ronald Dore, eds., *National Diversity and Global Capitalism* (Ithaca: Cornell University Press, 1996).

4. Peter J. Katzenstein, eds., *Between Power and Plenty: Foreign Economic Policies of Advanced Industrialized States* (Madison: University of Wisconsin Press, 1978); Peter Gourevitch, "The Second Image Reversed: International Sources of Domestic Politics," *International Organization*, 32 (4), Autumn 1978, pp. 881-911.

However, examining the long-standing, and supposedly durable institutions of the German political economy through this prism will illuminate a crucial "branching point," a term used in a different context in the 1980s.[5] Will the forces of a globalizing economy override the capacities of nation-states to determine domestic priorities, or will nation-states respond to global challenges by shaping and influencing these priorities through reinvigorated or newly developed institutional structures?

The subsequent argument is organized around three different dichotomies that characterize the tensions between German organized capitalist prevailing patterns vs. the realities of the new Europe, exemplified as it is by a neoliberal, deregulatory economic policy model with roots in Anglo-American economic theory. These dichotomies are:

1. *Individualism vs. Collectivism.* This distinction refers to a basic characteristic of the German economy, namely the absence of laissez-faire and the presence of large, centralized institutions, private and public. This collectivist pattern has stunted liberal impulses since industrialization in the 19th century[6] and has encouraged the formation of a pattern of political participation that was biased in favor of groups, often to the detriment of the development of an Anglo-American style individualism.
2. *Exit vs. Voice.* A second point of tension draws on Albert O. Hirschman's famous model outlining patterns of response by actors within organizations and institutions.[7] This section of the article will contrast the voice-based model of organizational behavior within German institutions that differs greatly from the more exit-based pattern more common in U.S. organizations, and appears

5. Michael Piore and Charles Sabel, *The Second Industrial Divide* (New York: Basic Books, 1984).

6. Alexander Gerschenkron, *Bread and Democracy in Germany*, 2nd ed., (Ithaca: Cornell University Press, 1989).

7. Albert O. Hirschman, *Exit, Voice and Loyalty* (New Haven: Yale University Press, 1970).

to be encroaching on prevailing German organizational practice in other European states and in the EU.

3. *Deals vs. Relationships.* The third dichotomy analyzes specific examples of how negotiations take place within Germany, in the primary institutions of corporatism: business, labor, and the state. This section will contrast the more common Anglo-American pattern of "one off" deals with the more common German pattern of long-standing relationships.[8] Transactions in the former instance often take place with no expectation that the parties to any one deal will ever consummate another. The German pattern expects partners to a given transaction to be one with whom they have done business in the past – often over many years – and expect to do so in the future.

Much of the best Modell Deutschland literature during the past several decades concluded that, on each of these three pairs of dimensions, issues of collectivism, voice, and relationships have tended to prevail over individualism, exit, and dealmaking.[9] However, the 1990s have seen each of the three "German-style" dimensions eroding in favor of their respective Anglo-American opposite numbers.[10] The most likely external causes of this erosion are the strains produced in the 1990s due to unification, Europeanization, and globalization.

The major portion of this article is comprised of three main sections examining the tensions within each of these conceptual dyads (individualism vs. collectivism, exit vs. voice, deals vs. relationships) through which German policy makers struggle with the

8. Kirsten S. Wever and Christopher S. Allen, "Is Germany a Model for Managers?" *Harvard Business Review*, 70 (5), September-October, 1992, pp. 36-43; Kirsten S. Wever and Christopher S. Allen, "The Financial System and Corporate Governance in Germany: Institutions and the Diffusion of Innovations," *Journal of Public Policy*, 13 (2), 1993, pp. 183-202.

9. Andrei S. Markovits, ed., *Modell Deutschland: The Political Economy of West Germany* (New York: Praeger, 1982); Andrei S. Markovits and Simon Reich, "Modell Deutschland and the New Europe," *Telos*, 89, 1991, pp. 46-65; William E. Paterson and Gordon Smith, *The West German Model: Perspectives on a Stable State* (London: Cass, 1981).

10. Wolfgang Streeck, "German Capitalism: Does it Exist? Can it Survive?" in Colin Crouch and Wolfgang Streeck, eds., *The Political Economy of Modern Capitalism: Mapping Convergence and Diversity* (London: Sage, 1997), pp. 33-54.

three-pronged exogenous challenge. The article will then conclude with an argument about why the German pattern of institutional adaptation has atrophied in the face of these three external pressures. Finally, it will suggest that only if conceived differently could a renewed German model be reconceptualized and reinvigorated, but only at a European level.

Individualism vs. Collectivism

Any discussion of this issue that compares American and European differences must begin with their remarkably different patterns of land settlement.[11] Quite simply, feudalism's presence in Europe and its absence in the United States had profound effects on the way that land was used. More importantly for this article, this distinction shaped the way individuals and groups developed and reinforced political relationships.

In European feudalism, land was not free to be distributed to individuals, it was owned by powerful forces that maintained tight control over its use. For European peasants – and later, oppressed industrial workers – this produced a socio-political environment of individuals working and living in close proximity to their neighbors. Moreover, the powerful forces that these individuals confronted generally embodied both economic and political concentrations of power. The political response to these forms of oppression, best suited to oppose them, was not individual initiative, but a collective response based on the only source of potential power these individuals possessed, namely their superior numbers. In contrast, in the United States, a land devoid of feudal strictures and limitations, there was a much greater opportunity for free citizens to redress grievances on their own initiative, without having to band together with similarly situated individuals. The mere presence of available land from the earliest colonial times to the Oklahoma land rush is evidence of the premium placed on individuals to settle and tame the land, Native Americans notwithstanding.

11. Louis Hartz, *The Liberal Tradition in America* (New York: Harcourt, Brace and World, 1955); Seymour Martin Lipset, *American Exceptionalism: A Double-Edged Sword* (New York: Norton, 1997).

In summary, the abundance of available land in the United States, and its absence in Europe created national predispositions toward individual or collective action and should not be underestimated. These legacies impart powerfully different perspectives about what kind of behavior and response to economic and political impulses are appropriate. For example, depending on which prevailing set of perspectives is on the table, what can we assume about such basic issues as freedom, the appropriate forms of economic activity, and the relationship of business to government? A society steeped in an individualist tradition will have one range of responses to these questions, while one embedded in collective actors and institutions will likely have a very different perspective.

The important point here is that Germany – since the onset of industrialization over a century ago – has had an economic policy model that is very different from U.S.-style laissez-faire policies. From the state-led, rapid industrialization of the late nineteenth century, to the catastrophic excess of the Third Reich, to the postwar Wirtschaftswunder, to the modern organized capitalist Modell Deutschland, the Germans have found individualist forms of capitalism inappropriate, if not irrelevant. Even well-developed economic policy options that evolved from liberal forms of capitalism – i.e., Keynesianism – have not developed strongly in Germany.[12]

Much more important in Germany than any forms of Keynesianism has been the "Social Market Economy."[13] It was called the Freiburg school, due to the development of these economic policies at the University of Freiburg in the 1930s. This set of economic ideas tried to avoid both the boom-bust cycles of laissez-faire policies and the heavy-handed state centered politics of both the Third Reich and the Soviet Union. It envisioned using the state, but only for the specific purpose of providing a framework within which organized groups and collective interests could interact and produce stable economic growth. Perhaps the most illus-

12. Christopher S. Allen, "The Underdevelopment of Keynesianism in the Federal Republic of Germany," in Peter A. Hall, ed., *The Political Power of Economic Ideas: Keynesianism Across Nations* (Princeton: Princeton University Press, 1989), pp. 263-289.

13. Ludwig Erhard, *Deutsche Wirtschaftspolitik: der Weg der sozialen Markwirtschaft* (Düsseldorf: Econ, 1962).

trative quotation embodying the organized capitalist philosophy of the social market economy is the following:

> [Our program] consists of measures and institutions which impart to competition the framework, rules, and machinery of impartial supervision which a competitive system needs as much as any game or match if it is not to degenerate into a vulgar brawl. A genuine, equitable, and smoothly functioning competitive system can not in fact survive without a judicious moral and legal framework and without regular supervision of the conditions under which competition can take place pursuant to real efficiency principles. This presupposes mature economic discernment on the part of all responsible bodies and individuals and a strong impartial state.[14]

Based on this set of economic ideas – which themselves were derived from patterns and policies formed in the late and rapid industrialization of the nineteenth century – the postwar West German economy developed the following distinctive features:

1. A highly integrated organized capitalism in which large and small firms developed interest associations that concentrated on the health of the industry, rather than a primary concern with individual firms. In fact, individual firms were often forced to conform to industry mandates as determined by these "parapublic"[15] institutions.
2. A universal banking system in which banks – large and small – could own stock, vote proxy shares, engage an large amounts of debt financing of private industry, and sit on the boards of directors of other firms.[16] Although this bank-dominated system has eroded in recent years,[17] it remains a powerful force in German capitalism, especially

---

14. Wilhelm Röpke, "The Guiding Principles of the Liberal Programme," in Horst Friedrich Wünche, ed., *Standard Texts on the Social Market Economy*, (Stuttgart and New York: Gustav Fischer Verlag, 1982), p. 188.

15. Peter J. Katzenstein, *Politics and Policy in West Germany: The Growth of a Semi-Sovereign State* (Philadelphia: Temple University Press, 1987).

16. Andrew Shonfield, *Modern Capitalism* (New York: Harper, 1965).

17. Richard Deeg, *Finance Capital Unveiled: Banks and Economic Adjustment in Germany* (Ann Arbor: University of Michigan Press, 1998).

for smaller firms, and represented one more collective actor in an economy that underplayed individualistic forms of capitalism.

3. A large, powerful trade union movement that sought to incorporate and integrate the German workforce into organizations that could speak collectively for workers.[18] Not only did these powerful forces of organized labor recruit members, they also encouraged – and took an active part in – the formation of works councils inside almost all German workplaces.

4. An extensive welfare state which built on the legacies of Bismarck's creation which both provided collective benefits as it simultaneously marginalized organized labor for two decades.[19] The leaders of the first Christian Democratic governments of the postwar era, Konrad Adenauer and Ludwig Erhard, realized the value of providing collective benefits to citizens at a time when wages were slow to recover in the early years of the Wirtschaftswunder (economic miracle).

The major point to take from the discussion of this first dyad is that individualistic, laissez-faire U.S.-style policies have never had a firm foothold in Germany. Thus, one should not expect German policy-makers to respond instantly to the kind of incentives and ideological incantations that dominate contemporary economic policy discussions. Even given the apparent hegemony of Anglo-American policy models in a marketizing, globalizing world, the Germans have been wedded to a model that makes much greater use of collective institutions than individual initiative. What observers should be waiting to see is not an instant embrace of Anglo-American policy models, but how and whether the firms, organizations and interests of the German economy respond – or attempt to respond – to these pressures using these collective insti-

---

18. Andrei S. Markovits, *The Politics of the West German Trade Unions: Strategies of Class and Interest Representation in Growth and Crisis* (Cambridge: Cambridge University Press, 1986).

19. Fritz Stern, *Gold and Iron: Bismarck, Bleichröder and the Building of the German Empire* (New York: Knopf, 1977).

tutions. Any embrace of individualistic patterns in German economic policy making would not take place without the full and complete exhaustion of traditional collective patterns.

Exit vs. Voice

When the image of an ideal-typical successful U.S. firm is considered, it often takes a form that reflects basic American values and virtues. One of the most prominent of these images is that of the individual entrepreneur, inventor, or tinkerer who – acting alone – produces a spectacular invention, innovation, or foundation for a new industry. One need only peruse the biographies of such individuals as Bell, Edison, Carnegie, and Rockefeller, among many others, to confirm this impression. In the modern age, such individuals as Andrew Grove (Intel) and Stephen Jobs (Apple) are touted as exemplifying these virtues. One common theme that emerges from these biographical sketches – accurate or not – is that these individuals broke away from larger firms or institutions and struck out on there own to start new firms. In one intriguing way to look at this phenomenon, they chose to "exit" from their original firms rather than using their "voice" to develop their innovation or invention within their original workplace. Given the preference for individual initiative outlined above, this development is neither surprising nor unexpected. It is simply the dominant and most widely publicized model of American economic innovation.

In contrast, the model of an ideal-typical successful German firm looks very different. Rather than the names of heroic individual "captains of industry" one hears the names of large firms such as Siemens, Daimler-Benz, Volkswagen, Bayer, BASF, Hoechst, as well as the Deutsche, Dresdner, and Commerz banks. In addition to not celebrating the individual leader or founder of these firms (Daimler-Benz excepted), these firms also have one other feature in common: most have been in existence for the past century. Throughout the turmoil of the late-nineteenth and twentieth centuries in Germany, these firms found a way to maintain themselves as functioning organizations. How did they do this? One important way is that they somehow imbued their organizations with an organizational dynamism that enabled them to withstand the "gales of creative destruction," to borrow a phrase from Joseph Schumpeter, during much of twentieth century Germany.[20] Oddly, many observers touting the individualistic-centered American model mistakenly cite Schumpeter as a justification for preeminence of small firms. A more careful reading of this work – particularly the chapter on monopolies – suggests just the opposite. Namely, it is more often the larger firms that have the resources necessary to adapt in turbulent times while smaller, more fragile firms often fail. From a Hirschman's perspective, what these large German firms have done is to capture via the voice of their employees, a dynamic force that has enabled these firms to adapt and thrive.

At the heart of Hirschman's formulation is the impact of exit or voice on an existing organization. Rather than celebrating the innovative capabilities of the individual who has "exited" and struck out on his own, Hirschman examines the impact for the existing firm if the innovative potential of a talented employee is allowed to leave. In other words, what impact does it have on a firm or organization if the choice for exit is easy? What is the impact if exit is difficult? In the latter case, voice is likely encouraged and its effect enhanced. In so doing the skills of the individual that would have left the firm have been retained by that firm, to the benefit of the firm's organizational dynamism.[21] If systematically repeated – and if the firm has the organizational resources to manage the retention of talented individuals – such firms will likely maintain a higher degree of adaptation and innovation than the supposedly "sclerotic" firms of Mancur Olson's formulation. Using Hirschman's framework, the question to ask of the German economy is this: given the triple pressures of unification, Europeanization, and globalization, has the efficacy of voice within German firms and organizations decreased, and the likelihood of exit increased?

To operationalize the exit vs. voice concept within the specifics of German firms and organizations requires us to think about it in the

20. Joseph Schumpeter, *Capitalism, Socialism, and Democracy* (New York: Harper and Row, 1975).

21. Robert Axelrod, *The Evolution of Cooperation* (New York: Basic Books, 1984).

context of two other paired concepts: instability vs. flexibility and stability vs. stagnation. One of the virtues which adherents of the German model of organized capitalism have always touted is its ability to achieve organizational flexibility within the context of institutional stability.[22] To the extent that voice – as manifested in such institutions the Betriebsräte, Mitbestimmung, and the Verbände – enhanced economic performance within German firms, stability and flexibility were maintained. The problem for this model during the 1990s, however, is that some of its essential foundational components have been eroded by increased opportunities for exit, which has destabilized organizational flexibility and institutional stability.[23] The destabilization of this virtuous circle (organizational flexibility and institutional stability) by unification, Europeanization, and globalization has caused many observers to offer new critiques of the "high everything" model of German industrial organization.[24] German unification is obviously part of this change, in the sense that the inability to deal with the structural unemployment of the 1990s has made this model less domestically acceptable. However, the more serious challenges in terms of increased exit for German firms and organizations is the EU and the globalized economy. Specifically, German firms and organizations can no longer count on the kind of bounded rationality, which enabled them to assume a stable set of institutional relationships. In other words competitive pressures from lower wage economies represented a much greater challenge to the efficiencies which formerly were present. In Hirschman's formulation, this has produced a much higher degree of "exit" opportunities for German firms. Not only does an expanding EU offer lower cost opportunities for German employers within Europe, but the global competition and the ease of locating production facilities abroad (literally exiting Germany) has substantially increased.

22. Kathleen Thelen, "Beyond Corporatism: Toward a New Framework for the Study of Labor in Advanced Capitalism," *Comparative Politics*, 27 (1), 1994, pp. 107-124.

23. Gary Herrigel, *Industrial Constructions* (New York: Cambridge University Press, 1995); Gary Herrigel, "Crisis in German Decentralized Production," *European Urban and Regional Studies*, 3 (1), 1996, pp. 33-52.

24. Kirsten S. Weaver, *Negotiating Competitiveness: Employment Relations and Industrial Adjustment in the US and Germany* (Boston: Harvard Business School Press, 1995).

The significant question to ponder with respect to the exit vs. voice dichotomy is how large an effect will it have on the adaptive capabilities of German firms and organizations? To the extent that the virtuous circle of voice-based forums within German firms are displaced by such phenomena as management-led "flexibilization," two-tiered wage structures, and part-time workforces, then German firms would begin to look like the structures of those from more liberalized states. Consistent with the individual vs. collective dyad discussed above, exit-oriented institutional patterns in Germany have been more the exception than the rule. To expect German firms and organizations to adapt quickly to such practices would be premature, if not unwise. Rather, a more likely expectation would be for such institutions to attempt to repair and reinvigorate more voice-like patterns and practices.

In the absence of a clear conception of what a voice-based organizational structure would be like, a turn to the exit option by default is possible. In essence, one great advantage that exit has over voice in this context is that it is much more the path of least resistance. In other words, it is much easier for individuals within firms or firms within Germany to exit as individual actors than it is for voice-based collective structures to be created or maintained. The latter requires clear and coordinated cooperative action among multiple organizations, the former relies primarily upon individual choice. And as exit options increase – to the detriment of voice – then organizational sclerosis rather than organizational dynamism becomes much more likely since the innovative individuals no longer have positive incentives to remain within the existing organizations. This is the crucial issue that German firms and organizations must address at the end of the 1990s.

Deals vs. Relationships

There are two primary models of transactions in business enterprises. One is a "deal" the other is a "relationship."[25]

25. O.E. Williamson, *The Economic Institution of Capitalism* (New York: Free Press, 1985).

A deal is a "one off" transaction in which there is no expectation that the parties to any one deal will ever consummate another. The incentive structure in such a bargain is for each of the parties to the deal to try to extract as much as possible from the other. In this sense, it is a classic zero-sum game in which one party's gain takes place at the expense of another. In any such deals between different firms, there is no expectation that one party has any interest in seeing the survival or prospering of the counterpart to the deal. When one is looking for empirical evidence of such practices, it is not surprising that such transactional relationships are more often found in countries where an individualistic ethos and/or an exit option is present. In fact, the presence of a "dealmaking" culture tends to reinforce both. Not surprisingly, countries at the forefront of liberalization and deregulation tend to have a much greater tendency to embrace and celebrate such transactional practices.

A transactional structure based on relationships contains fundamentally different assumptions. Rather than assuming that the parties are isolated actors, a relationship structure expects parties to any single transaction to be one with whom they have multiple transactions and believe that this relationship will continue. In this institutional arrangement the incentive structure is as much concerned with maintaining a conducive climate for future relationships than it is for striking a good bargain, in some cases even more. The parties to an ongoing or long-standing relationship often see this arrangement in positive sum terms. Not surprisingly, organized capitalist countries such as Germany have evolved a transaction model much more attuned to the rhythms of relationships rather than deals. As is the case with collectivist institutional patterns and voice-based organizations outlined above, relationship-based transactional patterns tend to reinforce – and be reinforced by – mutual interaction.

The most common examples of a relationship-based pattern rather than a dealmaking pattern in Germany are obvious. Among the most prominent are:

1. Industry associations (Verbände) which have as their primary function nurturing and reinforcing the

relationships among firms in specific industries.[26] In a feature common to both countries that industrialized late and/or place strong emphasis on exporting goods, these institutions have helped define economic competition differently than countries characterized by "dealmaking" patterns. In Germany competition is seen not primarily as between individual firms in the same domestic industry, but between the respective German industry and a counterpart industry in another country.

2. Works councils (Betriebsräte) and codetermination (Mitbestimmung) which have as their express purpose the aggregating of the interests of all employees within a given firm.[27] By fostering the development of dialogue among different groups of workers within specific firms and industries, these corporatist institutions strengthen the relationships among these groups and head off the "every man (or union) for himself" more characteristic of pluralist forms of organized labor.

3. In the absence of a state-led, dirigiste policy model, Germany has fostered a set of quasi-public institutions that perform many of the public functions performed by state bureaucracies in other countries. By developing a strong set of relationships among private and public sector actors, the Federal Republic was often able to avoid some of the more contentious state vs. market debates that plagued both Britain and France during the past two decades.

4. Framework regulation and self-regulation, which also developed in the absence of a strong centralized state, have generated an environment for developing and enhancing relationships among private and public sector actors. The banking industry is perhaps the most relevant example for demonstrating this pattern.[28] Rather, the German system has relied on a set of strict, but very

26. Ulrich von Alemann and Rolf G. Heinze, eds., *Verbände und Staat* (Opladen: Westdeutscher Verlag, 1980).

27. Kathleen Thelen, *A Union of Parts* (Ithaca: Cornell University Press, 1992).

28. Christopher S. Allen, *Domestic Politics and Private Investment: Financial Regulation in West Germany and the United States* (Washington, DC: American Institute

general, framework regulations (Rahmenbedingungen) that created high barriers to those wishing to enter the financial arena, but offered tremendous freedoms to those who crossed the hurdles and could function within the broad regulatory framework. For example, to start a bank in Germany, it is necessary to both have substantial capital reserves – generally higher than the international average – and to prove to regulatory authorities that bank officers have had sufficient experience in positions of authority in the financial industry.

These patterns of relationship formation and maintenance became deeply developed and solidified throughout the German political economy during the postwar period. In so doing, they effectively pre-empted the emergence of a dealmaking culture within the Federal Republic. As an indicator of the conceptual absence of the later concept, there is no exact translation of the word "deal" in German. *Handel* is not quite sufficient, since it more accurately translates as "trade" and thus fails to capture the "one off" gambling nature of the concept of the deal. To the extent that the word is used in German at all, the English word deal is preferred. In an interview with the former Chairman of the Deutsche Bank, the phrase "we don't do deals, we establish relationships" was the explanation of prevailing German industrial practice.[29] Yet even these deeply held practices were not immune from challenges.

As the processes of Europeanization and globalization intensified during the 1990s, the relationship culture – like the collectivist and voice-based patterns discussed above – also faced profound threats. As German and European businesses were forced to address wider horizons, they necessarily had to break out of the familiar world of long-standing relationships, nurtured over decades. What these actors had to contend with was the influx of dealmakers in an environment previously dominated by persons looking for business rela-

---

for Contemporary German Studies, Johns Hopkins University, 1990), Research Report No. 2.

29. Personal interview with F. Wilhelm Christians, Member, Board of Managing Directors, Deutsche Bank, 23 May 1989.

tionships. In other words, as the ground on which these relationships were based eroded, the dominant German pattern began to give way.

Believing in the German Model?

The preceding exposition of the tensions within each of the three sets of dyads – individual vs. collective, exit vs. voice, and deal vs. relationship – is at the root of the pressures plaguing the eroding German model. Clearly the exogenous shocks of unification, Europeanization, and globalization remain significant factors, but the three sets of conceptual tensions suggest something deeper and more troubling is involved for the German political economy. Clearly there has been tremendous pressure for German policy makers to adapt to the liberalizing, deregulating U.S.-U.K. model, but why? If one were to develop the wider European policy making agenda after a particular pattern, what country would Europe best model itself after: one that emulated that of the U.K. – the poorest performing of the major European nations during the postwar period – or Germany – the best performing one?

The easy answer to this question would be the German pattern rather than the U.K. one.[30] But the issue is far more complicated than that. The advantage that proponents of a liberalizing, deregulating Anglo-American system have is that the individual/exit/dealmaking model is both intuitively simple and instantly and obviously beneficial to those who can move into the new economic terrain and strike while the iron is hot. The organized capitalist German system based upon a collectivism/voice/relationships axis is both interpenetrated and complicated. In that sense it would require conscious and purposeful effort to construct such a system throughout all of Europe if it were to work at all. Moreover it would have to be encompassing in the sense that it would need to incorporate all of the major economic actors within Europe to work as it did within the Federal Republic in the past. Perhaps as

30. Christopher S. Allen, "Institutions Challenged: German Unification, Policy Errors, and the 'Siren Song' of Deregulation," in Lowell Turner, ed., *Negotiating the New Germany: Can Social Partnership Survive?* (Ithaca: Cornell University Press, 1997), pp. 139-156.

the introduction of the euro continues to preempt the role of national political actors in favor of more market-oriented practices, debates over the "democratic deficit" in Europe will prompt a call for more encompassing political institutions. However, as a more market-oriented model develops significant strength, it challenges the more cumbersome encompassing model.

There is also one more fundamental problem with developing and extending a reinvigorated Modell Deutschland for the EU. While the Germans clearly know their model in an intuitive sense, few can actually articulate the fundamental principles that underpin it. When asked, most German policy makers understand it in the context of "that's the way we have always done it" without reflecting on its theoretical underpinnings. Many German policy makers have indeed been heavily influenced by Anglo-American patterns of domestic policy. American based consulting firms like Arthur Andersen and increasing numbers of young German capitalists who have attended U.S. business schools or worked on Wall Street are making their presence felt. Furthermore, these patterns have been reinforced by the increased internationalization of all economies and the largest and most internationally-oriented of the German firms have already departed from the core practices of the old German model.

The previous success of the German-organized capitalist model is that socially constructed institutions of the political economy were interposed between the free market and the parties interacting within it.[31] These institutions foster relationships rather than deals. Deals cannot tolerate changes in the environmental circumstances in which they are made. That is why they must be subordinated to legally enforceable rules. Relationships, on the other hand, can be sustained by ongoing negotiations and trade-offs, allowing for what Kathleen Thelen calls "negotiated adjustment." But these relationships can only survive in the presence of a coherent framework that recognizes and supports distinct and frequently conflicting social and economic interests.

While many countries stress the need for adaptive institutions, effective ones are not created easily. For many countries that might

---

31. I would like to thank Peter Katzenstein for suggestions that have helped refine the exposition of this concept.

try to emulate competitive institutional patterns from Germany – at public, private, local, state-level, regional or national levels – they will be new creations.[32] But German patterns of framework regulation, institutionalized worker participation, vocational education, coordinated organized capitalism, and long term oriented investment developed over decades.

Thus, a more likely explanation can be advanced that an unintended departure from previous German form has been at work. As the best of the new institutionalist literature has argued, institutions are not just fixed structures.[33] They are dynamic entities which – at their best – are embodied by purposeful policy makers and patterns of understood responses to a wide range of policy outcomes. Yet these responses are not spontaneously-occurring phenomena. They need to be understood, reinforced, and continually tested against new challenges if they are to retain the capacity to produce suitable economic policies.

Because the German model of organized capitalism has seldom been touted as an explicit ideology, the German policy makers who have internalized this pattern of behavior – but rarely discussed it explicitly – may be unable to defend its merits when attacked by adherents of deregulation and laissez-faire. In numerous interviews with German officials in both the private and public sectors, researchers have reported that patterns of responses are often more intuitively understood than explicitly discussed. In one sense, this might suggest a beneficial shared understanding of a range of suitable responses. However, it also might indicate an inability to actually understand how to use past, prevailing institutional patterns with contemporary problems. In short, for Germany to build – or rebuild – institutional coherence to make policy choices demanded by residual structural problems concerning unification, European imperatives, and a globalizing economy, the precise role of these institutions must be discussed and understood, not just intuited.

32. David Soskice, "The Institutional Infrastructure for International Competitiveness: A Comparative Analysis of the UK and Germany," in A. B. Atkinson and R. Brunetta, ed., *Economics for the New Europe* (New York: New York University Press, 1991).

33. Sven Steinmo, Kathleen Thelen, and Frank Longstreth, *Structuring Politics: Historical Institutionalism in Comparative Perspective* (New York: Cambridge University Press, 1992).

Chapter 5

THE "STORM BEFORE THE CALM"
Labor Markets, Unemployment, and Standort Deutschland

Michael G. Huelshoff

Germany today is in the grip of self-doubt. Doubts about German democracy – one of the postwar manifestations of the "German Question" – have long troubled Germany and its partners. The one stabilizing factor, indeed the factor most often claimed to be propping up German democracy, was the economy. Today the situation is reversed. No one takes seriously the notion that a post-Cold War, post-unification Germany might pursue an aggressive and non-democratic Sonderweg yet again in Europe – and certainly not the Germans themselves. The debate, such as it is, focuses instead on how "normal" a state Germany can be. The source of self-doubt that seems foremost in Germany today is the economy.

The causes of this striking reversal are found in the very events that have marked the last two decades in Europe – the end of the Cold War and German unification. While these events mean that Germany must rethink its role in the world and in Europe, as Markovits and Reich point out, this is taking place in a context largely determined by Germany's past.[1] Yet German unifi-

1. Andrei S. Markovits and Simon Reich, *The German Predicament: Memory and Power in the New Europe* (Ithaca: Cornell University Press, 1997).

cation and the collapse of socialism in central and eastern Europe have also placed heavy burdens on the German economy. Transition in the new Länder has proven much more costly and time-consuming than was hoped in 1990. The German government can not, however, focus its time and money just on the new Länder – it must also address the transitions among its eastern neighbors. If Germany is to avoid economic and political instability to the east, including such destabilizing effects as immigration, slower growth, and the like; the government must take the lead among Western countries in helping the new democracies in Central and Eastern Europe.

If this is the dramatic dimension of the challenges facing the German economy, there is a more subtle yet equally significant challenge. For some time now, the German model of economic organization – described below – has faced growing pressure. The current jargon for this challenge is "globalization," yet the pressure for change in Germany goes back much further than the currency of this word.[2] Beginning at least in the late 1970s, the German model of economic organization has faced growing demands for change and adjustment to new conditions. Sometimes hidden by fluctuations in economic growth, this debate about German competitiveness – about Standort Deutschland – has never quite been resolved.

In this chapter, I examine one dimension of the Standort Deutschland debate, the question of labor market flexibility and unemployment. To be sure, this is a central element in the criticism leveled at the German economic model, but it is not the only problem. The chapter begins with short descriptions of the German model and the Standort Deutschland debate, followed by a discussion of three of the alternative labor market models being discussed in Germany today, the Anglo-Saxon model, the Dutch model, and Europeanization. I argue that none of these approaches can resolve the perceived Standort crisis. I then turn to what I see happening in Germany, a modified version of the old Modell Deutschland, that places greater emphasis on local actions guided

---

2. See Peter Katzenstein, ed., *Industry and Politics in West Germany: Toward the Third Republic* (Ithaca: Cornell University Press, 1989).

by principles of controlled conflict and gradualism to address Germany's problems. In the process, the role of regional and national politics is being redefined. This model necessitates a lessened role for national institutions and actors, but does not mean that they are as irrelevant as in other states.

The model I develop here, which I call the "storm before the calm" in German political economy, emphasizes the role of public debate in changing definitions of interest among social actors. The current Standort Deutschland debate has a considerable history, and that it is only now beginning to have significant practical implications needs to be explained. Too much of our analysis of German political economy has focused upon institutions and actors, and not enough on the political economic culture in Germany. This culture, I argue, often has its application at local levels, and is shaping Germany's adjustment to globalization in a reasonably consistent direction, toward greater flexibility in work hours and toward enhanced compensation in exchange for job guarantees. These adjustments constitute, I argue, a particularly German response to the collective problems of advanced industrial states. In conclusion, I discuss the implications of these developments for our understanding of the German political economy.

The German Model

As Germany's social market economy has transformed from what Ludwig Erhard described as a relatively unencumbered social market to a modern and extensive welfare state, academic analyses have tended to focus more and more on the interlocking nature of economic decision-making in Germany. With its roots firmly planted in the work of Alexander Gerschenkron, Shonfield's *Modern Capitalism*, one of the first postwar and post Wirtschaftswunder studies of political economy that included Germany, pointed to many of the elements that have come to be thought characteristic of the German political economy. These included the role of peak associations representing capital and labor, the banks as guarantors of the public good, and worker representation at the plant and firm levels. Shonfield also emphasized the importance of consultation among major social actors, including the government, business, and the trade unions.[3]

This consultation quickly became the focus of most analyses of the German political economy. A Modell Deutschland was proposed. As Markovits pointed out, this "Model Germany" had many characteristics, including a compliant political culture, relatively peaceful industrial relations and moderate wage demands, codetermination, a societal consensus favoring both an anti-inflationary policy bias and extensive social safety nets to protect those who suffered under the resulting austerity measures, an export-oriented economy and state, a pluralist and centrist political climate, and competent leadership.[4] Much attention focused upon institutional arrangements. Notions such as "organized capitalism," "managed capitalism," "corporatism," "policy networks," "interlocking politics," "multiple consensus requirements," and "ideology of social partnership" became common in academic discourse. Despite the collapse of informal national-level concertation among capital, labor, and the government in 1976, many analysts found evidence of continued consultation, cooperation, and joint decision-making in Germany, first at the macro, and later increasingly at the meso and micro levels in the German economy.[5] There was a general consensus that in Germany economic decisions were taken (at least in part) with the interests of the collectivity in mind. Major social actors expected to have to bargain, formally or informally, with each other to a greater extent and with more significant results than was common in most other advanced industrial societies. In sum, while academic analysis tended to focus upon the more easily observable institutional dimensions of Modell Deutschland, due note was taken of the ideological elements of the German political economy as well.

3. Andrew Shonfield, *Modern Capitalism: The Changing Balance of Public and Private Power* (London: Oxford University Press, 1965).

4. See Andrei S. Markovits, "Introduction: Model Germany – A Cursory Overview of a Complex Construct," in Andrei S. Markovits, ed., *The Political Economy of West Germany: Modell Deutschland* (New York: Praeger, 1982), pp. 1-11.

5. For a review, see Christopher S. Allen, "From Social Market to Mesocorporatism to European Integration: The Politics of German Economic Policy," in Michael G. Huelshoff, Andrei S. Markovits, and Simon Reich, eds., *From Bundesrepublik to Deutschland: German Politics After Unification* (Ann Arbor: University of Michigan Press, 1993), pp. 61-76.

The accomplishments of Modell Deutschland were indisputable. For most of the two decades after the oil shock in 1973, the German economy maintained high rates of growth, low inflation, and steadily growing productivity when many other economies were floundering. The German standard of living remained among the highest in the world. Given Germany's high degree of dependence on energy and raw material imports, and consequent need for exports to pay for them, this performance was indeed remarkable. It is not surprising, then, that many of Germany's competitors looked to emulate parts of Modell Deutschland, including the British during their experiment in the 1970s with corporatism, or the U.S. during the Carter and later the Clinton administrations.

These successes make the current difficulties in Germany all the more distressing. Modell Deutschland, so it is believed, has fallen on hard times. Now the Germans are debating whether they can learn anything from the very countries that they outperformed for the past two decades.[6] In the next section, I briefly explore this debate about Standort Deutschland.

The Standort Deutschland Debate

The debate about the competitiveness of the German economy rests on several points. First is the relatively high level of unemployment in Germany over the past few years – well over ten percent. In the spring of 1997, the seasonally unadjusted unemployment rate topped 12.2 percent and 4.5 million were out of work – the highest total since Hitler came to power in 1933.[7] This unemployment is also unevenly distributed across Germany, approaching 20 percent in the new states. Additionally, the relatively poor job creation performance of the Germany economy during the last boom, and the

---

6. See, for example, "Henkel: Deutsche können von Briten lernen," *Frankfurter Allgemeine Zeitung,* 28 November 1997, p. 17.

7. The unemployment rate dropped slightly thereafter, but Germany finished the year with the unemployment rate climbing from 11.3 percent in November to 11.8 percent in December, an increase of 373,400 people. The head of the *Bundesanstalt für Arbeit*, Bernhard Jagoda, expected little change during 1998. See "Arbeitslosigkeit in Dezember über 4,5 Millionen," *Handelsblatt Internet Edition*, 9 January 1998.

continued high level of unemployment during the current period of growth, indicate that much of this unemployment is structural – not subject to much change during upswings. Indeed, if the last few rounds of the business cycle are any indication, each recession seems to be adding to the rolls of the permanently unemployed.

Related is the perception that the German economy remains technologically behind the U.S. and Japan, especially in high tech sectors such as computers and telecommunications. To be sure, this is a Europe-wide problem. Part of the reason for the completion of the internal market in Europe was the perception that Europe was falling behind technologically.[8] Despite the Single European Act (SEA), the public perception in Germany is that Germany and the Europeans continue to lag behind the U.S. and Japan in key high-tech sectors, while others are catching up in the sectors where Germany maintained competitive advantages such as heavy engineering or automobiles.

Additional factors fueling the Standort Deutschland debate include the decline in investment in Germany. Between 1970 and 1979, 16.7 percent of all direct foreign investment in the European Union (EU) took place in Germany. This fell to 6.2 percent between 1980 and 1989.[9] Further, the German economy has not posted a surplus in direct investment (German direct investment abroad minus foreign direct investment in Germany) since 1974, and the deficit has accelerated through the 1980s and 1990s, topping DM 30 billion in 1995.[10] Between 1986 and 1995, the German economy attracted $26.8 billion in direct foreign investment, less than the U.S., the U.K., France, Spain, the Netherlands, Sweden, or Italy.

8. Robert O. Keohane and Stanley Hoffmann, "Institutional Change in Europe in the 1980s," in Robert O. Keohane and Stanley Hoffmann, eds., *The New European Community: Decision-Making and Institutional Change* (Boulder: Westview, 1991).

9. It must be noted that direct foreign investment figures are very unreliable, as corporate ownership is increasingly complex, and data collection methods often do not differentiate among types of investment. Yet the public perception is that Germany is an increasingly less attractive place to invest, fueling the Standort Deutschland debate.

10. These data are from the Deutsche Bundesbank's Monthly Report, as reported in Franz Bertsch, *How Competitive is the German Economy? Globalisation is Making Competition Tougher*, Inter Nationes Basis-Info 3-1997, Code No. 770Q8416.

Increasing numbers of German firms are directing their attention, and investment, overseas.[11] For example, Daimler Benz and
Deutsche Telecom listed their stock on the New York Stock
Exchange for the first time in 1997. Veba chairperson Ulrich Hart-
mann stated that "The economic growth we need won't be found in
Germany at the moment – but instead overseas in the Anglo-Saxon
world" when announcing that Veba would do the same.[12] Unlike
the wave of German foreign investment in the 1970s, these firms
seem to be successful, due to relatively low world inflation, improvements in production standards overseas, and better market access
via international and regional free trading regimes and the liberalization of capital markets. In a nutshell, German firms are losing the
sense of nationalism that used to keep them at home. There is an
uncoupling of German commercial interests from domestic politics
that is fueled by the globalization rhetoric.

This is not to say that the German economy is collapsing. There
are pluses as well as minuses for Standort Deutschland.[13] On the
positive side, a highly developed infrastructure, a well-educated
work force, high-quality production standards, political stability, relative social peace, a central geographic location, and a high level of
technological development in many manufacturing sectors all continue to strengthen German competitiveness. Yet, it is argued, the
minuses are beginning to grow for the German economy. In 1991,
Germany had the highest wages among advanced industrial states,
with the third highest personnel costs (after Italy and France). In
1996, German wages rose to DM 47.98 per hour, up 3.2 percent
over 1995.[14] Traditionally, high German wages have been offset by

11. See "Abwanderung der Produktion verstärkt," *Handelsblatt Internet Edition*, 10 April 1997.

12. "German Gridlock," *The Financial Times*, 26 September 1997, p. 12. Hart-
mann added East Asia would also be a likely locale for increased investment, a position that probably no longer holds.

13. See Josef Weindl, *Europäische Gemeinschaft* (Munich: R. Oldenbourg Verlag GmbH, 1996), pp. 233-245.

14. These data are from the BDA. An Institut der deutschen Wirtschaft (IW)
estimate put labor cost increases at 3.9 percent over 1995. See "Deutschland Spitzen-
reiter bei den Arbeitskosten," *Handelsblatt Internet Edition*, 1 July 1997. While the
yearly increase in percentage terms remained below the five percent average posted
between 1990 and 1996, the IW still found that Germany led all other industrial

very high rates of productivity growth. By the mid 1990s, France, Belgium, and the Netherlands surpassed Germany in productivity growth. As high-quality training spreads among Germany's competitors, the competitive compensation that high productivity growth generates for high German wages has begun to erode.

Germans also work among the fewest hours per year, compared to other advanced industrial states. Factory usage is also among lowest in the advanced industrial world, despite the relative infrequency of strikes. Standort minuses are thought to include high wages, a short workweek, and relatively low factory utilization rates, in addition to high taxes, restrictive work laws, high environmental protection costs, and high costs for energy, transport, and communication.

These factors, along with the perception that German capital markets remain weak and inflexible, have contributed to a belief that the German economy is lagging behind its international competitors. The Standort Deutschland debate of the late 1990s has much in common with earlier debates, often seen when the economy was in a slump.[15] That Standort Deutschland might be in

states on this measure. Additionally, Eurostat data show that non-wage labor costs in the EU grew dramatically between 1985 and 1995, from 28.7 percent of labor costs to 42.1 percent. The increase in non-wage labor costs was fastest in Germany, up from 39.5 percent in 1985 to 44.1 percent in 1995. Yet Germany still lagged behind Sweden (56.2 percent) and Finland (53.7 percent) in the EU. See "Abgabenlast auf Arbeit in der EU auf Rekordstand," *Reuters Internet Edition*, 14 November 1997.

15. See, for example, the concluding comments of Willi Semmler in "Economic Aspects of Model Germany: A Comparison with the United States," in Markovits, *The Political Economy of West Germany*; Jeremy Leaman, *The Political Economy of West Germany, 1945-85* (New York: St. Martin's, 1988), especially the conclusion; Graham Hallett, *The Social Economy of West Germany* (New York: St. Martin's, 1973), p. 83; D.M. Gross, "The Relative Importance of Some Causes of Unemployment: The Case of West Germany," *Weltwirtschaftsarchiv*, 124 (3) 1988, pp. 501-523; M. Hellwig and M. Neumann, "Economic Policy in Germany: Was there a Turn-around?" *Economic Policy*, No. 5, 1987, pp. 105-145, and K. Sauernheimer, "Die Standortqualität der Bundesrepublik Deutschland," *Fortbildung*, 35 (1), 1990, pp. 3-5. A more recent treatment with several contributions pointing out weaknesses in the German economy is William D. Graf, ed., *The Internationalization of the German Political Economy* (New York: St. Martin's, 1992). See also K. Seitz, "Die Japanisch-Amerikanische Herausforderung – Europas Hochtechnologieindustrien kämpfen ums Überleben," *Aus Politik und Zeitgeschichte*, B10-11/92, 28 February 1992, pp. 3-15.

trouble is nothing new. What is new is that the debate seems to have captured much more public attention than in the past.

In May 1993, Economics Minister Günter Rexrodt summarized the changes the government saw as necessary to correct the problems faced by the German economy: tax reduction for business; more research and development spending; more flexibility in labor markets; greater emphasis on technical, rather than academic, training; greater stability in energy policy, including greater reliance upon nuclear power; and accelerated privatization of transport and communications.[16] The federal government has floundered about trying to meet these goals, especially in such areas as taxes and pensions. A sharp debate has erupted among trade unionists over how to respond to globalization, while business leaders attempt to expand their independence and flexibility by raising fears that Germany is falling behind. Even Bundespräsident Herzog has issued warnings about Germany's economic future.[17] Irrespective of the reality of an economic crisis in Germany today, there is a perception that globalization exists and requires a fundamental rethinking of Modell Deutschland. In the following sections, I explore three solutions to the labor market and unemployment dimension of this perceived crisis, the Anglo-Saxon model, the Dutch model, and the potential for collective action at the European level.

The Anglo-Saxon Model

The success of the United States, and to a lesser extent Great Britain, in generating new jobs is a frequent theme in discussion about unemployment in Germany. The so-called "jobs machines" of the Anglo-Saxon countries rest on several policy choices, some of which can be emulated in Germany. Yet the underlying philosophy of the Anglo-Saxon model is incompatible with the German tradition. Hence, there is relatively little that the Germans can learn from the experience of the U.S. and the U.K.

16. Eric Owen Smith, *The German Economy*, (London: Routledge, 1994), pp. 515-516.

17. See "Herzog verlangt radikale Reformen," *Handelsblatt Internet Edition*, 28 April 1997.

The Anglo-Saxon model has several dimensions.[18] First are low non-wage labor costs. Taxes and welfare spending are kept low, to minimize personnel costs and to encourage the unemployed to find new work. Worker participation in business decision-making is discouraged, to further minimize non-wage labor costs and maximize entrepreneurial flexibility. Tax relief is used to stimulate investment and private consumption, which is thought to generate new jobs. Large and flexible venture capital markets are linked to new job creation. Finally, labor market flexibility is maintained via comparatively low minimum wages, little in way of wage regulation, and few regulations concerning hiring and firing. In principle, then, the Anglo-Saxon model rests on the argument that individual choice – to offer, or to accept, a job – must be maximized. If labor markets are so organized, according to the logic of this approach, the length of time workers are unemployed will be kept short, and new job creation will be encouraged. Firms therefore maximize their flexibility, a value thought to be crucial in a global economy.

One supposed consequence of this form of labor market organization is low unemployment. The U.S. unemployment rate is about half the German rate. While real wages in the U.S. have fallen in the past decade, the economy has added millions of new jobs. In the German case, real wages have stagnated or slightly increased in the recent past, and comparatively few new jobs have been added. Yet changing the rules of the game to coincide more with the U.S. is not likely in Germany.

Implementing the Anglo-Saxon model in Germany would require significant changes in German industrial relations. No one in Germany today, even on the side of capital, seriously proposes the elimination – or even reduction – in worker representation, a cornerstone of German industrial relations that is the culmination of decades of bargaining and political conflict among capital, labor, and the state. Indeed, these structures are thought to constitute an important Standort plus. Non-wage labor costs have received

---

18. Much of this section is drawn from Thomas Eger and Hans Nutzinger, *The Labor Market Between "Exit" and "Voice": Can the American Model be Applied to Germany?* Inter-Nationes Basis-Info 7-1997, Code No. 770Q8816.

significantly more attention, but action at the macro level has been blocked by the political weakness of the governing coalition (micro level changes are addressed below). Tax cuts have been equally as difficult to negotiate, as has the introduction of more flexibility in hiring and firing (with the notable exception of the 1985 Job Promotion Act).

The Anglo-Saxon model clashes with the German model not just in terms of the translation of its details, but in its basic philosophy. The German model rests on long-term cooperation among workers and managers. The rules that protect German workers from dismissal, guarantee relatively high wages even for those beginning a new job, and provide generous non-wage compensation for workers (vacations, holiday pay, etc.) also tie workers to firms, giving them a greater stake in the firm's success or failure. Thus, firms are more likely to develop institutional structures, and improve the skills of their work force, to emphasize quality in production – another Standort plus. This is not the case in the U.S. or U.K., where workers move freely from one firm to the next and managers organize the firm around simple and easily monitored tasks that can be accomplished by semiskilled (and hence easily replaced) labor.

Some Anglo-American policies can be used in Germany, including the freeing up of venture capital.[19] Yet this too can have only limited effect on Germany's international competitiveness. The traditional conservatism of German investors suggests that it will be a long time before venture capital markets in Germany play the sort of role they play in the U.S. Lowering wages for unskilled workers is another alternative, so as to create incentives for employers to hire them. Lower minimum wages can only be of limited usefulness, however, as most of these proposals are coupled with wage subsidies to guarantee adequate income levels for unskilled workers – a further drain on already tight public coffers. As this last example shows, it is difficult to conceptualize the application of policies developed for a society based on individualism in a society based upon collective values.

---

19. Which, it would appear, was a goal of the CDU/CSU/FDP governing coalition for 1998. See "Koalition Plant Umfassende Finanzmarktöffnung," *Frankfurter Allgemeine Zeitung*, 3 December 1997, p. 17.

The Dutch Model

If the Anglo-Saxon model can be of only limited utility in Germany, then the Dutch model, drawn as it is from a society much more similar to Germany, might seem a better fit. In Germany today, there is much discussion of the utility of the Dutch model to address Germany's economic problems. Yet there are elements of the Dutch model that would be difficult to transfer to Germany.

The core of the Dutch model is a compromise struck between capital and labor in November 1982 that traded off improvements in profits and redistribution of work for wage restraint.[20] This agreement linked restraint in wage demands to reduction in work hours. Further, reduced work hours were also linked to reduction in pay. The state, which had worked before 1982 to prop up wages, reduced its role in the national bargaining among capital and labor. Local deviation from national standards was permitted, especially for wages. As a result, and in the context of high unemployment and falling international competitiveness, trade unions weakened. The balance of political power, once the state had removed itself from direct participation in collective bargaining by allowing local independence, shifted to capital.[21] One consequence of this development is a fall in real wages in the Netherlands in the past decade.

An additional part of the Dutch model is moderation in social spending. Through the 1980s, and even prior to the reduced hours for less pay compromise in 1982, Dutch governments worked to cut back the welfare state (from, admittedly, a very high level). Public and semipublic sector pay cuts were instituted, and unemployment benefits were curtailed. The state also encouraged broader use of early retirement schemes, which became common in the Netherlands. Finally, a key element of the Dutch model is the increased use of part-time work. Beginning in 1984, part-time employment schemes grew, often targeted at school-leavers and other young workers. By 1996, 38.1 percent of all employed per-

20. A.F. van Zweeden, "The Netherlands," in B.C. Roberts, ed., *Industrial Relations in Europe* (London: Croom Helm, 1985), p. 171.

21. Jelle Vesser, "Continuity and Change in Dutch Industrial Relations," in Guido Baglioni and Colin Crouch, eds., *European Industrial Relations: The Challenge of Flexibility* (London: Sage, 1990), p. 221.

sons had part-time jobs, a much higher share than in the U.K. (24.6 percent), or Germany (16.3 percent).

The Dutch model is debated in Germany today primarily because it seems to have led to uncommonly low unemployment, and macroeconomic stability. In April 1997, the Dutch unemployment rate stood at 5.3 percent, one of the lowest in Europe. The number of people at work rose over 16 percent between 1982 and 1997. Similar figures for Germany and the EU are three and four percent, respectively. Additionally, macroeconomic performance has been strong. Between 1987 and 1994, real GDP rose at an annual average of 2.84 percent, significantly higher than the 2.1 percent EU average. Real GDP growth is projected at three percent for 1998. The 1998 projected budget deficit is 1.8 percent of GDP, down from 2.6 percent in 1997 – and well within the criterion of the European Monetary Union (EMU).

Can, as many advocate, this model be translated to Germany? As with the Anglo-Saxon model, there are things the Germans can learn from the Dutch. Yet there are hidden aspects of the Dutch model that suggest that its utility in addressing Germany problems will be limited.

On the plus side, there is no doubt that easing the availability of part-time work would cut into Germany's unemployment rate. That less than half as many (in percentage terms) Germans hold part time jobs than do the Dutch suggests some room for job creation via part-time work. Especially important is the targeting of young workers. Getting part-time work off the ground, however, has proven difficult. Encouraged by the 1985 Job Promotion Act, generation of more part-time work is currently mired in the so-called "DM 630 jobs" debate. At issue is the payment of social security fees for workers whose weekly wages fall below DM 630, the cut-off for mandatory employee and employer contributions. Resolving these issues will ease the use of part-time work. Data from early 1998 indicates that part-time work is growing in Germany.

Yet the negatives are also significant. A close look at the Dutch case suggests that the unemployment success is a bit misleading. While some of the reduction in unemployment is attributable to part-time work, work times have also fallen significantly. The average hours worked per worker per year in the Netherlands fell from seventeen hundred in 1991 to fourteen hundred in 1996. This means the economy is producing fewer goods. Since Germany already ranks at the bottom among advanced industrial countries in hours worked, there is limited room for squeezing more jobs out of reduced hours. Further, the utility of reduced work hours in generating new jobs is not supported by the Dutch case. As Vesser points out, the reduction in work hours negotiated between 1982 and 1985 in the Netherlands generated little new employment, in part due to chronic over-staffing in many Dutch firms.[22] Management responded to reduced work hours by cutting operating time, not by hiring new workers. Thus, it is unlikely that the low rates of unemployment in the Netherlands were generated by reduced work hours, or that lowering work hours will automatically reduce the unemployment rate in Germany. I return to this issue below.

Additionally, the low rates of unemployment have been partially generated by keeping large numbers of people out of the work force. In 1996, labor force participation in the Netherlands stood at 62.4 percent, much lower than the 68.8 percent in Germany, 73.7 percent in the U.K., or 77.3 percent in the U.S. Most of this is due to spouses who choose to stay at home, and to early retirements. While there is, in principle, nothing wrong with reducing the active work force in this way, it does raise social issues, especially for women (the usual stay-at-homes). Early retirement may not be suitable for all workers, especially those who value work for more than just its wages. These social costs must be addressed in schemes to reduce the active labor force. Additionally, the Netherlands and Germany currently vary very little in the percentage of women between the ages of 25 and 54 who work, nor do they vary much in the percentage of males between 55 and 64 who work.[23] Clearly, there is little for the Germans to learn from the Dutch here.

The liberal application of disability is another way the Dutch have reduced labor force participation. Beginning in 1967, the

22. Jelle Vesser, "Continuity and Change," p. 216.

23. Additionally, in comparative terms the Germans and Dutch lag significantly behind most other advanced industrial countries in employing both women aged 25 to 54 or men aged 55 to 64, suggesting little room for further reductions in the active labor force from these categories of workers. See Martin Wolf, "Europe's Real Insiders," *The Financial Times*, 18 November 1997, p. 16.

Dutch government gradually liberalized its definition of disability and the administration of disability regulations. First, the definition of disability was expanded to include a broad range of psychological illnesses including stress; and for those partially disabled, part-time work was required to be in the disabled worker's former profession. The former move greatly increased the total number of workers claiming disability, to over four times of expectations, in just a few years. By 1988, stress-related illnesses and disabilities accounted for about a third of new disability cases, up from 13 percent in 1970.[24] Disability payments were fixed at 80 percent of prior income (70 percent after 1987), indexed to wage increases, and continued until retirement. Unemployment benefits, in contrast, tailed off after two and a half years (now six months, after reforms in the late 1980s), making a disability claim more financially attractive than an unemployment claim. Further, disability adjudicators were required to take into consideration the difficulties that the partially disabled would face finding similar work, effectively making partial disability total. Even a finding of partial disability, then, could result in full payment.[25]

Despite reforms in the early 1990s designed to take new and young recipients off the disability rolls, Dutch disability rates are still much higher than the OECD (Organization for Economic Co-operation and Development) average. In 1994, 40.1 percent of all workers falling in the OECD's broad unemployment definition (which includes those on unemployment schemes, social assistance, early retirement, and subsidized employment, as well as disability) were categorized disabled.[26] It is doubtful whether the Germans should want to replicate this program, and unlikely that they could afford it.

The Dutch unemployment success comes with some significant hidden costs. How, then, have the Dutch been able to maintain such strong macroeconomic performance? Some suggest that

24. Rudy B. Andeweg and Galen A. Irwin, *Dutch Government and Politics* (New York: St. Martin's Press, 1993), pp. 204-205.

25. Organization for Economic Co-Operation and Development, *The Labour Market in the Netherlands* (Paris: OECD, 1993), p. 18.

26. Organization for Economic Co-Operation and Development, Paris: OECD, 1996.

it has come via a 10 percent decrease in the Dutch guilder's trade-weighted exchange rate between 1981 and 1996.[27] Germany's trade-weighted exchange rate grew 50 percent during the same period. Exchange rate policy will no longer be available to Germany – or the Dutch – with EMU. Additionally, real wage decreases have helped to maintain strong macroeconomic performance and low unemployment. In 1997, real wages in the Netherlands were lower than they had been in 1990. Replicating this performance is a less than optimal solution for German workers. While the Dutch model suggests that the Germans might well benefit from greater use of part-time work, the other ways the Dutch have reduced their unemployment may not be acceptable in Germany.

Europeanization

A third strategy to address problems with German competitiveness is Europeanization. Much of the logic behind the SEA and EMU is to make Europe more competitive in the global economy. While the SEA did not have its projected effects on European competitiveness, and while EMU probably will also not radically change the situation, collective action remains an option. Again, while some things can be accomplished at the European level, the Standort crisis will not be resolved there. In this section, I will examine three issues, the regionalization of labor markets, collective action to address unemployment, and the fit between German and European economic and social preferences.

One strategy to address European, as well as German, competitiveness problems is to develop European-level labor markets. Indeed, of late there has been increased attention on issues such as

27. Wolfgang Münchau and Gordon Cramb, "Debunking the Dutch Myth," *The Financial Times*, 18 September 1997, p. 13. Trade-weighted exchange rates are the average of the exchange rates of all countries with whom a nation trades, weighted by the volume of trade between the two. Thus, the trade-weighted exchange rate gives a measure of the likely impact of exchange rate fluctuations on trade flows. See Robert E. Hall and John B. Taylor, *Macroeconomics*, fifth edition (New York: W.W. Norton, 1997).

European collective bargaining, common company statutes, and increased labor market flexibility. Yet the room for change here is limited. On some issues, German interests seem quite out of line with those of its European partners. The Germans vetoed a draft company statute regulation in the fall of 1997 because it failed to protect German codetermination adequately. The level of worker participation in firm decision-making common in Germany was unacceptable to most of Germany's European partners. There are limitations in other areas as well. European-level collective bargaining has long been debated in the EU's Economic and Social Council and the European Trades Unions Confederation, with little success. In the face of globalization, some unions have reiterated the need for European-level coordination. Yet the old problems of cooperation across Europe remain – huge differences in union organization, philosophy, and scope; vastly different legal environments; and significant language and resource barriers. While it may be moving forward, it will be a long time before European-level collective bargaining begins to reshape national politics.

The German veto was even more evident and effective over collective action to address unemployment. At the Amsterdam summit in June of 1997, and the follow-on jobs summit in November 1997, the Germans blocked a more active European role fighting unemployment. German opposition was based on several points. First, the Germans argued that unemployment is best addressed at the local level, and not at the national or regional levels. Thus, unemployment programs in Germany are decentralized, and most of the management of German unemployment is taken out of the government's hands and placed in those of the para-public Federal Labor Office. Second, the proposals to fund European-level unemployment programs were unacceptable to the Germans.[28] These proposals included pooling of existing funds, transfers within the EU budget, and the redirecting of spending within existing budget lines. Only the latter was acceptable to Germany, since the pooling of funds would have redistributed German unemployment funds to other states,[29] and transfers within the

28. Much of the following is taken from the author's interviews, Bonn, May-June 1997.

budget would have generated opposition from the current recipients. Since the unemployment problem and its solutions were defined as local by the Germans, and since there was no way to find the resources for new European-level programs, the Germans would accept only small steps and minor shifts in existing programs at the Amsterdam and jobs summits. These included some loose guidelines for job creation and regular reporting on their achievement, a pledge to offer training for young workers and the long-term unemployed, a commitment to ensure that at least 20 percent of the unemployed are in training after five years, the commitment of ECU 1 billion from the European Investment Bank for start-up and venture capital loans for small- and medium-sized firms, and consideration of tax reforms to encourage job creation.[30]

Behind these positions on labor market harmonization and unemployment policy were two fundamental elements of the German approach to Europeanization. The first is a preference for market solutions that has characterized the German position on Europe from the founding of the Common Market. There has long been tension in the EU between market tendencies and dirigiste tendencies, between preferences for private action versus public intervention. The Germans have, for the most part, emphasized the market. Hence, the generation of European-level labor law must pass through a German market filter that is often alien to other governments (such as the French). This is not to suggest that the Germans always prefer freeing labor markets along Anglo-Saxon lines. As was suggested, the German government often wants to see its comparatively rigid labor market replicated at the EU level. Rather, the tension lies in the extent to which the state should be involved in labor markets, especially in job creation schemes.

29. This would have resulted in a net loss for Germany, at a time when there were almost uniform demands in Germany, from Chancellor Kohl on down, for a fairer distribution of the German contribution to the EU budget, and for reductions in the overall German contribution. See "Kohl: Deutsche EU-Beiträge zu Hoch," *Handelsblatt Internet Edition*, 16/17 August 1997.

30. "Special EU Jobs Summit," *European Voice*, 27 November-3 December 1997, p. 31.

Second, there was dissatisfaction with the trajectory of European social policy generally in Bonn.[31] There was a growing perception in the Kohl government that the EU had developed as far as it should in the social field. Policy makers spoke more of the need for maintaining national flexibility and independence in social policy making than in the past. This seemed to be driven by a perception that European Court of Justice rulings unduly limited the government in addressing social policy problems. In short, some in the German government were increasingly less interested in codifying European social law, and wished to keep social policy on an intergovernmental agenda.

The Schröder government is decidedly warmer toward European-level cooperation to fight unemployment. The government's January 1999 program for its six-month tenure as Council president raised unemployment to the very top of the European agenda. The departure of Oskar Lafontaine from the coalition, however, was widely interpreted as a shift back toward the right on economic questions. The full scope of German policy toward Europeanization of unemployment, however, remains unclear. German positions are likely to remain at least partially constrained by some of the factors that the former government also faced.

The scope for addressing Germany's perceived labor market problems at the European level is limited. It is difficult to find a consensus at the European level that would also protect Modell Deutschland. Further, the Germans are firmly opposed to a more activist role for the EU in fighting unemployment. Finally, all EU initiatives must pass through a peculiarly German market filter, and the government is beginning to define its preferences away from more EU social law, and toward more German intergovernmental action. Thus, it seems unlikely that a solution to the Standort Deutschland problem can be found at the EU level. Regardless, European-level politics and political developments are of growing concern for all members, including the Germans. For example, the introduction of part-time work was eased by the passage of an anti-discrimination regulation by the Council of Ministers in

---

31. Author's interviews, Bonn, May-June 1997.

December 1997,[32] and the monitoring program put in place by the Economic and Social Council should help to further the goals of the jobs summit.[33] The inclusion of unemployment in the Amsterdam Treaty also raises the saliency of the issue at the European level. The options the Germans have to affect the competitiveness of the Germany economy are limited, and will be further limited, by the development of EU law and policy competence.

The Uniquely German Solution

Neither the Anglo-Saxon model, nor the Dutch model, nor Europeanization offer single and unique solutions to the Standort Deutschland debate. Each may help to reduce unemployment in Germany, but none is satisfactory in and of itself. The Anglo-Saxon case suggests the need for limited labor market deregulation, and for programs to encourage venture capital. Labor market deregulation is also a lesson of the Dutch model, especially in the creation of more part-time work opportunities. Europeanization can help in a more general fashion, by finding points of coordination with other EU states, and exploring new ideas. None of these examples, alone or taken together, offer satisfactory or coherent solutions to the perceived Standort Deutschland problem.

I have emphasized the perceived nature of the crisis in German competitiveness for a purpose. Much of the data presented here suggests that the Germans are indeed lagging behind their competitors on some – but not all – economic indicators. Yet there is an underappreciated part of Modell Deutschland that helps, I argue, to clarify the nature and severity of the Standort Deutschland crisis, and to resolve it. This is what I call the "storm before the calm" element of German economic culture: the propensity for the Germans to complain loudly about how bad they have it, and

32. Yet even this step may prove of limited value, since the generation of minimum standards for the treatment of part-time workers is left to the member governments. See "EU-Minister über Teilzeitarbeit einig," *Handelsblatt Internet Edition*, 15 December 1997.

33. See "ESC Preparing to Follow Up Jobs Summit," European Voice, 6-12 November 1997, p. 29.

then come together to resolve their problems in an almost coordinated, but ad hoc fashion. That is, the storm of public complaint comes first in Germany, followed by the calm of social adjustment to new economic conditions. While much of the earlier analysis of Modell Deutschland correctly pointed to the importance of the economic culture ("ideology of social partnership," for example) in the study of German political economy, these arguments help to understand the recent developments in Germany.

The social adjustment that follows public outcry in Germany, I argue, is often of an ad hoc character. Social actors at relatively low levels of aggregation find local solutions to what are perceived to be aggregate problems. These solutions are copied elsewhere in the economy if they seem to work. In the case of this latest round of the Standort debate, this is manifest in the large number of deals cut at the industry level to reduce costs, and in the growing localization of collective bargaining, often at the firm and plant level. These processes are long run – they entail gradual change and social consensus that predate this latest round of the Standort Deutschland debate. What is important here is the element of social consensus. While imperfect, there seems to be a growing consensus in Germany that the economy can not address the problems of globalization using the old means. Without this growing consensus, it would be difficult for the German political economy to adjust to changing international conditions. While the competitive pressures have existed for some time, it is the growth of this consensus, I believe, that is leading to a renegotiation of the postwar compromise that is Modell Deutschland.

On the surface, public debate before social or political action can be said to characterize all modern democracies. There are two factors that make the German case different. The first is the reluctance to engage in large-scale social experimentation, as opposed to, for example, the United Kingdom under Thatcher, or the Netherlands. Gradualism has long been noted in analyses of political change in Germany since 1945, as in other countries. The changes I describe here, however, are all happening fairly quickly – what has developed gradually is the social recognition that change is needed. Second, what makes the German debate about globalization and Standort Deutschland unique is the fevered pitch at which it takes place. All sides of the debate use catastrophic predictions to make their case. In this way, the German "calm before the storm" stands out in comparison to many other societies.

There are a number of indicators that suggest that German workers and managers are slowly adjusting to global pressures, and are doing so on their own and without coordinated governmental policy. First, compensatory cuts were negotiated in a range of wage agreements that were negotiated in the year after the passage of a new federal law limiting sick pay. This law, pushed heavily by business, sought to lower the non-wage tax burdens on employers by limiting sick pay. The law quickly became a cause celebre among the unions, leading to angry exchanges between managers and unionists, and some short-term strikes when employers tried to write the new sick pay law into existing and new collective bargaining agreements in the fall and winter of 1996. The employers were forced to back down.

Yet in the collective bargaining agreements reached between November 1996 and the summer of 1997, compensatory reductions in non-wage compensation were negotiated. In exchange for maintaining sick pay at one hundred percent of wages in the rubber, metal and electrical, cement, chemicals, clothing and textile, ceramics, paper, construction, mining (Rheinland-Pfaltz and Bayern only), plastics (Bayern only), and food (Hesse and Rheinland-Pfaltz only) industries, cuts were made in a range of related benefits. These cuts included excluding overtime work from the calculation of vacations, limitations in payments for short-term illnesses, and reductions in vacation and spa benefits.[34] If sick pay cuts were unacceptable, the unions recognized that cuts were necessary elsewhere in order to maintain jobs. This pattern is similar to the agreement between IG Metall and Volkswagen in 1993 to introduce a four-day work week with cuts in fringe benefits in lieu of cuts in basic monthly wages, and the agreement with Mercedes

34. These were among a large variety of additional cuts. A significant amount of regional variation was also allowed in some of the cutbacks for the industry-wide agreements. See "Tarifvertragliche Umsetzung des Entgeltfortzahlungsgesetzes mit Auswirkung auf den Krankenstand," Bundesverband der Deutschen Arbeitgeberverbände, *Tarifarchiv*/Wy, nd.

to locate its new mini-car facility in Germany in exchange for restructuring early retirement regulations in favor of the firm.

Even more significant was the outcome of collective bargaining in the chemical industry in the spring of 1997. Negotiators for the unions and the chemical industry trade association agreed to a new contract that allowed for wage cuts of up to ten percent, and adjustment of work hours in exchange for no layoffs, when firms faced serious economic distress. Further, the new contract encouraged greater independence from industry-wide rules, allowing local union councils to negotiate deals independent from national unions, and decentralizing collective bargaining. The latter provisions are similar to those negotiated by IG Metall for workers in chemical plants in eastern Germany. Other examples of flexibility at the firm level include the agreement at Opel in 1997 to introduce work hour "corridors" that allow managers to raise or lower work hours in response to changes in demand, an expansion of early retirement possibilities at VW negotiated in June of 1997 to open up jobs for young workers, and the agreement by Ford and its workers to keep jobs in exchange for $120 million in benefit cuts. Finally, Opel was able to lower high rates of worker absenteeism by linking holiday bonuses to absenteeism rates at the factory level.[35] While many of these agreements were made possible by the passage of the 1985 Job Promotion Act, it was the growing sense of crisis a decade later that has led to these agreements.

These developments at the local level have not come without controversy. The bypassing of collective bargaining agreements often results in wages significantly lower than those reached under traditional collective bargaining. This has led to a sharp conflict in the construction industry in Berlin, for example, where construction firms operating under locally negotiated wage agreements in Brandenburg have been able to win contracts away from firms operating under collective bargaining constraints in Berlin.[36] Local autonomy has also led to controversy in the union movement. Many unions have found it difficult to find consistent responses to localization. IG

35. See Graham Bowley and Frederick Stuedemann, "Job Evaluation Needed," *The Financial Times Survey: Germany*, 18 November 1997. p. IV.

36. A counter-trend is seen in the East German steel industry. See "Ost-Stahlindustrie steht Streik bevor," *Handelsblatt Internet Edition*, 15 December 1997.

Metall, for example, was split into three rival camps at its November 1997 Darmstädter Kongress zur Reform des Flächentarifs during a debate on how to respond to loss of control over local negotiations. One camp emphasized maintaining the existing system and ignoring local deviations, a second preferred to essentially eliminate wage scales and embrace localization, and a third to develop a system of alternative wage scales that might rein in localization.[37]

An additional controversy is the proposal, reiterated in April 1997 at the Berlin DGB Employment Summit, to further reduce work hours to thirty-two per week, with or without full pay. Business reaction was overwhelmingly negative, without regard to the issue of compensation.[38] The president of the Federal Labor Office, Bernhard Jagoda, predicted that a reduction in work hours would produce few new jobs. The controversy continues, and has been fueled by some voices in the CDU calling for a return to a forty-hour week.[39] Yet survey data suggest that there is little support among workers for the thirty-two-hour week as a means to fight unemployment,[40] and the head of the DGB, Dieter Schulte, backed away from the proposal in November 1997.[41]

On the surface, the localization of wage bargaining, particularly in light of the collapse of national initiatives such as the Bund für Arbeit in 1996, suggests that Germany may well be going the

37. Rainer Hank, "Die IG Metall unter Schock," *Frankfurter Allgemeine Zeitung*, 24 November 1997, p. 17. That the union movement remains uncertain over reforms is seen in the continuing debate at all levels. See "DGB Warnt vor Atomisierung der Tarife," *Handelsblatt Internet Edition*, 23 October 1997.

38. See "Zwickel will 32-Stunden-Woche", *Handelsblatt Internet Edition*, 10 April 1997; Peter Thelen, "Falsche Fährte," *Handelsblatt Internet Edition*, 10 April 1997; "Harte Debatte um 32-Stunden-Woche," *Handelsblatt Internet Edition*, 11 April 1997. Most economic analysis suggest that a reduction in work hours will have only a slightly positive impact on unemployment. See Owen Smith, *The German Economy*, pp. 315-317. Much the same was found by the OECD in studies of reductions in France, and in studies of some sectors of the German economy. See "Slight Effect of Work Week Cuts," *The Financial Times*, 16 December 1997, p.4.

39. "Streit um Rückkehr zu 40-Stunden-Woche," *Handelsblatt Internet Edition*, 4 August 1997.

40. "Wenig Interesse an 32-Stunden-Woche," *Handelsblatt Internet Edition*, 26 August 1997.

41. "Schulte gegen 32-Stunden-Woche," *Handelsblatt Internet Edition*, 18 November 1997. Schulte expressed a preference for cuts in hours worked per year and early retirement.

Anglo-Saxon route. Yet it is important to note that in each case noted above, plant-level agreements to cut costs were possible only because management agreed not to cut jobs. Further, there are signs that trade unionism is not dying in Germany. Buttressed, no doubt, by reports that demand stimulation would help to pull the Germany economy out of recession and generate new jobs, many unions entered the fall of 1997 calling for four to five percent wage increases in future bargaining. In his annual New Year press conference, Schulte indicated that in 1998 the unions will push a more aggressive campaign for wage increases than in the recent past, while his vice-chair, Walter Reiser, spoke of the need for wage reform.[42] At this writing, it seems as if the unions have hardened their bargaining positions. In sum, reform of labor markets goes hand-in-hand with continued trade union activism.

The Germans, therefore, seem to be groping toward a redefinition of the postwar compromise between capital and labor. The trend toward labor market flexibility is likely to continue, but this has not (yet) resulted in the relative collapse of trade unionism seen in the U.S. or the U.K., nor the seeming permanent weakening of trade unionism in the Netherlands. The Standort Deutschland debate has clearly risen to crisis proportions in Germany, but the Germans are finding their own solutions to the problems posed by globalization, and they are doing so in an ad hoc fashion emphasizing local-level adjustment. The full dimensions of this new compromise are not yet apparent, but cutbacks in wage and non-wage compensation will not mean that trade unionism is threatened. What appears to be developing is a new consensus that provides for flexibility in working hours and, occasionally, in pay, in exchange for job guarantees. This trend is coupled with reductions in non-wage compensation. The pattern looks little like the Anglo-Saxon or Dutch models, and does not rely upon European-level institutions or processes. As the storm of public debate fades, what will be increasingly clear is that the Germany economy is finding its feet – in a uniquely German way.

42. "DGB kündigt härtere Gangart an," *Handelsblatt Internet Edition*, 13 January 1998; "Riester fordert grundlegende Tarif-Reform," *Handelsblatt Internet Edition*, 13 January 1998.

Conclusion

The debate about Standort Deutschland reflects, I argue, underlying tendencies in the German political economy that emphasize collective decision-making and a culture of compromise. In this chapter, I have explored three solutions to the perceived problems of the German economy: a greater reliance upon unregulated labor markets, an adoption of the Dutch model, and a regionalization of German labor markets. In each case, the alternatives being debated in Germany today offer only partial solutions to the perceived problems facing Germany. What is developing in Germany is, I argue, a uniquely German solution, one that matches localization of collective bargaining with continued active trade unionism at the national and regional levels. Greater flexibility in work hours and pay, and cuts in non-wage compensation, are being exchanged for job guarantees. In other words, while the relationship between capital and labor is being redefined, this redefinition is taking place in the traditional postwar German political culture of cooperation, controlled conflict, and gradualism.

Academic analyses of the German political economy usually blend together the interest, institutional, and ideological bases of German politics. What this analysis suggests is that the ideological bases may well prove more important to understanding German politics, especially in times of stress and change. Ideology, it seems, provides initial guidelines or rules of the game when there is considerable risk and uncertainty. These guidelines and rules shape, but do not determine, the resulting compromises in interests that are institutionalized. Yet ideology itself is subject to rival interpretation, and can adjust when objective conditions change.

Chapter 6

THE BUNDESRAT, INTEREST GROUPS, AND GRIDLOCK

German Federalism at the End of the Twentieth Century

Stephen J. Silvia

Over the course of the 1990s, the Bundesrat (Federal Council) – the second house of the German parliament – has come to play an increasingly important role in German politics. Prominence, however, has brought the Bundesrat far more admonition than approbation, particularly from the German business community, because the opponents of former chancellor Helmut Kohl's governing coalition have used the second house to hinder the passage of most proposals for economic reform.

Starting in the mid 1990s, the president of the Federal Association of German Industry (Bundesverband der Deutschen Industrie, BDI), Hans-Olaf Henkel, repeatedly denounced the role of several components of the German political order – in particular, the Bundesrat – as detrimental to the German economy because they impede quick decision-making. Henkel argued that if the Federal Republic continued to take only slow and at best incomplete steps toward deregulation and tax relief, it would quickly slide into the economic minor leagues.[1] Similarly, Hans Peter Stihl, president of the German Chambers of Industry and Commerce (Deutscher Industrie- und Handelstag, DIHT), said that he "worried" about the Bundesrat impeding economic reform.[2] Corporate leaders, such as Wolfgang von Pierer from Siemens and Wendelin Wiedeking from Porsche, as well as prominent pro-business politicians, such as Otto Lambsdorff, have all called for reforms that include reducing the role of the Bundesrat in German politics.[3]

In order to assess the significance of the intense mobilization against the current role of the Bundesrat, it is essential to answer the following question: Why did the Bundesrat, after spending the first decade of Helmut Kohl's government in obscurity, suddenly become one of the most important institutions in German politics? Two contending arguments can be distilled out of the hundreds of analyses of the Bundesrat undertaken over the decades as the best potential explanations for a rise in the importance of the Bundesrat in German politics: a "political conjuncture" hypothesis[4] and a "structural secular" analysis.[5] Celestial analogies capture the essence of each of these arguments.

From the perspective of the political-conjuncture argument, the Bundesrat resembles a comet. The second chamber journeys along an elliptical orbit within the German political universe. Whenever the political constellation at the federal and state (Land) levels produces majorities comprising different political parties in the two houses of the German parliament, the Bundesrat swings deep into the heart of German politics. The Bundesrat blazes

1. *Handelsblatt*, 29 July 1997; and *Wirtschaftswoche*, 7 August 1997.

2. *Welt*, 15 September 1997.

3. *Spiegel*, 23 June 1997; *Süddeutsche Zeitung*, 8 August 1997; and *Welt*, 22 September 1997.

4. For example, Hartmut Klatt, "Forty Years of German Federalism: Past Trends and New Developments," *Publius* 19, no. 4 (Fall 1989), pp. 185-202; Peter Pulzer, "Responsible Party Government and Stable Coalition: The Case of the German Federal Republic," *Political Studies* 26, no. 2 (June 1978), pp. 181-208; and Hans-Georg Wehling, "The Bundesrat," *Publius* 19, no. 4 (Fall 1989), pp. 59-60.

5. Fritz W. Scharpf, "Der Bundesrat und die Kooperation auf der 'dritten Ebene'," in Bundesrat, ed., *Vierzig Jahre Bundesrat.* Tagungsband zum wissenschaftlichen Symposion in der Evangelischen Akademie Tutzing vom 11. bis 14. April 1989 (Baden-Baden: Nomos, 1989), pp. 121-61.

brightly, capturing considerable public attention during these periodic occultations of the traditional centers of elected political power, that is, the chancellor and the Bundestag (Federal Diet). Nonetheless, this dazzling display of political pyrotechnics has little lasting impact on the underlying German political institutions and practices. Eventually, Landtag or Bundestag elections shift the German political constellation once more. The first and second houses of the German parliament come back into a harmonious political alignment and the Bundesrat is tossed once again into the remote outer depths of the German political solar system until the cycle repeats itself. Moreover, just as observers in ancient times believed that the appearance of a comet heralded the dawning of a new era, some contemporary political prognosticators claim that a divided German legislature portends an imminent change of government.[6]

A second argument takes a structural-secular approach. The proponents of this perspective assert that the combination of strong, competitive political parties and the expansion of "policy interdependence" (Politikverflechtung) both horizontally (i.e., among the Länder) and vertically (i.e., between the Länder and the federal government) has increasingly immobilized German politics.[7] Immobilism has grown steadily since at least the late 1960s. Today, policy makers in the Federal Republic have extreme difficulty implementing even the most modest reform, because an ever widening circle of public institutions and political jurisdictions – each with particularistic concerns – can block it. Consequently, over the years, Germany has enacted increasingly fewer reform proposals. Fritz Scharpf's depiction of the German polity evokes the image of the Bundesrat as an asteroid hurtling toward a collision with a planet representing Germany's democracy and economy. A continual strengthening of institutional "gravity" in the form of Politikverflechtung makes it increasingly difficult for German policy makers to change the course of the Bundesrat in order to avert an economic and political cataclysm.

The first forty years of the Federal Republic of Germany, which include one instance of divided government, served as the empir-

6. *Welt*, 27 September 1997.
7. For example, Scharpf, "Der Bundesrat," pp. 131-132; and Konrad Hesse, *Der Unitarische Bundesstaat* (Karlsruhe: Müller, 1962).

ical foundation for both the political-conjuncture and structural-secular analyses. This chapter tests the power of these models by applying them to the decade of German history that has transpired since their development, which contains a second round of divided government. The chapter begins with an overview of the role of the Bundesrat in the German political system since 1949 followed by an analysis of the two periods of divided government. It concludes with an appraisal of the political-conjuncture and structural-sectoral schools in light of the most recent experience with divided government in the Federal Republic. The chapter finds that today's "reform gridlock" (Reformstau) is largely a product of political conjuncture rather than any secular trend. Nonetheless, the intensity of the last cycle *is* greater than in the past largely owing to a secular trend toward increasing the structural reach of the Bundesrat, which Scharpf identifies.

The Bundesrat: Structure

A thorough understanding of the structure of the Bundesrat and its place in the German polity is an essential prerequisite to assessing the strengths and weaknesses of the political-conjuncture and structural-secular arguments. This section undertakes that task.

The Basic Law (Grundgesetz, GG) distributes seats in the Bundesrat roughly in proportion with population. Each Land receives at least three votes in the Bundesrat. Since 1990, Länder with more than two million inhabitants have four votes, Länder with a population of more than six million have five votes and Länder with more than seven million have six votes. The total number of seats in the Bundesrat is currently 69.[8] This distribution of Bundesrat seats favors the smaller Länder, but it prevents a coalition of small Länder from passing a bill against the will of the larger Länder.[9]

There was widespread consensus among drafters of the Basic Law, the de facto constitution of the Federal Republic of Germany,

8. Hesse gained a fifth seat in 1996 as a result of an increase in its population. This increased the number of *Bundesrat* seats by one to sixty-nine.

9. Arthur B. Gunlicks, "German Federalism after Unification: The Legal/ Constitutional Response," *Publius* 24, no. 2 (Spring 1994), p. 97.

in favor of a bicameral legislature. Germany had a tradition of bicameralism; both the Second Empire and the Weimar Republic had second houses. Second, providing the Länder with a voice in national affairs through a second chamber would enhance the political stability of the republic by broadening the foundations of its political legitimacy. Third, many of the delegates to the German constitutional convention hoped that a Bundesrat consisting of Länder representatives would put their region before party and interest-group concerns, thereby counterbalancing the considerable power that the Basic Law grants to political parties, especially in the Bundestag. In practice, however, the second chamber has not fulfilled this expectation. Party considerations have come to play a prominent role in defining and shaping the crucial votes that come to the Bundesrat.[10]

Uwe Thayson rightly points out that federalism as it has evolved in Germany since 1949 "reflects two specific and lasting components of German political culture: an ideology of proficiency and a distinct aversion to conflict."[11] In contrast to federalist arrangements throughout much of the world, postwar German federalism is not arranged like a "layer cake" of fully autonomous political units with distinct functional and geographical jurisdictions. Germany's interwoven system of federalism resembles a "marble cake" instead. The federal and the Länder governments are both involved in the drafting of federal legislation, the collection and distribution of revenue, and the administration of federal laws in a complex division of labor *within* each functional and geographical sphere. The result is a substantial degree of policy interdependence and coordination that brings substantial uniformity to a federal system of governance.[12]

---

10. Wehling, "The Bundesrat," p. 58; and Hans Hugo Klein, "Parteipolitik im Bundesrat?" in Dieter Wilke and Bernd Schulte, eds., *Der Bundesrat. Die staatliche Entwicklung des föderalen Verfassungsorgans* (Darmstadt: Wissenschaftliche Buchgesellschaft, 1990), p. 353; and Albert Pfitzer, *Der Bundesrat. Mitwirkung der Länder im Bund*, third revised edition (Heidelberg: Decker and Müller, 1991), pp. 150-51.

11. Uwe Thayson, *The Bundesrat, the Länder and German Federalism*, German Issues no. 13 (Washington, DC: American Institute for Contemporary German Studies, 1994), p. 8.

12. Konrad Hesse, *Der unitarische Bundesstaat* (Karlsruhe: Müller, 1962); and Uwe Leonardy, "The Working Relationship between *Bund* and *Länder* in the Federal Republic of Germany," in Charlie Jeffery and Peter Savigear, eds., *German Federalism Today* (New York: St Martin's, 1991), p. 52.

German federalism virtually eliminates the autonomy of public institutions at all levels, thereby reducing the Federal Republic
to what Peter Katzenstein has called a "semi-sovereign state."[13]
Instead of following the model of the United States constitution,
which contains power by pitting three powerful and autonomous
branches of government against one another in a series of contained conflicts, the Basic Law keeps power in check by dispersing
it. Dispersion forces the various branches of government to consult
and to coordinate if they are to get things done, promoting cooperation over conflict.

German federalism promotes proficiency through a system
that many call "executive-led" or "administered" federalism. This
form of federalism assigns a powerful role to the Land chief executive, thereby excluding the Landtage. The prime ministers of the
sixteen individual Länder select Bundesrat delegates without having to attain ratification from their Landtage. Each Land delega-
tion at the Bundesrat must vote as a bloc and is bound by an
imperative mandate set by the Land government. The party leaders in coalition governments rather than the Landtage hammer
out the Land imperative mandates. There is no case in which the
Länder parliaments have a formal say over the choice of delegates
or imperative mandates. The reasoning behind the concentration
of powers in the hands of the Land executives is to encourage the
Bundesrat to place "objective" *(sachlich)* over "political" *(politisch)*
concerns in an effort to depoliticize public administration. This
construction has frustrated interest groups – such as businesses
and their associations – precisely because it provides so few opportunities to influence Bundesrat decisions directly. It has not, however, stopped national political parties from exerting considerable
influence, which has exasperated interest groups even more.[14]

The Bundesrat is not co-equal in power to the Bundestag, but
it does have more power than any other contemporary second

13. Peter J. Katzenstein, *Policy and Politics in West Germany: The Growth of a
Semisovereign State* (Philadelphia, Pa.: Temple University Press, 1987), pp. 349-53.

14. Thayson, *The Bundesrat*, p. 8; and Gerhard Jahn, "Bundesrat gegen Bundestag – Gesetzgebung im Spannungsfeld zweier Verfassungsorgane," in Dieter Wilke
and Bernd Schulte, ed., *Der Bundesrat: Die staatliche Entwicklung des föderalen Verfassungsorgans* (Darmstadt: Wissenschaftliche Buchgesellschaft, 1990), pp. 370-71.

chamber in the world, except for the United States Senate.[15] Any amendment of the Basic Law requires approval from two thirds of the Bundesrat members. The Bundesrat has the right along with the Bundestag to initiate bills. In practice, however, the vast majority of bills begin in the Bundestag. Two types of bills move from the Bundestag to the Bundesrat: "approval laws" (Zustimmungsgesetze) and "objection laws" (Einspruchsgesetze). Approval laws are the class of bills that affect either Land revenue or the administration of legislation by the Länder in any way. The Bundesrat has an absolute veto over approval laws. The Bundesrat has prevailed with an expansive interpretation of which bills are approval laws. If at least one part of any bill potentially affects a Land or any activities administered by one or more Länder, the entire text of that bill is subject to absolute veto. This typically amounts to slightly more than one half of all the bills that come before the Bundesrat.[16]

When the Bundesrat vetoes an approval law, the bill is automatically remanded to the joint Bundestag-Bundesrat mediation committee (Vermittlungsausschuss). The task of the mediation committee is to craft mutually acceptable compromise language for the bill in question or to declare the two houses at an impasse. Each Land prime minister chooses the Land representatives to the Bundesrat mediation committee as well as alternates for a term concurrent with the Bundestag legislative period. Since German Unification on 3 October 1990, the mediation committee has included sixteen representatives of the Bundesrat (i.e., one from each Land) and sixteen representatives from the Bundestag, distributed in proportion to the number of seats each party has in the first chamber. In order to facilitate agreement, the Basic Law forbids using an imperative mandate to bind the vote of any mediation committee member and requires the mediation committee to hold all of its meetings in private. Interest groups, therefore, find it exceedingly difficult to influence directly the actions of the mediation committee.[17]

15. Wehling, "The Bundesrat," p. 53.
16. Thayson, *The Bundesrat*, p.16.
17. Klaus Lange, "Die Legitimationskrise des Bundesrates," in Dieter Wilke and Bernd Schulte, eds., *Der Bundesrat. Die staatliche Entwicklung des föderalen Verfassungsorgans* (Darmstadt: Wissenschaftliche Buchgesellschaft, 1990), pp. 242-43.

All bills that are not approval laws are considered objection laws; the Bundesrat has a "suspensive" veto-power over them. If the Bundesrat approves a suspensive veto, the Bundestag can either amend the bill in question until it satisfies a majority of the Bundesrat or override the suspensive veto with a "chancellor's majority" (i.e., a majority of the entire membership of the Bundestag). If two thirds or more of the Bundesrat delegates veto an objection bill, the Bundestag must obtain at least a two-thirds majority vote of those present, which must also amount to at least an absolute majority of the entire membership of the Bundesrat, to overturn the veto (GG, Article 77).

When a single political party or coalition has a majority in both houses, the considerable strength of German political parties plays a positive role. The common political bond tends to facilitate coordination and to dampen (but not completely eliminate) the number and intensity of conflicts between the Bundestag and Bundesrat.[18] The chancellor of the dominant party sets the political initiative in the Bundestag, and the Bundesrat plays at best a minor role, just as the drafters of the German Basic Law intended. In contrast, if the government's majority in the Bundestag is thin and the "opposition" governs a preponderance of the Landtage, the Bundestag opposition can actually hold majorities in both the Bundesrat and the mediation committee. Control over the Bundesrat and the mediation committee gives the opposition considerable power to frustrate the majority in the Bundestag.[19]

How have the political parties and interest groups dealt with such a contradictory constellation of political power when it has occurred? The following historical section addresses this question.

18. Kai-Uwe von Hassel, "Der Bundesrat zwischen Länderinteressen, gesamtstaatlicher Verantwortung und Parteipolitik," in Bundesrat, ed., *Vierzig Jahre Bundesrat.* Tagungsband zum wissenschaftlichen Symposion in der Evangelischen Akademie Tutzing vom 11. bis 14. April 1989 (Baden-Baden: Nomos, 1989), pp. 74-75.

19. Leonardy, "The Working Relationship," p. 56; and Pulzer, "Responsible Party Government," p. 201.

The Bundesrat in Historical Perspective

The importance of the Bundesrat in German politics has ebbed and flowed twice since 1949. Throughout the 1950s and into the mid 1960s, the Bundesrat proved to be weaker than the drafters of the Basic Law had anticipated. The creation of a federal government, including a full array of ministries, and the recovery of domestic and then national sovereignty inevitably reduced the relative importance of the Länder on the West German political scene, especially in comparison to the late 1940s when the Länder were the highest and most powerful indigenous governing authorities. The formidable chancellorship of Konrad Adenauer and the dominance of the Christian Democratic parties at both the federal and Land levels also weakened the relative weight of the Bundesrat in German political affairs.[20]

The German public, moreover, had a relatively low regard for the Bundesrat during those years, which further diminished the influence of the second chamber. A broadcast of a portion of the Bundesrat debate over the 1953 European Defense Act produced this initial negative impression among Germans. It featured Länder bureaucrats engaged in a confusing technical exchange of contradicting interpretations of the Basic Law that the press dubbed a "maze of competency articles" (Paragraphenzuständigkeitsgewirr).[21] For years thereafter, the dominant image of the Bundesrat among German citizens remained one of Länder bureaucrats using technicalities to obstruct the work of the Bundestag and the federal ministries.

Scholars traditionally rely on the number of instances when the joint Bundestag-Bundesrat mediation committee is summoned as a rough indicator of the relative independence of the Bundesrat and the number of bills that failed as an approximate measure of the Bundesrat's strength. The mediation committee was called into action in seventy-five instances during the Federal Republic's first legislative period (1949-1953) and in sixty-five cases during the second legislative period (1953-1957). Eight approval bills failed after a Bundesrat veto in the first legislative period and six failed during the second.

20. Thayson, The Bundesrat, p. 27.
21. Pfitzer, Der Bundesrat, p. 150.

The Bundesrat issued one objection veto both in the first and the second legislative periods. The Bundestag overrode the veto in the second period, but not in the first. Since the Bundesrat passed more bills in each of the Federal Republic's first two legislative periods than in any subsequent one (549 and 518), this record hardly qualifies as legislative gridlock. Initial testing of the contours of the new West German constitution was both inevitable and politically healthy. The number of instances requiring the assembly of the mediation committee declined thereafter. During Adenauer's last two administrations (1957-1961 and 1961-1965), the mediation committee was summoned less often (49 and 39 times).[22]

The number of instances requiring the use of the mediation committee fell further during the "grand coalition" between the Christian Democratic Union (Christliche Demokratische Union, CDU) and the Social Democratic Party of Germany (Sozialdemokratische Partei Deutschlands, SPD). Ironically, the mediation committee was summoned thirty-nine times (i.e., no less than in the previous legislative period), despite the fact that a party participating in the Grand Coalition was at the head of every single Land government at the time. The new Keynesian demand-management measures and the *Ostpolitik* were the main targets of Bundesrat vetoes. Only two initial Bundesrat vetoes culminated in the death of bills, however.

The formation of the "social-liberal" coalition between the SPD and the Free Democratic Party (Freie Demokratische Partei, FDP) marked a turning point in the use of the Bundesrat. The CDU and the Christian Social Union (Christliche Soziale Union, CSU) were in opposition for the first time, but still controlled a majority of the Landtage. The mediation committee intervened thirty-three times during the abbreviated sixth legislative period, which ran from 1969 to 1972. Although the absolute number remained low, the ratio of summonses per bill passed in the Bundestag reached a level not seen since the 1950s. CDU and CSU officials at the time described the active use of the Bundesrat to blunt if not block government initia-

22. Idem, p. 153.
23. Pulzer, "Responsible Party Government," pp. 201-202; Wehling, "The Bundesrat," p. 59; and Hans Koschnick, "Der Bundesrat zwischen Länderinteressen, gesamtstaatlicher Verantwortung und Parteipolitik," in Bundesrat, ed., *Vierzig*

tives as "creative opposition" and a "duty,"[23] whereas many Social Democrats, Free Democrats and their supporters denounced the Christian Democratic tactics as "ruthless exploitation," and the Bundesrat as a "counter-government," a "blockade instrument" and a "naysaying machine."[24]

The use of the Bundesrat to thwart the agenda of a government reached an all-time high during the seventh, eighth, and most of the ninth legislative periods (1972-1976, 1976-1980, and 1980-1983). Helmut Schmidt's first full administration was unusually active. From 1972 to 1976, the Bundestag passed more than 500 bills. These bills produced a record 104 summonses of the mediation committee. The Bundesrat vetoed 19 percent of all the bills that came before it. Eight approval bills died as a result of Bundesrat vetoes. The Bundesrat vetoed an unprecedented five objection bills, four of which were ultimately overturned by the Bundestag. The orgy of rejection in the Bundesrat was a product of the unusually active legislative agenda of the Bundestag, which was in turn the result of economic crisis, the sizable majority of the SPD-FDP coalition and the SPD's attempts to make good on a number of long-standing promises made to organized labor and other groups sympathetic to the social democratic party.

Christian Democratic successes in the 1976 federal and Landtag elections gave the CDU-CSU an unfettered majority in the Bundesrat. Consequently, the Christian Democrats took the aggressive use of the Bundesrat to new heights. In 1976, CDU leader and prime minister of Rhineland-Palatinate Helmut Kohl justified his party's aggressive tactics, stating that he had no intention of "pursuing a stimulatory economic policy (Konjunkturpoli-

---

Bundesrat. Tagungsband zum wissenschaftlichen Symoposion in der Evangelischen Akademie Tutzing vom 11. bis 14. April 1989 (Baden-Baden: Nomos, 1989), p. 87.

24. Philip Blair, "Law and Politics in Germany," *Political Studies* 26, no. 3 (September 1978), p. 355; Friedrich Karl Fromme, "Die beiden 'Kammern' in Widerstreit. Gegensätzliche Mehrheiten in Bundestag und Bundesrat," in Dieter Wilke and Bernd Schulte, eds., *Der Bundesrat: Die staatliche Entwicklung des föderalen Verfassungsorgans* (Darmstadt: Wissenschaftliche Buchgesellschaft, 1990), p. 381; and Wolfgang Knies, "Der Bundesrat: Zusammensetzung und Aufgaben: Zum Schlussbericht der Enquête-Kommission Verfassungsreform," in Dieter Wilke and Bernd Schulte, eds., *Der Bundesrat*, p. 221.

tik) for the 'Sozis'."[25] The Christian Democrats used their veto on a full 20 percent of all bills (77 times) between 1976 and 1980, and a record nine approval bills eventually died. The Bundesrat also issued a record seven suspensive vetoes, five of which were overridden by the Bundestag. SPD and FDP officials, as well as representatives from organized labor and other groups sympathetic to the SPD denounced the Christian Democrats' aggressive tactics in the Bundesrat, but to no avail.[26] The CDU-CSU Bundesrat strategy reached a crescendo in October 1982. The impact of the aggressive tactics of the CDU-CSU contributed to the FDP leadership's decision to shift its allegiance from the SPD to the CDU-CSU and form a new governing coalition under the leadership of Helmut Kohl.

The formation of the conservative coalition brought the Bundestag and the Bundesrat back into political alignment for several years, improving relations between the two chambers of the German legislature. During the first full administration under Helmut Kohl (1983-1987), the mediation committee was summoned only a record-low six times (for only 1.9 percent of all bills passed) and none of the six bills vetoed failed ultimately to pass through both houses in a modified form. No suspensive vetoes were cast. Bundesrat challenges increased in the second Kohl administration (1987-1990), rising to 13, but this still remained far below the typical number of vetoes cast in the 1950s and 1960s, despite a gradual increase in the size of the SPD minority in the second chamber. Only one approval veto failed to pass in a modified form. The Bundesrat also voted in favor of one suspensive veto, but the Bundestag overrode it.[27]

The relationship between the Bundestag and Bundesrat became more contentious throughout Helmut Kohl's third term in office. The SPD steadily gained a larger share of the Bundesrat seats. Moreover, German unification added to the tensions between the two

25. Gerhard Lehmbruch, *Parteienwettbewerb im Bundesstaat* (Stuttgart: Kohlhammer, 1976), p. 150.

26. For example, IG Chemie, *Protokoll*. 11. ordentlicher Gerwerkschaftstag. Mannheim – 7. bis 13. September 1980, vol. 1 (Hannover: Buchdruckwerkstätten Hannover, 1980), p. 92.

27. Pfitzer, *Der Bundesrat*, p. 153.

houses of the German legislature because it dramatically increased the degree of heterogeneity across Länder and raised a completely new set of concerns. Initially, four of the five eastern German Länder voted the CDU into power, which briefly bolstered the position of the Christian Democrats in the Bundesrat, but the SPD continued to score political successes in western German Länder, which improved the Social Democrats' overall position in the Bundesrat.

Especially contentious debates revolving around German unification and the 1992/93 economic downturn led the mediation committee to be summoned more than eighty times during the twelfth legislative period, which ran from 1990 to 1994. By 1991, the SPD either alone or in a coalition with the Alliance Greens held 26 seats in the Bundesrat. In contrast, the CDU-CSU either alone or in coalition with the FDP controlled just twenty-one seats. A grand coalition between the SPD and CDU effectively nullified ten additional seats. Two so-called "traffic light" coalitions (i.e., SPD-FDP-Alliance '90/the Greens, or "red," "yellow," and "green") in Brandenburg and Bremen accounted for seven additional seats, and an SPD-FDP coalition in the Rhineland-Palatinate held the remaining four seats. Thus, the SPD led Land governments of various coalitional configurations that held a total of thirty-seven of the sixty-eight seats in the Bundesrat, but the participation of the FDP in three of these governments rendered fourteen of those votes unavailable for use against the Kohl government. The remaining thirty-one votes did not comprise a majority. The SPD occasionally managed to produce a Bundesrat majority in opposition to the Kohl government when an issue arose that was particularly contentious to easterners, regardless of party. Similarly, Helmut Kohl at times offered special concessions to the SPD-led coalitions that also contained the FDP, the Kohl government's junior party at the federal level, to gain a working majority on important legislation.

The 1994 federal and Landtag elections reduced the Kohl government's plurality in the Bundestag to just ten seats and produced the first ever SPD-Alliance Greens Bundesrat majority. This new political landscape enabled the SPD and Alliance Greens to take control of the mediation committee for the first time. The total number of bills vetoed during the thirteenth legislative period increased from 26 to 33; the SPD in the mid-1990s has proved no less hesitant than the Christian Democrats were in the 1970s and early 1980s to exploit majorities in the Bundesrat and the mediation committee as fully as possible.

Assessing the Contending Arguments in Light of the Evidence

How do the two contending arguments fare when they are assessed relying on the historical record? If the political-conjuncture argument were correct, we would expect to see the relative importance and contentiousness of the Bundesrat fluctuate directly with the political fortunes of German parties. If the opposition in the Bundestag gains control of the Bundesrat, it will use it aggressively to advance its interests and even to leverage its way back into the chancellor's office, if possible. Indeed, the record of the activities of the Bundesrat and the mediation committee follow a cyclical pattern that is closely related to the strength of the opposition in the Bundesrat rather than to the character of external events in the economy or society. Hence, the bulk of the evidence confirms the political conjuncture argument.

Nothing in the political-conjuncture argument, however, accounts for the far more extreme swings in the cycle of Bundesrat activity in the 1980s and 1990s when compared to the 1950s and 1960s.

If the structural-secular hypothesis were correct, one would anticipate a relatively steady rise in both the total and the relative numbers of absolute and suspensive vetoes and fewer overrides of those vetoes over time as the policies of federal and Land governments became increasingly interwoven. Expanding policy interdependence should draw an ever-larger number and wider variety of participants into negotiations about increasing numbers of issues. The more groups and issues become involved, the less likely they are to reach a common position. Consequently, the status quo becomes increasingly difficult to change.

The Bundesrat data do not confirm the structural-secular hypothesis. The sharp drop in independent activity of the Bundesrat during the 1980s could not have occurred if political immobilism had set in. The dearth of independent activity in the Bundesrat and in the mediation committee during the 1980s is truly remarkable, particularly in comparison with the 1950s and early 1960s. A political conjuncture alone does not account for it. Nonetheless, the structural-secular argument does help to account for the increasing intensity of the political cycle of the Bundesrat. Increasing policy interdependence does extend the impact of most political phenomena, be they positive or negative. Hence, a secular rise in policy interdependence could account for the greater fluctuations.

Conclusion

The cyclical dynamics of party competition within a federal, bicameral political order largely account for the onset of periodic bouts of political gridlock. Consequently, two of the reforms proposed by Hans-Olaf Henkel could reduce the likelihood of gridlock in the Federal Republic: the reduction or elimination of the power of the Bundesrat to enact absolute vetoes, and the replacement of Germany's hybrid system, which includes both proportional representation and direct mandates attained through single-district elections, with a pure first-past-the-post system for converting votes into seats in legislatures. The likelihood of these reforms ever being adopted is minimal, however. The first reform would seriously reduce cooperative federalism in Germany because the Länder – regardless of the party in power – would have a substantially diminished say over policy. The Länder would fight this change to the bitter end and, under the current system, could block such a constitutional change.

The second reform, namely, the adoption of first-past-the-post electoral rules, would be at least as controversial as the first. A pure first-past-the-post system tends to eliminate smaller parties with no regional stronghold, because such small parties rarely can gain any seats in the legislature. This reform would increase the odds that a single party could attain a majority of the seats in the Bundestag, eliminating the need to form multiparty coalitions in order to govern. A first-past-the-post system also produces wider swings in the distribution of parliamentary seats than Germany's current hybrid electoral system. Still, repeated razor-thin majorities that allow one party to control the Bundestag and another to control both the Bundesrat and the mediation committee are no less likely to result. Besides, such a change in the electoral regime is highly unlikely. Both the FDP and the Greens would fight vigorously against a first-past-the-post system. In practice only a grand-coalition government would be in a position to enact such legislation, and the odds of one forming any time soon are quite low.

When all the rhetoric is stripped away, it becomes clear that the German business community was frustrated that the Kohl government was not able to deliver the tax cuts and the selective deregulation that business wants. In other words, the central concern of the business community is policy, not constitutional efficiency. Since the SPD-Alliance Green government came to power as a result of the September 1998 federal election, business leaders have all but dropped their campaign to reduce German federalism. The best way to change policy in a democracy is through elections, not constitutional reform and lobbying. The business critics would be better served focusing on these latter, more conventional means.

Chapter 7

FAHRVERGNÜGEN ON THE DATENBAHN

Germany Confronts the Information Age

Beth Simone Noveck

The German political reaction to the information age can be encapsulated in former Chancellor Kohl's answer to a journalist's question about German policy toward the Datenautobahn. In a pithy and telling reply, Kohl said: "The condition which we today have on the highways is such that we can already envision when it will be only stop and go."[1] Enough said.

Clearly, Germany is not advanced in its assimilation of cyberculture nor is the polity embracing the promise of electronic democracy. Yet it is still worth examining Germany's response to the information and communication revolution[2] at this early junc-

---

1. *Der Spiegel* 52/1994.
2. The information society heralds not only an era of more information faster, but of new forms and opportunities for communication among individuals and among citizens. It is this communications potential arising from networked technologies, in particular, rather than the access to more data, which is highly political and likely to change the shape of public life in the next century. See W.B.H.J. Van de Donk, I.Th.M. Snellen and P.W. Tops, eds. *Orwell in Athens* (1996). The democratizing effects of new technologies has been extensively discussed. See, e.g. "A Magna Carta for the Knowledge Age" at http://www.dds.nl/~n5m/texts/charta.htm and "Munich Statement" at http://www.akademie3000.de.

ture for what it says about contemporary German politics and political culture. The reaction by an entrenched elite to what is regarded as a potentially revolutionary movement, promising radical change in all spheres of public and private life, creates a window illuminating the contours of this purported revolution and the current political climate in Germany. For example, in the United States the daily panegyrics in the press about electronic commerce, or the equally fervid inveighing against cyberporn, come as no surprise to even the casual observer of American life. Similarly, the clichéed French whining about American cultural imperialism on the Internet and the search for an electronic equivalent to the "Loi Toubon" to stave off a digital ambush of French culture are to be expected. Given the uniqueness of Germany's recent past, the preoccupation with Datenschutz – data privacy and protection – fits the pattern of the nation's traditions.[3] Similarly, Germany is spearheading the effort in Europe to impose greater restrictions on the proliferation of pornography and hate speech. That Germany is the first country to pass a national Multimedia Law[4] (Establishing the General Conditions for Information and Communication Services – Information and Communication Services Act, IuKDG) is also typical for a nation prone to hyper-regulate.[5] But the puzzle here is that, in both word and deed, the attitude toward new media is dramatically liberal and deregulatory

3. It is also a legal necessity under EC law, which requires all member nations to conform their national laws to the European Directive 94/EC on the "Protection of Individuals with Regard to the Processing of Personal Data and on the Free Movement of Such Data" and Directive 95/EC on the "Protection of Individuals with Regard to the Processing of Personal Data and on the Free Movement of Such Data." Available at http://www.privacy.org/pi/intl_orgs/ec/final_EU_Data_Protection.html.

4. On 13 June 1997 the Bundestag enacted one of the world's first legislative attempts to regulate comprehensively the new communications media of the information age. This legislation creates a new legal framework for multimedia B defined separately from broadcast, telephony or print media. It also sets rules for the liability of Internet service providers, fixes requirements for provider transparency and data privacy, and establishes the legal infrastructure for a digital signature system. The Multimedia Law consists of three new federal statutes and six additional articles that adapt existing legislation to new media. The framing law went into effect on 1 August 1997.

5. Elizabeth Neuffer, "Germany lays down the law, and then some," *The Boston Globe*, 13 October 1997.

in character – in other words, very un-German.[6] The Telecommunications Law of 1996[7] which laid the groundwork for the Multimedia Law of 1997, has been hailed as one of the most liberal and modernizing pieces of telecommunications legislation to date. The Multimedia Law, in reality an umbrella encompassing three distinct new laws and various updates to existing legislation, at least formally, impedes excessive regulation.[8] The slogan used is "*Ordnung in Freiheit*" (Order through Freedom). The chief proponent of this legislation, Jürgen Rüttgers, former Minister of Education, Science, Research and Technology (BMBF), and christened semiofficially the "*Zukunftsminister*" (the Minister of the Future), was on the stump, promoting the legislation and bragging about Ger-

6. See Stephen Vogel, *Freer Markets, More Rules* (Ithaca: Cornell University Press, 1997).

7. The reform of telecommunications regulation in Germany unfolded in three stages (1989, 1994, 1996), culminating in the Telecommunications Law of 1996 (Telekommunikationsgesetz). All communications services had previously been owned, maintained, and operated by the Deutsche Bundespost. In 1985, a commission was created to develop a plan for the future of privatized telecommunications. Private television in Germany came onto the scene at this point as well. But the first wave of competition did not arrive until 1989, when the German telephone company loosened its monopoly, introducing competition into the communications sector in all areas except basic telephone service. The idea at that point was to liberalize the market in end-user products rather than in ownership and operation of the infrastructure. In other words, prior to 1989 only modems purchased from the state-monopoly would function in the German phone system. At this point, legislation split the postal monopoly into three separate operating units: Deutsche Bundespost Telekom, Deutsche Bundespost, and Postbank. In 1994, in the second stage of reform, the Bundestag amended the constitution to enable the conversion of Deutsche Bundespost Telekom into a private corporation, Deutsche Telekom Aktiengesellschaft. In 1995, Deutsche Telekom AG began as a one hundred percent state-owned company, but in 1996, shares in it were sold off to private investors. The Telecommunications Law has thrown open the voice telephony market to competition, including foreign entrants to the German market. In 1996, the government granted three licenses for alternative telecommunications provision.

8. The trend in European media policy is increasingly away from information society toward information economy. The liberal ideal has shifted the emphasis toward the need for deregulation to promote wealth generation. Government regulation is seen by many as the impediment to the unfolding of economic progress. See Shalini Venturelli, "The Information Society in Europe: The Passing of the Public Service Paradigm of European Democracy," in Cafruny and Lankowski, *Europe's Ambiguous Unity: Conflict and Consensus in the Post-Maastricht Era* (Boulder, Colo.: Lynne Rienner Publishers, 1997).

many's new deregulatory, liberal posture, like a proud father, touting his child's proficiency with computers at a tender age.

Deregulation, Reregulation or Status Quo

The question is what does the uncharacteristic departure from regulatory rhetoric-as-usual say about this recent legislation and the state of politics in Germany. The answer – sadly – is that despite the rhetoric of cowboy capitalism and free market euphoria which has seized the German debate over the Information Society, what happened here is less a strengthening of market power than a consolidation of political power by the federal government in opposition to the German states (Länder). This was achieved by a shift in emphasis from speech rights, linked to the culture of broadcasting, to free competition rights – from information society to information economy. There were a number of political factors motivating this departure, most prominently, a challenge to the federalist balance of power as underpinned by the current constitutional order of media law. The government of Germany was orchestrating a disavowal of the legal tradition, under the old Bundesrepublik and its Constitutional Court, of using media to promote and support free speech and democratic political culture, a special tradition which grew out of a unique past of which this government would like to be free.

"Tradition!"

This special tradition, which forms an important backdrop to understanding the story, emerges from the highly politicized and ideological nature of media policy in the immediate postwar.[9]

9. Christoph Wagenleitner, *Coca-Colonization and the Cold War* (Chapel Hill: University of North Carolina Press, 1994); Nicholas Pronay and Keith Wilson, *The Political Re-Education of Germany and her Allies after World War II* (London: Croom Helm, 1985); Harmut Lehmann, *Culture and Politics in Nineteenth and Twentieth Century Germany* (Washington, D.C.: German Historical Society, 1992).

Informed by its fascist past[10] – that lived experience out of which the cultural theories of the Frankfurt School about the interrelationship between media, cultural, and fascist politics emerged – the fathers of the Republic knew that mass media had an important role to play in safeguarding democracy.[11] The early entry of fascist ideology through the stage door of culture and the use of mass media to spread fascism signaled to the Allied occupiers that democratization could be accomplished partly through the manipulation of culture, especially media.[12] They used all media – print, broadcast, and film – to delouse Germany of the Nazi bug.[13]

The clearest evidence of the perceived linkage of media and political culture is manifested in the postwar jurisprudence of Germany's Constitutional Court (Bundesverfassungsgericht) which itself solidified this interrelationship in the way it shaped and legitimated the structure of broadcasting in the immediate aftermath of the war. The dozen cases that comprise the court's broadcasting cases (Rundfunkentscheidungen) have been the blueprint for the design, operation, and even content of the dual broadcasting system in Germany up until today. This is the epitome of the term "Rechtsstaat," where law molds policy. Article Five of the Basic Law ("Everyone has the right freely to express and to disseminate

10. In the 1933 broadcasting became an instrument of National Socialist propaganda. The Minister for Popular Education and Propaganda was responsible for it though the technical aspects remained part of the Postal Service. Constitutional Court Decision BVerGE 12, 205 (210) (Deutschland Fernsehen).

11. From the Manifesto of the Kulturbundes in 1946: "A new spiritual community must be created in order that we can pass the tests we have set for ourselves as a result of our own guilt and can attach ourselves once again to the community of free and truly democratic peoples."

12. Even before Hitler's rise to power, Alfred Hugenberg's right-wing newspaper empire prepared the way for the abuse of the media by the National Socialists after 1933. See J. A. Leopold, *Alfred Hugenberg: The Radical Nationalist Campaign against the Weimar Republic* (New Haven: Yale University Press, 1978).

13. They established the Allied Publicity and Psychological Warfare Division to effect denazification through cultural policies. See Pronay and Wilson, *The Political Reeducation of Germany and her Allies after World War II*. The occupiers saw culture, especially in the form of media as a means to bestowing a new sense of corporate identity, common morality, and social cohesion This notion was in keeping with the German tradition of Kulturstaat where cultural, rather than political, affinities constituted a large part of self-identity, in particular in an era where cultural heroes were still untainted by the scourge of fascism.

his opinion by speech, writing, and pictures and freely to inform himself from generally accessible sources. Freedom of the press and freedom of reporting by broadcast and motion pictures are guaranteed. There shall be no censorship.") has given rise to a positive-right tradition of free speech whereby the government must take affirmative steps to guarantee freedom of opinion formation, not merely safeguard negative liberties as in the American system.[14] The legal doctrine of Grundversorgung (universal service) stands for the principle that there exists a minimum informational and educational diet to nourish democracy.[15] Sports, for example, is an integral part of universal service. For this reason, Leo Kirch's purchase of the broadcast rights to World Cup Soccer led to a legal furor in Germany and Kirch's acquiescence to the broadcast of the games on public television in addition to his pay-per-view station.[16] Because the German Constitution mandates the freedom of opinion formation, rather than mere free speech, the Court took upon itself to forge a strong public broadcasting system which, unlike many of its European counterparts, was meant to be separate from the state and from the private sector.

The result of the legacy of this past has been two-fold. On the one hand, since the advent of private television, German broad-

14. See Peter Quint, "Free Speech and Private Law in German Constitutional Theory," *Maryland Law Review*, vol. 48 (1989): 247; David P. Currie, "Positive and Negative Constitutional Rights," *University of Chicago Law Review*, vol. 53 (1986): 864; David E. Weiss, "Striking a Difficult Balance: Combating the Threat of Neo-Nazism in Germany while Preserving Individual Liberties," *Vanderbilt Journal of Transnational Law*, vol. 27 (1994): 899.

15. The expression encapsulates the guarantee by the Basic Law to a certain minimum provision of broadcasting for the entire German population. However, this minimum reflects more than mere technical provisions, it speaks to the content of television streaming into German living rooms. Public broadcasting therefore has a constitutional mandate to supply German viewers with the necessary content to live up to the broadcast freedom and freedom of opinion called for by Article Five. Not simply the broadcast of political events and educational programming, Grundversorgung covers everything which people need to know and experience to participate in social communication. A comprehensive diet of television can nourish the informational hunger of the individual, broadly understood. See inter alia, BVerfG 83, 238 (6th Broadcasting Decision).

16. Jürgen Krönig, "Sport als Rambock: Vor allem der Fußball soll dem digitalen Bezahl-Fernsehen zum Durchbruch verhelfen," *Die Zeit*, Nr. 3, 10 January 1997, p. 41.

casting has been of a high quality and also highly diverse within each channel's programming and across the spectrum of channels. At the same time, whatever the theoretical strengths of the legal foundation of German media, it would be misleading to idealize a system that suffers, in practice, from various shortcomings. For example, since the advent of private television, that famed quality, especially critical journalism, is in the process of declining. The system suffers from woeful economic inefficiencies as the result of the requirements that private broadcasters obtain fifteen separate licenses[17] and be supervised by non-democratically elected bodies representing, not individual citizens, but entrenched social interest groups.[18] Finally the oligarchic tendency toward concentration in this industry, dominated by a handful of rich and influential players, such as Leo Kirch and Bertelsmann, plagues Germany as much as it does any country.[19]

The Information and Communication Services Act (IuKDG)

The stated purpose of the IuKDG is to create a reliable legal foundation for the construction of a free market in information and communications services. Analogous to the philosophy underlying traditional intellectual property law, its twin aims are to (1) stimulate investment in multimedia by creating a stable and reliable legal environment for this industry, and (2) guarantee innovation

17. Each state has its own broadcasting regulatory authority except for Berlin and Brandenburg, which share one.

18. The Interstate Broadcasting Agreement §25 provides that the most important representative social groups should be able to input into the programming process. They do this in the form of the Medienräte of the state broadcasting regulatory authorities, which oversee private broadcasting. These citizen boards, with members from the two major churches, the Jewish community, the major unions and women's groups etc. are selected by the state parliaments but not directly elected.

19. Bertelsmann and Kirch are waging a all-out legal and financial attack against public television. For example, they are seeking to exclude Austria's public station, ORF1, from the Bavarian cable spectrum by challenging its legal basis for inclusion. In addition, the public stations are having financial difficulty competing with the privates.

and creativity in the field through free market competition. In addition, the law attempts to protect the civil rights of individual users and safeguard the interests of the public. To this end the framework law includes separate laws for the use of teleservices, a law on data privacy in teleservices, and a law on digital signatures.

The IuKDG lays down a carefully drafted and controversial definition of those "information and communications services" subject to the new regulations of the Teleservices Act. It applies to "those electronic information and communication services which are designed for the individual use of combinable data, such as characters, images, or sounds and are based on transmission by means of telecommunication." In other words, all forms of individual communication, such as telebanking, data exchange, and Internet services are covered under this definition. Anything intended for an individual's use and control would be covered even if used on a common network.[20] This definition does not include information and communications services consisting of editorial material whose primary purpose is to influence public opinion (i.e., broadcast, pay-per-view, on-line magazines, or web-pages with strong editorializing). These services remain the domain of the states and covered by the Interstate Agreement on Media Services (Mediendienstestaatsvertrag).

The drafters, in laying out this definition, chose not to emphasize the technological form of new media but, their function. The distinction is not drawn between mass communication media and individual communication, per se. Rather, the law governs everything that, from a user's perspective is to be considered an individualized form of communication. This supposed groundbreaking scheme is ambiguous in its sparseness and begs the question of how it will be administered rationally in its current form. How, after all, are media which have so-called "strongly editorial

20. "Multimedia services make it possible in the arena between broadcast and individual telecommunications for the everyman to offer information anytime to anyone or to call up information by individual selection and thereby combine or switch between several technical or substantive means of superindividual as well as individual communication." Martin Bullinger and Ernst-Joachim Mestmäcker, *Rechtsgutachten: Multimediadienste, Aufgabe, und Zuständigkeit des Bundes für Multimedia-dienste* (6 April 1996), p. 21.

content meant to influence public opinion" reasonably supposed to be distinguished? And how does this phrase define areas of regulatory competence?[21] However, the drafters regard this language as a success because it effects a deliberate differentiation between "new" individualizable technologies and those which target a mass audience. Traditional broadcasting, which remains within the constitutional purview of the state, is thereby clearly set apart. This takes into account rapidly converging forms of media but, as we shall soon discuss in more detail, also attempts to strike at the heart of the states' legal competence to regulate media.

The new framework legislation contains provisions outlining the liability of Internet service providers for the provision and distribution of potentially illegal content[22] and sets out transparency obligations for service providers, limiting their ability to collect and disseminate personal user data.[23] Article Three is the

21. Broadcasting is defined as "für die Allgemeinheit bestimmte Veranstaltung und Verbreitung von Darbietungen aller Art in Wort, Ton und Bild unter Benutzung elektrischer Schwingungen ohne Verbindungensleitung oder längs oder mittels eines Leiters." Rundfunkstaatsvertrag § 2 ¶ 1 (1991 as amended, 1997).

22. Article One, the Teleservices Act, legislates that service providers would be subject to liability under the applicable law for the provision of their own unlawful (i.e. pornographic or Holocaust revisionist) content. They *might* also be responsible for foreign content, which they make available for users, only if they are cognizant of the material and if they are in a technical position to prevent its use. In other words, if a service provider offers someone else's content, the owner of that content remains primarily responsible. Yet if the provider was specifically aware of the particular content and would be, technically, in a position to prevent its dissemination then the provider will share responsibility. However, service providers are not responsible for foreign content to which they only provide access. If the service provider, after taking into account the telecommunications secrecy rules of the Telecommunications Act, is still aware of the content and is in a technical position to stop it and could be expected to do so then he or she will be held responsible even for foreign content.

23. Article Two, the Teleservices Data Protection Act, governs the use of personal data obtained by service providers. The provider must inform the user about any data being collected unless the user waives the right to know. Data may be collected only to the extent necessary for billing and for market research if done anonymously and with explicit user consent. The service provider must facilitate anonymous usage and payment as well. However, the service provider is obligated to turn over personal data to the authorities as needed for "purposes of criminal prosecution, to prevent danger to public security or for the fulfillment of the legal responsibilities of the Federal Office for the Protection of the Constitution."

Digital Signature Act, which, in conjunction with the Ordinance on Digital Signatures of 8 October 1997, creates an administrative infrastructure for the issuance and administration of secure digital signatures (electronic seals) within the private sector under government supervision.

From Broadcasting to Multicasting

In light of the particularly dirigiste style of German broadcasting management and legislation, as promulgated by the Constitutional Court and the states, and given that Germany is not a nation known for a regulatory *nonchaloir,* the deregulatory rhetoric of the Multimedia Law resonates dissonantly. This is a risk-adverse government presiding over a nation where only ten percent of the population invests in the stock market.[24]

The German population largely opposed telecommunications reform despite its paying some of the highest tariffs in Europe. Protection of employees was considered a greater good than cheaper prices, and reform was perceived as potentially costing jobs. Even the Verein der Postbenutzer, the Association of Postal Users, was only reluctantly in favor of change. Reforms in telecommunications and multimedia have been entirely top-down[25] because large seg-

24. Stock market participation rates went from 4.6 million at the beginning of 1996 to 5 million. This increase of 400,000 is due, in large part, to the Deutsche Telekom sell-off. However, many of these new shareholders received their stock as employees of that company, rather than as the result of voluntary participation in the capital markets. Despite the rise there is no indication of any change in attitude towards stock trading. "Schutzgemeinschaft der Kleinaktionäre," *Frankfurter Allgemeine Zeitung,* 16 April 1997, p. 17.

25. In June 1989, the Federal Cabinet promulgated a position paper entitled, "Concept of the Future of Information Technology." Kohl established a Council for Research, Technology and Innovation, which was preoccupied with questions of the Information Society, and published a handbook entitled, *The Information Society: Opportunities, Innovations, Challenges.* The government has embarked on several major initiatives, which are designed by small commissions sometimes in cooperation with representatives of large industry. The end user, however, is conceived of as a test case and not a full-fledged actor in the process. See Herbert Kubicek, *Allgemeiner Zugang und informationelle Grundversorgnung,* in Tauss, Kollbeck and Mönikes, p. 157.

ments of society are technophobic and wary of anything which might jeopardize the status quo. The rhetoric of *schlanker Staat* – the leaner, meaner state – is all the rage in word, though not in deed. Despite a negative economic prognosis, the government will not effectuate pension or labor reform, preferring instead to protect the traditional German Sozialstaat. Yet lip service is paid in the telecommunications and multimedia arena to Thatcherite capitalism.

These contradictions have multiple origins. First, there has been a fundamental failure in Germany to recognize the political nature of new media akin to the old tradition and, instead, to perceive them as purely the creatures of the free market.[26] Those in power simply do not realize that the media they are dealing with have potentially as much influence over political culture as television did for the last generation. They do not grasp, for example, that these technologies can be implemented to crack open bureaucracies and render government more responsive, transparent, and accessible to its constituency. Germany does not offer electronic tax filing nor is Internet penetration at anything like the level it has reached in the United States. The former Federal Ministry of Education and Technology (BMBF) responded to an electronic mail request for a publication relating to new media by mailing a document via post at a cost of DM 24 and three weeks shipping time. In a country without a Freedom of Information Act, the panoply of uses of the Internet beyond shopping has not been thoroughly appreciated.[27]

Secondly, the communication and information revolution in Germany is not a grassroots movement, spurred on by the likes of the Center for Democracy and Technology, the Electronic Frontier Foundation, and millions of individual, addicted university users.

26. On the political nature of new media, including the Internet, see Michael E. Kraft and Norman J. Vig, *Technology and Politics* (Durham: Duke University Press, 1988); Robin Mansell, *The New Telecommunications: A Political Economy of Network Evolution* (London: Sage, 1993) and Neil Postman, *Technopoly* (New York: Knopf, 1992) or *Amusing Ourselves to Death* (New York: Viking, 1985).

27. Jörg Tauss, Member of Parliament, tells the story of how, when he began his tenure in Bonn, he installed a modem and a PC in his office. One day a technocrat appeared to confiscate the modem. He informed Tauss that whereas Members of Parliament were entitled to unlimited free telephone calling, they are not allowed to have a modem!

This revolution has its origins in part, in the uniqueness of 68er culture in Germany, whose legacy is a noticeably absent American-style grassroots culture. Rather, the information superhighway has been paved by a chain gang of conservative politicians and big business interests, joined together after a successful partnership of fifteen years of center-right domination and no different since the change in government. Media czar Leo Kirch paid for the cabinet's private flight to the United States for the World Cup. The government's slogan was "*Wir werden Multimedia möglich machen!*" or "*We will make multimedia possible!*" The government, not the people, will usher in the new era.

Third, the contradictions surrounding multimedia are a function of the personalities involved. Rüttgers as well as politicians like Staatssekretär Siegmar Mosdorf, also formerly head of the parliamentary Enquête Kommission for New Media, and Jörg Tauss, SPD member of parliament, are all relatively young and up-and-coming politicians, trying to distinguish themselves against the gray backdrop of politics-as-usual in Bonn. The American-style rhetoric of greater liberalization sets them apart and enhances their image as modernizers and reformers in an era of stagnation and Reformstau.

Finally, the central and most important key to understanding the Sturm und Drang pulling between the rhetoric of economic liberalization and the etatist impulse toward regulation and resistance to change is the desire to wrest control over media from the states. This is nothing to do with Internet-and-politics or a genuine shift in economic ideology towards a new liberalism. Rather, this is a pure legal competence struggle. In the ensuing effort to ensure that lucrative new media will be the legislative and legal domain of the federal authorities in Bonn, the German government is also attacking indirectly the states' power to regulate broadcasting.

The State vs. the States

In the process leading up to the ratification of the new Teleservices Law, the states continuously demanded that jurisdiction over new media be ceded to them. The states already had in place the Medien-dienstestaatsvertrag, which harmonized and streamlined regulation of broadcasting, and were already in the process of preparing a draft of a new version to include new media regulations.

In its draft legislation intended to make a resounding statement to the Länder that new media would belong to it, the federal government created a specially worded definition of new media – or so-called Teledienste (teleservices) – that declared the federal government's power to regulate telephony. To insure federal authority and to avoid any power grabbing by the states, the authors of the legislation were careful to make sure its wording would not trigger review by the Bundesrat and thereby delay the process of its passage. The states and the federal government, however, eventually reached a compromise, agreeing to sign on to the new legislation while also approving an almost verbatim version in the form of a Medienstaatsvertrag. It is worth noting that the State Agreement still refers to Mediendienste and the federal law calls the same technologies, Teledienste, in a word game intended to reinforce constitutional authority. This compromise was reached, however, at the expense of the legislation's coherence and effectiveness.

The states and the federal government were at loggerheads over this legislation, not merely because of routine infighting, but because with over 4.5 million unemployed in Germany, the highest level since 1933,[28] there existed the genuine hope of creating more jobs in this new sector; any regulation in this arena was regarded as of the utmost importance and sensitivity. Given the Reformstau in other branches of the economy, progressives in Bonn continue to hope that new media can be protected from invasive and hyperregulatory measures on the part of the states. Liberalizing this sector and doing away with excessive Länder regulations[29] are meant to attract badly needed investment, stimulate growth, create jobs and inspire confidence.[30]

28. "Calls Emerge for New German 'Alliance for Jobs,'" *The Reuter European Business Report* (1 April 1997).

29. At the most extreme, the Länder debated whether or not to tax every PC in every office under their power to impose fees on television sets and radio under the rationale that a PC can be used to watch television. Home computers are covered by the household tax on televisions. But the idea of taxing office PCs was regarded by many as a cash cow.

30. Multimedia in Europe is predicted to be a $37 billion dollar industry by the year 2000 with 10 million new jobs created by that time. Already the German telecommunications market alone is worth $80 billion dollars.

There are further political reasons for the federal government's salvoes against the states (and the states' obstreperous resistance to the federal government's new media legislation). Because of the lack of input from grassroots, civil liberties, or other public interest groups in this arena, such political factors have an unusually strong impact on federal media policy.

First, desirous of investment in the German economy, the Bund wants to curry favor with the media and telecommunications conglomerates by eliminating or minimizing the right-of-way fees and other licensing requirements which the states and municipalities extract for the use of the public cable and telecommunications architecture running through local territory. With the opening of the German telephony market to private competitors, including foreign service-providers, the state has agreed to lease use of the extensive Deutsche Telekom infrastructure to these newcomers in order to reduce barriers to entry and facilitate true competition. However, the municipalities may still extract Weggelder – right of way payments – for piggybacking off the local routes. This is a distinct disincentive to foreign investment and a source of contention between the two political levels. In the new media arena, especially, excessive regulation is not only inefficient but impossible to enforce and only causes uncertainty and confusion among investors.

Secondly, with the slippage of Germany's hegemony in the new Europe and the rise of an era of "new federalism," in which regions are increasingly powerful – economically, politically, and culturally – through their representation in Brussels and their own maneuvering on the world stage, Bonn is seeking to consolidate its power base and prevent the states from gaining an undue foothold in an arena of increasing importance. Slowly, but markedly, the power of the nation-state in Europe is receding as a united Europe achieves greater prominence and actual strength. The unit of decision-making is, at once, enlarged and reduced as the regions become more important within Europe.

Linked to new federalism is the perceived threat posed by the "crown princes" of the Länder and the broadcasting empires that they dominate. The power of rich and populous states, especially Bavaria and Baden-Württemberg, are not to be underestimated in the analysis of German political culture and contemporary political climate. Because television is regulated on a state-by-state basis, the state governments can bring pressure to bear on the broadcasting authorities within the state and influence their decisions, especially the receptivity to Bonn. Whereas Bavaria was known in the Kohl era for its SAT1-promoted *"Kanzlerfernsehen,"* North Rhine-Westphalia's TV, in particular, RTL, is more *"Kanzlerfern."* Furthermore, the regional banks (Länderbanken) finance the media industry on the state level and are themselves repositories of great power outside the purview of the federal government. Leo Kirch and other media moguls have built their power bases squarely in their home region from which they have proceeded to conquer all of German media and thereby play a tremendous role in shaping public political opinion through their command over broadcasting.

The Bund-Länder rivalry during the Multimedia Law debate was, to some extent, party-political, a holdover from the last administration. The CDU had been susceptible to attack and was therefore concerned about ceding power to the states, which were two-thirds social democratic and controlled the lower house of Parliament. If the federal government could dilute the political power of the states by taking media out of their grasp, it could weaken their base whose foundation is partly in the mandate to legislate culture/education and broadcasting.

The features of the new Multimedia Law which would create a new legal category for multimedia and interactive media came about, not because the Germans better understand that, in an era of convergent technologies, old models of broadcast and common carrier simply do not suffice, but because of *Realpolitik.* The desire to seize political power from the Länder motivated the institution of these legal changes. The deliberate decision at this juncture to create regulations for a specifically non-broadcast sphere of individualizable technologies based on economic rationales has two effects. First, these economic rationales are replacing freedom of expression and similar democratic ideals as the primary constitutional value underpinning media regulation.[31] Secondly, the inven-

---

31. The constitutional underpinning justifying the new law is Basic Law Article 73 (federal government's power to regulate the economy), rather than Article 5 (guarantee of the freedom of expression and opinion formation).

tion of a new regulatory regime, not only repudiates state power over multimedia, but undermines the legitimacy of the old system of broadcast regulation, which is slowly being eroded. The federal government – and many others – would like to kill the hydra of German media, with its one weighty head in Karlsruhe and fifteen heads in each of the state broadcasting authorities. The oracles in Bonn portend that with the move to pay-per-view and TV-on-demand, television will come to look less and less like broadcasting and more and more like one of the new media subject only to regulation by the federal government.

Broadcast regulation in Germany undoubtedly has its terrible shortcomings and flaws like any regulatory system which cannot simultaneously please fans of the free market, fans of governmental control and consumer protection, and devotees of civil liberties. But the recent trend toward wresting power from the states, accomplished via tricks of legal semantics and constitutional reinterpretation, serves less to redesign the current structure of broadcasting than it does to eviscerate the values of free speech, diversity, and democracy by replacing them with the liberal ideal of free market over all else.[32]

For better or for worse, this trend could mark the end of the postwar era of media regulation as we have known it. After years of conservative government, the alliance between big capital and those in power is relatively open and uncriticized. These groups encourage the turn away from the constitutional ideals of the broadcasting era because, not only does the government get to consolidate its political power, they get much wanted freedom from state regulation and the onerous albatross of Article 5.

---

32. Another explanation for the about-face from the traditional values of broadcast regulation might be the desire to shed the legacy of the Holocaust. One could argue that the German Federal Government wants to begin a new era where maintaining free markets is the guarantee – as in the U.S. – that media serve the goals of democracy. The older way, where the State proactively takes steps to assure that freedom of speech and freedom of broadcasting are maintained, a doctrine intimately tied into denazification and the beginnings of the postwar, are viewed by many as outdated. An excursus into what Amos Elon termed, "the politics of memory" and the linkage between media policy and Shoah is, however, outside the scope of this paper.

Alleviation of the burdens imposed by the overregulation of the broadcasting industry in Germany is a good thing. The broadcasting structures that have evolved out of the Constitutional Court's interpretation of Article 5 into a behemoth of administration on the state level need trimming and reform if public television is to be economically viable. However, many who are pushing most strongly for (de)regulation of new media according to the principles of free market competitiveness and weakening the broadcast model are also not promoting strongly political technologies, like the Internet, in the name of civil liberties. They are pushing digital television and other high stake technologies, using the rhetoric of deregulation to further monopolistic goals (as opposed to true competition and a genuine free market).[33] Whereas in the United States deregulation and privatization are ends unto themselves, in Germany it would seem that deregulation is merely a tool used to serve other political interests.

In the debate over the theory and practice of new media regulation, which implicates the future of old media regulation, the traditionally vociferous opposition from the Left has been absent. This is partly a function of the personalities involved, charismatic younger politicians who were vying for a future cabinet seat and therefore were not anxious to rock the boat too much. Mainly, however, the Left started out fighting technological innovations in the name of saving workers' jobs and preserving the social safety net. Now that it has become clear that the information society means more jobs for German workers, the Left finds itself defining its agenda too little and too late in the game. Though Mosdorf, Tauss, and others distinguish themselves as the leading players on the Left in this arena and, whereas they have party members who work with them in their parliamentary committees, there are not enough politicians on the Left committed to the issues of the information society and media regulation.

The tradition of treating media differently in deference to their special political power has not vanished. Rather, competing impulses

---

33. "Kartellamt will Pay-TV-Bündnis verhindern," *Süddeutsche Zeitung*, 9 January 1998 (European Cartel Commission expected to outlaw Kirch-Bertelsmann joint-venture in digital television).

between the democratic potential of media and their economic usefulness coexist and are at odds. Because of the current political climate, the trend in media regulation policy appears to be a decision to treat information as an economic good, rather than as a public merit good with special political qualities. This embracing of the free market does not represent a sudden shift to American-style capitalism. It is largely dictated by Brussels and enhanced by the motivation to wrest political power from the German states in an effort to jump-start the economy. It is likely that this impulse will have to be reconciled with the older traditions of protecting free speech, guarding data privacy as a fundamental human right, and translating the principles of the broadcasting regime into policies applicable to new media. This struggle, however, has a distinctive resonance in German politics because of its unique legal tradition.

Modernization and reform are much needed. But the sacrifice of a noble ideal as embodied in Article 5 comes at a point when it is most needed to take advantage of the political potential of new media. The Internet promises to transform the face of political society to an even greater extent than the television did forty years ago. The failure to recognize the political nature of these interactive technologies should perhaps be recharacterized as a not-wanting-to-recognize them in order to seize power from the states and the Constitutional Court. To place new media securely under the constitutional and regulatory authority of the federal government comes dangerously close to upsetting a long tradition of constitutional jurisprudence. In many respects, this represents progress. However, the complete absence of any sense of new media as a public institution – the failure to create public spaces and places in cyberspace – leaves the citizen in the information society vulnerable to the pull between the Scylla and Charibdis of the all-powerful state and the all-powerful market. It leads to politically passive consumers of information widgets and opens the door for regulatory interventionism by the federal government albeit not by the states.

This situation does not bode well for the future of political culture in Germany in the next century or for the future of global cyberpolitical culture. In the rush to deregulate and to reregulate the legal arena to accommodate new media, the Germans risk losing a German tradition of great value.

Chapter 8

ENGINEERED LIKE NO OTHER

German Society and the Automobile

Carolyn Höfig

It was something of a desecration, coaxing my Trabant – the plastic-bodied, two-stroke automotive emblem of East German technical and social engineering – through the heart of Ludwig Erhard's home territory, Upper Franconia. After all, Erhard, the father of the social market economy, presided over the postwar recovery that brought West Germany, among other things, these assiduously maintained streets and the sleek, solid cars that roared by me on them. A sky-blue Trabant 601, a shabby relic of the financial failure that was state socialism just over the border, hardly fit into the scene.

But I had to get to Würzburg somehow, so I took to the trunk roads above Bayreuth, where my little car could travel at the speed limit, alternately 80 or 100 clicks. The Trabi did not smoke much at these speeds. Nonetheless, everyone who came up behind us passed at the first opportunity, and the displeasured expressions that registered on their faces as they did increased my sense of profanation.

Suddenly, into a patch of sunlight in the opposite lane drove another Trabant. It was that chemical green color. It was also a more recent model than mine, and it bore new license plates from a locality somewhere in the restored state of Mecklenburg. (Mine still had the old-days designation for the socialist administrative district of Halle on narrow aluminum plates.) I saw the driver's face light up even before he flashed his head lamps at me. I flashed back. We waved out the window to each other as we went by, and when the other Trabi disappeared into the Franconian forest behind me, I felt as if I had taken leave of a friend.

I turned off after that to pass the German coffee hour at a monastery-turned-inn outside of Bamberg, as did the Mercedes-load of locals who had covered the last few kilometers of their provincial-customary *Kaffeefahrt* behind me. They had also witnessed the encounter, I found out, for , as we all converged on the front step of the inn, one of the Daimler-women sniffed from under her hat, "I see that Trabi drivers greet one another on foreign streets."

"That's called 'solidarity,' madam," I replied. "We need it these days."

"These days" were the better part of a year into German unifi-cation, and one could read out of the episode the degree to which Germans had – or had not – come together in their hearts and minds. The Mecklenburger in the green Trabant needed to know nothing more about me than my taste in automobiles to inspire his show of camaraderie on the "foreign" roadways in the state of Bavaria. Similarly, the comment of the Mercedes-driving matron betrayed her infrequent contact and resulting discomfort with the other Germany, its inhabitants and their customs. Doubtlessly, she addressed herself to me by way of backhanded introductions because she took me for an Easterner, like my car. Indeed, who else would sputter through the countryside in such a conveyance?

Cars, as big-ticket consumer goods, betoken status and rela-tive wealth in most societies today. In Germany, however, the cor-relation of the automobile to social identity is particularly pronounced. The history of this relationship in the Federal Repub-lic mirrors the state's political, social, and cultural development since 1945 in important ways; motorization and stabilization in the postwar period were not merely simultaneous but mutually rein-forcing manifestations of the westernization and democratization of the FRG. Today, for instance, the German stock market responds not only to bears and bulls but to moose, at least when a hypo-thetical elk overturns a $100 million new release from Mercedes.

Similarly one might joke about the curious connection between a German and his car – a devotion that can transcend some human bonds, as the tabloids never tire of reporting – but one can also draw certain conclusions about the past and the future of German society in studying this connection. In a word, the question of what drives the Federal Republic follows from the determination of what the Federal Republic is driving. The present essay pursues this observation from the record of the recent past to the portents of the current circumstances.

German engineers and inventors figured vitally in the early development of the automobile, and the legacy of Messrs. Daimler and Benz, among others, accounts in a preliminary way for the pride Germans take in their cars. Motorized vehicles appeared on city streets with some frequency by the turn of the century, the picture of modernity and progress. But the private car remained the privilege of the richest Germans well into the Weimar democracy, despite increasing public interest in American-style mass-motorization.[1] The National Socialists, in accord with Adolf Hitler's express and abiding interest, moved first to introduce a widely available and affordable personal car, the Volkswagen.

The idea of a nation outfitted with the reliable bug-like "people's car" in egalitarian flat black appealed to the Nazis at various levels. By the time the vehicles rolled off the assembly line in 1938, they offered the NSDAP the prospect of a rapidly mobilizable populace. Before the war in Europe permeated Nazi planning and society, however, the Volkswagen fulfilled and furthered domestic propaganda, which depicted the party and the state as the guarantor of the little man's share of German prosperity.[2] Hitler himself compared the VW to the mass-produced radio sets that the Nazis distributed in the name of spreading the trappings of affluence and reinforcing the party's line in the private sphere.[3]

---

1. Hans Mommsen and Manfred Grieger, *Das Volkswagenwerk und seine Arbeiter im Dritten Reich* (Düsseldorf: ECON, 1996), pp. 53-54. See also Neil Gregor, *Star and Swastika* (London: Yale University Press, 1997).

2. Mommsen and Grieger, *Das Volkswagenwerk*, p. 56.

3. See Hitler speech at the opening of the 1934 International Automobile Exhibition in Berlin, reproduced in Max Domarus, *Hitler Reden 1932 bis 1945*, Vol. 1, Pt. 1 (Wiesbaden: Löwit, 1973), pp. 369-371.

The car fit neatly within the Nazis' Strength Through Joy campaign (*Kraft durch Freude* or KdF); in fact, early plans called it the KdF-Wagen. Strength Through Joy marked the NSDAP's program of industrial mobilization, initially directed toward increasing productivity in the armaments sector and soon expanded in principle throughout German industry. To this end, KdF posited a sixfold objective: social compensation; increased productivity through recreation and relaxation; enhanced national health, including the emotional and mental vigor of the work force; promotion of *Heimatliebe*, or the love of one's native soil; improving the self-esteem of German workers; and fostering the national community.[4] The KdF car fulfilled this mission, serving at once as a material linkage between the state and the working driver, as transportation to the leisure functions that would restore and motivate the worker and as the object of pride in workmanship and achievement.

In this same vein, the production of the VW meant more state-subsidized industrial jobs – as, indeed, did the construction of the highways on which the Nazi everyman would drive his Volkswagen[5] – which at once placated the restless unemployed and embroiled workers in the National Socialist system. If nothing else, the promise of an automobile of their own was also meant to buy worker acquiescence to the new societal order.

Nazi racial theory applied to the roadways of the Third Reich, as well. Specifically the tautology held that the genetic unreliability of foreigners – above all, of Jews – rendered them incapable of upholding Nazi traffic laws, just like all other conventions in Hitler's state.[6] Moreover, the linkage of National Socialism and the automobile lent the politicization of driving a particular charge. As one contemporary insisted, the image of "Jews at the wheel of a motor car on the city streets ... or even as the beneficiaries of

4. Bruno Fromman, *Reisen*, (Stuttgart: Historisches Institut der Universität Stuttgart, 1992), p. 110. See also Tim Mason, *Social Policy in the Third Reich*, trans. Jim Broadwin (Providence and Oxford: Berg, 1993), p. 160.

5. See Alfred Gottwaldt, *Julius Dorpmüller, die Reichsbahn und die Autobahn* (Berlin: Argon, 1995); and Erhard Schütz and Eckhard Gruber, *Mythos Reichsautobahn: Bau und Inszenierung der 'Straßen des Führers' 1933-1941* (Berlin: Christoph Links, 1996).

6. Fritz Kamm, *Die Versagung und die Entziehung der Fahrerlaubnis* (dissertation for a doctorate of law at the Ruprecht Karl University, Heidelberg, 1940), p. 59.

Adolf Hitler's roads, which German workers' hands built" marked a particular offense to Nazi sensibilities.[7] Jews, gypsies, and members of other "alien races" could no more participate in the community of German drivers than in the racial community at large. For in the Nazi state, in pointed contrast to liberal Weimar, an individual's willingness to obey the laws of the land counted for nothing against "German thinking" and "German feeling."[8] Thus, just as widespread motorization equaled societal mobilization in the Third Reich, the German car culture became joined to the national culture from the outset of its mass-phenomenon status.

The Nazi war effort swallowed up almost all of the material manifestations of popular automotion in Germany as readily as Hitler had bestowed them; the state confiscated private cars as the war began, and soon gasoline and rubber wheels no longer figured in the remnant civilian experience. (By the end of World War II, Germans had even seen their bicycle tires seized to supply the military.) The community of German drivers went down to the same defeat as the social order that spawned it.

The shortages persisted in the immediate postwar period, of course. But then, a car could hardly navigate in the rubble-strewn streets of bombed-out cities, and anyway, movement within or among the zones of occupation was a difficult proposition at best. In this phase of the nascent Federal Republic, the predominant automotive icon in everyday life was the Jeep, usually filled with GIs or some other representatives of the American (or at least Americanized) leadership. One rarely saw Germans in Jeeps, though one knew what to think of the young women who smiled at the occupants.

In the popular imagination, German taste ran toward American cars in these years, in part because this country's dawning automotive golden age gave rise to ever more elaborate, even poetical vehicles, and in part because the need for cultural realignment had left the Germans to uncertain imitations of the new power's conventions.[9] In many ways, a Studebaker represented a realm of

7. idem, pp. 60-61.

8. idem, pp. 59-60.

9. See Günter Bayerl, "Die Darstellung des Autos in der Literatur – ein Spiegel der Motorisierung?" in Hans Pohl, ed., *Traditionspflege in der Automobil-*

experience of which West Germans could hardly conceive in those days, a world of easy affluence and personal freedom. Could Germany ever aspire to such a society?

Even before the Marshall Plan got going in earnest, the western Allies encouraged the reconstruction of the German automobile industry in the name of recovery and stabilization.[10] The Volkswagen plant in Wolfsburg came first in line, if only because 15 percent of remaining undestroyed plant distinguished VW as the most functional facility left.[11] Under the British occupying authority, VW produced nearly 1300 cars by the end of 1945, the total automobile production for post-Nazi Germany's first year. The British returned Volkswagen to German responsibility on 2 January 1948. VW distinguished itself in the public mind as a successful convert to West German democracy.[12]

Daimler-Benz resumed production in 1946; Opel, in 1947; and BMW, without its plant in East German Eisenach, in 1952. As the Korean War gave further urgency to the western Allies' plans for a prosperous and productive FRG, German car makers, like other industries, took up the challenge. The automotive sector also led the Federal Republic in the integration of new technologies, new business models and new approaches to labor relations.[13] In all, the return of the native automobile industry boded well for the West German economy.

Not until January 1957, however, did the number of private cars surpass the sum of motorcycles and motorized scooters in the FRG;[14] economic recovery on the individual level took a while. As

---

industrie, a collection of papers delivered at the Stuttgarter Tage zur Automobil- und Unternehmensgeschichte vom 8. bis 11. April 1991 (Stuttgart: Franz Steiner, 1991), pp. 201-238, esp. pp. 212-214.

10. Compare Wolfgang Benz, *Die Gründung der Bundesrepublik: Von der Bizone zum souveränen Staat*, 3d. ed., (Munich: Deutscher Taschenbuch Verlag, 1989), pp. 81-97.

11. The statistics and the dates in this paragraph appear in Hermann Glaser, *Kulturgeschichte der Bundesrepublik Deutschland* (Munich and Vienna: Carl Hanser, 1986), Vol. 2, p. 146.

12. Bayerl, "Die Darstellung des Autos," p. 218.

13. See Volker Wellhöner, *"Wirtschaftswunder"-Weltmarkt-westdeutscher Fordismus* (Münster: Westfälisches Dampfboot, 1996).

14. Thomas Krämer-Badoni, Herberg Grymer, and Marianne Rodenstein, *Zur sozio-ökonomischen Bedeutung des Automobils* (Frankfurt: Suhrkamp, 1971), pp. 14-15.

the economy recovered, the German car industry demonstrated a vehicular pluralism to go along with the fledgling marketplace of ideas in the FRG, manufacturing something for any postwar sensibility. Old money, for instance, continued to buy the time-tested prestige models from Daimler-Benz. In a twist of the new socioeconomic order, the seamy shadow-side of the upper strata also identified itself with the Mercedes star; one thinks here of the storied Rosemarie Nitribitt, whose hallmark in a short life as a high-class prostitute was her 190 SL convertible. (As one writer observed of the callgirl whose fees equaled half the average worker's monthly wage in 1957, "From now on, everyone stared at the auto, and it occurred to no one that the car was just a bit better looking than its driver.")[15] The protagonists of pulpy doctor novels inevitably drove station wagons from reputable, old manufacturers – always a late model but never brand new. At the same time, a countervailing attitude held that the particular charm of the humble Volkswagen, for instance, stemmed from its "simplicity, utility, and sobriety."[16]

Additionally, there began to develop a purely Federal Republican car culture. It began in 1948 with the American-ish Hansa 1500, which emerged fully formed in chrome and white walls from the firm of Carl F. W. Borgward. The Hansa 1500 was the first entirely new postwar German automobile. It was small but "racy,"[17] German but without the troublesome prehistory of, say, the Beetle; it and its siblings – notably the stylish Isabella – made quite a hit in the FRG. Moreover, Borgward's cars posted impressive international sales. Here was the West German economic miracle summed up in one, pontoon-shaped consumer commodity. (The maker of the Hansa 1500 was similarly a creature of the era: although Borgward had produced three-wheelers and other small commercial vehicles before the war and acquired the majority interest in Hansa

15. Hoche, Karl, *In diesem unserem Lande* (Düsseldorf and Zurich: Artemis & Winkler, 1997), p. 108. The squalid life and 1957 murder of Rosemarie Nitribitt served as the substance for at least one television movie in the Federal Republic and countless fictionalized tellings in print.

16. Martin Beheim-Schwarzbach, *Der geölte Blitz* (Hamburg: n.p., 1953), quoted in Bayerl, "Die Darstellung des Autos," p. 219.

17. Glaser, *Kulturgeschichte*, 2, 148.

Lloyd shipping in the late 1920s, he stood out as one of the new rich entrepreneurs who shaped the early Federal Republic by sheer force of personality.[18] Just as tellingly, Borgward's company, the largest private employer in the city of Bremen, failed to survive the consolidating period of the West German economic recovery, and it closed its doors in 1961.)[19] Embodying the virtue of necessary frugality as well as the muted hopefulness of the FRG's builders, the Borgward Hansa 1500 heralded an age.[20]

In December 1961, VW could celebrate its sixteenth year of postwar production and its five-millionth auto produced in that spanse.[21] The latest "small wonders" from Wolfsburg shared the road with a bounty of tiny but widely available German cars: the Goggomobil, of which some 245,000 were assembled and sold between 1955 and 1967;[22] a three-wheeled single-seater produced by Messerschmidt; and BMW's puggish Isetta 300. An Isetta now graces a landing amid recovery-years exhibits at the Museum of the FRG in Bonn; the Museum of the Berlin Wall in the once and future capital also features an exemplar, this one modified to smuggle people across the German-German border. (Folding an extra human body into the Isetta was such an unlikely proposition that the midget contraption made several successful expeditions before the East German border guards caught on.) In a word, the Isetta and its *Zeitgenossen* (contemporaries) witnessed the concurrent recovery and remotorization of the Federal Republic of Germany. Cities changed, as did the patterns of social and geographical mobility, and industry expanded, all of which further reinforced the economic miracle.[23] The leisure and vacation culture began to take its familiar late-industrial-age shape.

18. idem, 87.

19. See Wilhelm Eberwein and Jochen Tholen, *Borgwards Fall* (Bremen: Steintor, 1987), esp. pp. 9-14.

20. Compare the similar argument about modernization and Americanization in France, in Kristin Ross, *Fast Cars, Clean Bodies* (Cambridge and London: MIT Press, 1995), esp. pp. 15-70.

21. Glaser, *Kulturgeschichte*, 2, 146.

22. idem, 147.

23. Compare Kramer-Badoni, Grymer, and Rodenstein, *Zur sozio-ökonomischen Bedeutung*, pp. 17-19.

German cars became larger and more powerful as the Federal Republic did. "Buying German" connoted one's social arrival, within the Federal Republic and, increasingly, overseas. The curious transformation of BMW in the 1970s from a debt-ridden producer of quirky rattletraps and the occasional race car to the world renowned manufacturer of the ultimate driving machines mirrored Germany's rise to international economic importance.

Domestically, too, the BMW came to represent the preferred conveyance for the status-anxious, upwardly mobile *Profilneurotiker*. Opel reverted to the doilied middle class, the eternal *Spießbürgertum*. Volkswagen continued to purvey its image as the car that transcended class, though the Beetle all but disappeared from the roadways by the 1980s while various models of VW touting power and performance took its place. West German prosperity had trickled into even the most rural reaches of the Federal Republic. The mid-range Benz – the same models that serve as taxi cabs – acquired the epithet "peasant Mercedes" in the popular idiom, reflecting the popularity of the reliable 200 and 300 series among increasingly wealthy farmers.

The often-stated manifest right of free Germans to drive freely – that is, as fast as the fruits of their labor could go on the ever wider, ever flatter autobahns – became the cherished and well-practiced West German equivalent of life, liberty, and the pursuit of happiness.[24] Western observers who believed that liberal democracy was a luxury item in Germany, which the Germans would support and embrace as long as it generated sufficient affluence for enough people, could look upon the West German automobile culture with some relief. Society in the Federal Republic looked – and drove – increasingly like a polity dedicated to its new political and social system.

East German party chief Walter Ulbricht attempted to make policy out of his own vision of modern German society: Automobiles parked in rows before every prefabricated apartment block in the workers and peasants paradise. To no small degree, this nod to

---

24. Compare Glaser, *Kulturgeschichte*, 2, 94. Glaser's characterization of the German take on the pursuit of happiness applies to consumption in general in the *Fresswelle* days and thereafter.

consumer concerns marked a countermeasure to the similar sym-
bols of West German affluence and their allure to the East German
workers.[25] Only partially recovered from the abortive 1953 popular uprising in the German Democratic Republic, Ulbricht and
other members of the ruling Socialist Unity Party reckoned that
the skilled and laboring classes – on whose productivity the political, economic, and social plans of the GDR depended – might be
less inclined to depart for the West if the East could offer them all
the material comforts *and* the moral-political high ground. This
policy stance derived from more than cynical power-political aspirations, however. Ulbricht sought to effect his own transformation
of German society by much the same mechanism as his West German counterparts, the western Allies, and even Hitler before
them; that is, if the leadership could make the new system work for
the people, the people would work for the new system.

By the late 1950s, the GDR generated sufficient wealth to sus-
tain its population in more comfort, despite war damage and the
subsequent years of expropriation of plant and resources to the
Soviet Union. In 1958, for example, Berlin did away with the
ration-coupon system for foodstuffs – admittedly a decade or so
after the Federal Republic's economic reform abolished rationing
but an encouraging milestone to the party leadership just the same.
In 1957, the state automobile factory in the Saxon city of Zwickau
began producing the Trabant, named to evoke images of satellites,
high technology, and the future. (After all, the birth year of the
Trabi also saw the launch of both Sputnik orbiters.)

The Trabant, like its cousin, the Wartburg, which the East Germans produced in the Eisenach facility that once made BMWs,
served a different kind of status aspiration than its West German
counterparts, namely national prestige. Through mass motorization, the East meant to show how it could keep material pace with
the West. Meanwhile, the popular psychology of automobile own-

25. See "Aus der Entschließung des V. Parteitages der SED über die weiteren
ökonomischen Aufgaben, 15. Juli 1958," reproduced as Document 136 in Hermann
Weber, *DDR: Dokumente zur Geschichte der Deutschen Demokratischen Republik*
(Munich: Deutscher Taschenbuch Verlag, 1986), pp. 237-239; see also Manfred
Jäger, *Kultur und Politik in der DDR 1945-1990* (Cologne: Edition Deutschland
Archiv im Verlag Wissenschaft und Politik, 1995), p.158.

ership was rather more straightforward in the GDR: One had either a car or a friend who did, and arranging transportation became one more manifestation of mutual coping at the everyday level.

The Sachsenring assembly line produced its one-millionth Trabant on 22 November 1973, just about the time that motor cars came to outnumber motorcycles and scooters on East German thoroughfares.[26] By then, Ulbricht had already ceded his post to Erich Honecker, who proclaimed the advent of consumer socialism while, at the same time, banishing the vestigial East German private sector that accounted for 14.4 percent of the national income, predominantly in food and textile production.[27] This move only exacerbated the existing tension in the economy. On the one hand, Honecker could already claim to preside over a society that had fulfilled many of Ulbricht's material goals: Average household income had trebled since 1949.[28] And this improvement in national fortunes did translate into a comparatively higher standard of living for everyday East Germans in some respects. For instance, every home in the GDR now had a refrigerator, and most were on their way to acquiring a freezer to match;[29] there was certainly no shortage of food to store in these appliances, either.[30] On the other hand, East Germans increasingly overspent on food because there was nothing else to buy.[31] The regime began to import limited num-

---

26. Statistics in Friedrich Drange, Richard Herzog and Klaus Kockel, "Vom Fortschritt durch Verstaatlichung zum Rückstand in der Produktivität – die Industrie als wichtigster Wirstschaftsbereich," in Egon Hölder, ed., Im Trabi durch die Zeit – 40 Jahre Leben in der DDR (Stuttgart: Metzler-Poeschle, 1992), pp. 163-174, esp. p. 166.

27. David Childs, The GDR: Moscow's German Ally, 2d ed. (London: Unwin Hyman, 1988), p. 85.

28. Margot Münnich and Erhard König, "Von der Not der Nachkriegsjahre zu geischertem Einkommen – die Entwicklung des Lebensstandards," in Hölder, Im Trabi, pp. 97-110, esp. p. 98 and p. 103.

29. Münnich and König, "Von der Not," p. 108.

30. Compare Hans-Ulrich Saretzki, Reinhard Schenke, and Günter Glende, "Von der Lebensmittelkarte zur Warteliste für das Auto – die planwirtschaftliche Entwicklung des Einzelhandels," in Hölder, Im Trabi, pp. 139-152, particularly p. 148, where the authors assert that by the early 1970s, foodstuffs – even such "luxury" items as butter, fruit and coffee – were readily available but the quality of the offerings began to fall noticeably.

31. Saretzki, Schenke and Glende, "Von der Lebensmittelkarte," pp. 145-147.

bers of Mazdas and Volkswagens against hard currency for sale in the GDR, just as it unveiled the Exquisit and Delikat specialty stores, which sold Western products for wildly inflated prices payable in East German marks. (A bar of West German chocolate, which sold for 1 Western Deutschmark in the hard-currency Intershop stores, fetched 7 GDR-marks in the Delikat.)[32] And, in an unconscious condemnation of their own system, the highest party officials had themselves driven around in black Volvos, which were incontrovertibly more comfortable than East bloc cars.

In a word, the state failed ever more glaringly to fulfill the expectations that its own propaganda raised. The automobile provides a ready example. Only by the late 1980s did more than half of East German households own a car,[33] a rate of motorization that the West Germans surpassed around 1970.[34] Of course, one might argue that the East Germans had fewer places to go, given the limited vacation options and poor road conditions. Gasoline shortages plagued the GDR from the oil crises of the 1970s until the state's demise, and repair work, for want of spare parts, remained an expensive and unreliable proposition for most East German drivers. (Berlin obligingly oversaw the production of a series of do-it-yourself repair books;[35] car owners in the GDR got by as they always did, hoarding whatever parts came their way, if only for barter, and improvising whatever they could not replace officially.) The indigenous car culture, then, ranged in experience from "arranging" a new windshield to cramming two weeks' worth of vacation equipment (including food, depending on the destination) into the back to sharing rides with colleagues. Like most aspects of life in the GDR, the car culture prompted both complaint and self-deprecating humor.

Despite the problems of owning and maintaining a motor vehicle, the East German public embraced the notion of mass-motorization. In fact, demand already outstripped production of cars in

32. idem, p. 152.

33. Münnich and König, "Von der Not," p. 110.

34. Krämer-Badoni, Grymer, and Rodenstein, *Zur sozio-ökonomischen Bedeutung*, p. 21.

35. See, for instance, Franz Meißner, ed., *Trabant: Wie helfe ich mir selbst?* 2d ed., (Berlin: VEB Verlag Technik, 1974).

the GDR by the early 1960s.[36] The resulting system of advance order sign-up assumed its most perverse proportions just as Honecker promised material improvements for his fellow citizens: anyone who put his name on the list for a car in 1974/75 could expect to wait until 1990 for his or her vehicle. Many East Germans did, indeed, aspire to their first car in 1990 – thanks to the economic union that preceded unification that year.

The Trabant, which until then, comprised more than half of the six million automobiles on the streets of the GDR, was taken out of production on 30 April 1991, mere months after receiving the title of 1990's Car of the Year.[37] A few green-arrow signs on traffic signals, admonishing eastern Germans of their remnant freedom to turn right on a red light if the way is clear, are today all that remain of the promise of East German car culture – a promise that never quite lived up to the party's hopeful slogans.

Now, one might question whether the automobile or the progress that it represents really amounts to that much good in Germany or, more precisely, whether the West German example merits much praise. Critical observers in the West linked the car culture with general social trends in the FRG – for better *and* worse. Friedrich Dürrenmatt wrote cars into such works as *Der Besuch der alten Dame* and *Die Panne* by way of attacking a money-mad society; Max Frisch took up the loss of autonomy to the rules and structure of the crowded city thoroughfares in *Stiller*; Heinrich Böll revisited the theme of automobiles and pernicious social stratification in *Ende einer Dienstfahrt*.[38] For a variety of reasons, the way forward for the Federal Republic was not the A3 or the turbocharged machines tearing along it.

As skeptics point out, automobile ownership hardly counted as a rational proposition, when the typical driver dedicated a relatively large sum to a piece of equipment with an indistinct purpose even though cheaper and, frequently, faster public transit was readily

---

36. Saretzki, Schenke and Glende, "Von der Lebensmittelkarte," pp. 148-149.

37. Karl-Heinz Pesch, "Von der Trümmerwüste zum Ausbau des Verkehrswegenetzes – Straßen, Schienen und Wasserwege auf 108,332 km2," in Hölder, *Im Trabi*, pp. 209-228, esp. p.218.

38. See Bayerl, "Die Darstellung des Autos," pp. 221-226.

available.[39] Transportation is a means, not an end; therefore the mode should not matter, in the efficiency model. Similarly, the drain on scarce natural resources that the car culture represented rendered the cost-benefit calculations of a happily motorized society more ambiguous. (The oil crisis of 1973/74 brought to the FRG the now-sentimentalized "car-free Sundays," when all driving was prohibited in the name of conservation.) And then there was the matter of pollution, an ever more widely held concern as the Green movement gained force in the Federal Republic. How could a responsible society justify its attachment to motor vehicles in these circumstances?

As for the deeper significance of automobiles in society, according to dissenting social scientists, the car culture obscured, if not promoted, the basic flaw in the West German social order: the unequal distribution of wealth and, hence, power in the FRG. In 1969, for instance, more than 12 million private cars were registered to travel the streets of the Federal Republic, but these were distributed among just less than 50 percent of all households.[40] At the same time, one in five of the households that belonged to the highest monthly income category owned a second car, suggesting a further concentration of wealth.[41] And while 48.5 percent of all working class households owned a car in 1969 – compared to nearly 70 percent of white-collar and public official households – a worker spent a significantly larger portion of his wages on the purchase of a (typically somewhat smaller) car.[42] The middle class had its car culture, then, *and* held the working class in thrall with these tokens of potential prestige.[43] In the gap between the promise of material reward and the reality of sociopolitical domination, critics feared, the fundamental inequalities would continue to fester. The shiny veneer of the car culture only encouraged complacency and competition in this scheme.

Further, the diffusion of cultural interest and participation into the commercialized car culture removed the Federal Republic that

---

39. Compare Krämer-Badoni, Grymer, and Rodenstein, *Zur sozio-ökonomischen Bedeutung*, p. 59.
40. ibid.
41. ibid.
42. ibid.
43. Compare Glaser, *Kulturgeschichte*, 2, 89.

much further from its founding ambition to be a *Kulturstaat* that would make high culture available to everyone.[44] In a word, the West German car craze meant popular culture in the worst sense, by these lights. The automobile aided and abetted Theodor Adorno's "culture industry" by propelling modern citizens between the increasingly disconnected public and private aspects of life and, thus, perpetuating the illusions of free time.[45] With a little reflection, for instance, the diligently consuming paterfamilias in the 1950s advertisement might have guessed that his example of packing the kids in the Ford Taurus and off to the Italian Alps – to the envy of his neighbors – would give rise to the days-long autobahn infarctions that herald the start and end of the school holidays in Germany today.[46]

This tidal cycle of traffic jams, as the whole country feels obliged to hit the same roads for the same destinations at the same time of each year, shows the extent to which consumption replaced contemplation in the cultural community of the FRG. Indeed, the ritual began with the purchase of an automobile: the whole construct of model years and body types could claim little practical application and less aesthetic richness. It served only to goad more people to buy more cars. In all, the cultural critic might conclude, the car helped make the modern West German a more efficient consumer without doing much to bolster his consciousness or his humanity.[47]

Instead, rugged individualism run – or driven – amok in cars led an increasing number of Germans to aggression against their fellows on the road, to reckless speeding, or at least to the small but cumulative acts of rudeness that appear in news stories on most days. (TÜV inspectors can require that a car have functional turn indicators but they cannot ensure that the self-absorbed driver will use them.) Whereas some vestige of politeness, or perhaps just cowardice, might keep the average German civil in his face-to-face

---

44. Compare Jost Hermand, *Die Kultur der Bundesrepublik Deutschland, 1965-1985*, revised ed. (Frankfurt and Berlin: Ullstein, 1990), p. 153.

45. Theodor Adorno and Max Horkheimer, *Dialectic of Enlightenment* (London: Verso, 1979). Compare also Krämer-Badoni, Grymer, and Rodenstein, *Zur sozio-ökonomischen Bedeutung*, p. 64. See also Hermand, *Die Kultur*, pp. 158-174.

46. See Glaser, *Kulturgeschichte*, 2, 145.

47. Compare Glaser, *Kulturgeschichte*, 2, 80.

affairs, the combination of power and anonymity bestowed by a car emboldened him to act out his repressed rage and impatience once he hit the pavement. Status competition, alienation, blind consumerism, hyper-individualism, technological tyrannization – the automobile visited all these plagues and more on the FRG, according to the car culture's detractors. For this superficial token of progress and wealth, the Federal Republic traded a sizable share of its genuine democratic potential.

On the other hand, these same musings on Germans and cars demonstrate the success of the FRG's social structures. Without question, the consumer culture of the Federal Republic did not satisfy expectations of many cultural critics; in this vein, one might have hoped, for example, that the personal mobility afforded by an automobile would have encouraged a more open and thoughtful community. But even the lowest-brow cultural expressions – including the excesses of some car owners – do not warrant such pessimism. A centripetal society in Germany remains preferable to one that tends to the extremes.

The whole program of the FRG sought to give a majority of West Germans a stake in maintaining the liberal democratic Federal German republic that brought about this transformation. Automobiles, like independent housing, vacations, and education, comprised part of the social-contract package that the FRG offered. It is true that this new middle class – oriented not toward property holding and autonomy like the old practitioners of the independent professions but rather toward income as a means of consumption – brought with it a certain tendency toward conformism and status hierarchy.[48] But it is also true that in the course of five strikingly peaceable decades, the "Land of the Great Middle," as cultural historian Hermann Glaser calls the Federal Republic,[49] has, for the most part, succeeded in ameliorating its social divisions and, thereby, stabilizing its political culture. The West German dream, as it were, has proven at once resilient and inclusive.

For instance, while the economic downturn of 1967 witnessed a slight flattening of the car-purchasing rates, as some West Ger-

48. ibid.
49. ibid.

mans postponed the acquisition of an automobile until the prevailing circumstances passed, the ranks of car owners in the FRG continued to grow steadily throughout the social turbulence of 1968 and the *Wendezeit* (transitional period) thereafter.[50] That is to say that ever more West Germans bought into their system's prospects for resolving the current tensions as they invested in motor cars.

The very fact of mass car-ownership signifies the transformation of the automobile from symbol of elite luxury to consumer product for all social strata.[51] Of course, both Hitler and Ulbricht could claim to have effected some degree of motorization in their respective Germanys, so widespread popular access to motor cars does not, in itself, guarantee a functioning civil society. But a breakdown of new-car acquisition patterns in the Federal Republic shows a clear concentration in the middle ranges of size and cost – and that across all class groupings.[52] Meanwhile, automobiles of all categories increasingly resemble the middle-range models, which bespeaks a self-conscious social norming, expressed in consumer behavior.[53]

One recent manifestation of this same inclination toward the middle is the new Mercedes models, which buyers may order without the numbers above the tail lights. These chrome or sometimes gold-toned characters identify the size of the engine in the car; from this bit of information, another driver might hone his guess as to the vehicle's cost and, thus, its owner's social position. Their absence from the back ends of the biggest new Daimlers may mark a stroke of coyness rather than modesty in some drivers. In either case, however, the car-culture doubters may take heart in this small retreat from the all-out, mine-is-bigger-than-yours competition inherent in automobile ownership.

Similarly, fuel efficiency and low emissions have become pegs on an alternative scale of automotive identity, with competitive energies directed toward maximizing gas mileage. The Daimler-

50. Krämer-Badoni, Grymer, and Rodenstein, *Zur sozio-ökonomischen Bedeutung*, p. 14.
   51. ibid. p. 25.
   52. ibid. pp. 37-39.
   53. ibid. p. 59.

Benz company now boasts a whole research and development department with an ecological mandate,[54] and Opel markets a Corso "Eco" model with scientific plaudits for the car's environmental friendliness.

By the late 1980s, West Germans could afford to fetishize their culture, as a classic-car trend announced a nostalgia for the early days of the Federal Republic. The Beetle was back, now as an automotive heirloom and prized show-off piece for Sunday putters through town. The truly hip among the well-moneyed mounted pilgrimages to the American West in search of pristine classic Cadillac convertibles, preferably in period pink or turquoise. In this case, the car – further divorced from its ostensible purpose as means of transportation – provided the link to the past, real or imagined. To some observers, this fashion represented a kind of rebellion against the relentless conformism of the present-day car culture, as well as a broader comment on the dubious aesthetic and ideological appeal of the contemporary period.[55] It certainly marked a shift in the German self-perception.

By this time, German society, like its automotive expression, had matured. The great personalities who had shaped the polity in the first years after the war had since given way to professional politicians who distinguished themselves principally through their assorted scandals. The Federal Republic achieved a comfortable role as one of a group of leading equals in the European Community. Relations East and West proceeded sanely. The economy motored on. It even opened some to foreign cars, which gained wider acceptance as the German automobile culture rolled toward multi-culturalism.

The now-settled shorthand of vehicular identity – with some humor added in – even provided a safe venue to address, identify and integrate, however negatively, the last, hard-core inassimilable elements in the West German system. A fad wave of jokes posited the quintessential counterpoint to middle-class striving as the trashy owner of a second-string muscle car, the Opel Manta. This fabled being not only resisted but reviled bourgeois gentility:

54. "Da wird mir schon Schwumrig," *Spiegel Spezial*, No. 9 (1997), pp. 116-117.
55. See Kurt Möser, "Massenverkehr und Oldtimerkultur," in *Traditionspflege in der Automobilindustrie*, pp. 110-117.

Q: What's left over after a fatal Manta accident?
A: A length of gold chain and a mourning hair dresser.

He was ill-connected to current events and the concerns of majority society around him:

First Manta driver: "Hey, dude, I bought the new Duden yesterday."
Second Manta driver: "Dude, did you install it yet?"

He was typically a racist, a jingoist, a drunk, a deadbeat, a complainer, and a rube, the very antithesis of the successful West German's self-conception. Most tellingly, he was utterly immune to upward mobility and status:

Q: What's the shortest Manta joke ever?
A: "A Manta is parked in front of the university."

In the climate of consensus that prevailed in the FRG in the late 1980s, aficionados of the Manta joke could yuk it up with some assurance as to the like-mindedness of their audience – right up until 9 November 1989. When the border between the Germanies collapsed that night, the herald of German unification, 16 million East Germans stepped up to try their hand at the West German dream. A western car topped the wish lists of thousands of eastern newcomers; thus did they articulate their desire to participate in the Federal German polity.

By their very numbers and their divergent experience, the East Germans changed society in the Federal Republic of which they are now citizens. Of course, the basic contours persist: the social market economy, liberal democratic governance, and that grand middle class. The infusion of new members of the polity and new demands on the system represented an incomparable strain, however. Most students of Germany wondered just how smoothly the transition might go.

At the wheel of the Trabant, I experienced the range of (literally) street-level reactions to unification in the summer and fall of 1991: the newly rich Easterner, menacing an apparent countryman with his freshly acquired West-Auto; the instant comrades-in-Trabis, ready to swap spark plugs or help push-start a fellow at a stop-light stall; the West German consultant, asking me, next to my car, for directions in the slow, sing-song tones with which well-meaning strangers speak to small children or the mentally disturbed. (He was relieved to find that Trabi drivers speak comprehensible German.) On the cobblestones of Wittenberg's market square or amid the ruts of my employer's parking lot – just like on Bundesstraße 22 between Bayreuth and Bamberg – Germans appropriated me first as the driver of a Trabant. The rest of the experience followed from there.

To their credit as sportsman-like humorists, the Germans stopped telling Trabi jokes almost as soon as the all-German traffic authorities moved to keep the plastic terrors off the roads. On the other hand, the general assumption held was that we Trabi drivers would switch to more suitable means of transport like any other German; that we too would join the crowd. To that end, Opel now works out of the Eisenach assembly line that formerly turned out Wartburgs after East German authorities stripped the facility from BMW's possession. As the drive-in Trabi conventions in Berlin and elsewhere in the new states of eastern Germany indicate, the united German car culture has already found a slot for the little machines. Their former drivers might welcome this classification as part of the identity-forging process in this next "model year" of the Federal Republic.

Chapter 9

GLOBALIZATION, GENDER, AND THE GERMAN WELFARE STATE

The Maldistributive Consequences of Retrenchment

~~

Patricia Davis and Simon Reich

Solidarity is not only demanded when it is a question of making demands and fighting for them, as in wage restraint and job conflicts. There is also a solidarity of workers with the jobless …. In the present situation in Germany, solidarity of workers in the west with workers in the east is also required. (Helmut Kohl, *Financial Times*, 1 May 1992)

In the aftermath of the Cold War, a vacuum emerged for policy makers, academics, and commentators. The solid foundation upon which international relations had been built had crumbled with surprising ease, leaving not only a fluid politics but intellectual disarray. Whether nature abhors a vacuum or not, those elites entrusted with influence certainly did. And so after a few intellectual and policy false starts – such as the "New World Order" – the term "globalization" emerged as the very cornerstone upon which our understanding of foreign affairs (economic and security) was to be built. No current political speech by national leaders is complete without a reference to the effects (pernicious or benign) of globalization. Correspondingly, a cottage industry has been cre-ated in the academic disciplines of political science, economics, and sociology built on studying the phenomenon of globalization. The fact that academic programs and centers have now been cre-ated to study it attests to its institutionalization as a key concept, complete with its own lexicon and embryonic paradigm, although careful consideration of its meaning, causes, and effects remain at a premium.[1]

Yet debate still rages over two sets of issues. The first concerns whether globalization is indeed a real phenomenon or simply a imaginative conception of elites seeking to justify their policy pref-erences. Those favoring the latter position argue that policy mak-ers use the supposed new constraints imposed by globalization to justify implementing policies that they have always preferred. For advocates of the skeptical approach, globalization provided a con-text in which such "reform" could take place. For them, the con-cept is not only overstated but its benign influences are overblown. Indeed, globalization is dangerous and perhaps nonexistent as a phenomenon. Furthermore, its invocation generates fear and resis-tance as a subterfuge, justifying often unnecessary cuts in employ-ment and welfare. As Paul Hirst and Grahame Thompson suggest: "Globalization is a myth suitable for a world without illusions, but it is also one that robs us of hope" leading to "the pathology of overdiminished expectations."[2] A second issue concerns the dis-tributive consequences of globalization. Has it indeed created new winners and losers, or are they historical and predictable – simply rearranging the chairs on the *Titanic* as those who sink do so with alarming familiarity?

We cannot possibly answer either or both of these questions in this paper with any certainty. What we can do is look at a critical case, that of the Federal Republic of Germany, whose leadership currently expresses public and repeated anguish over confronting the pressures of globalization. Our purpose is to argue that, regard-

1. "Globalisation and Sites of Conflict: Towards Definition and Taxonomy," Working Paper Number 1, Centre for the Study of Globalisation and Regionalisa-tion, Warwick University, June 1998.

2. Paul Hirst and Grahame Thompson, *Globalization in Question*, (Cam-bridge, UK: Polity Press, 1995), p.6.

less of whether the forces of globalization are real or imagined, the policy solutions bear a familiar ring in the German context. As has been historically the case, the supposedly sophisticated and progressive German welfare state has unduly burdened women in the reallocation of resources while cutting back its total social spending by a remarkably small percentage. While current debates rage over the allocation of burdens, and Germany's leaders consistently call for solidarity in accepting those burdens equitably, we suggest that state policy has sought to do exactly the opposite – identifying women as a weak political constituency who have traditionally generated little resistance in the face of economic discrimination. Gender has therefore once again emerged as a critical variable in the political economy of German social welfare in the 1990s. The chairs are indeed being rearranged with predictable winners and losers.

We argue that the explanation for this focus lies in the gendered norms common to Germany since unification, norms institutionalized in the Basic Law of the Federal Republic.[3] Furthermore, not only is the discriminatory nature of current German institutions disposed towards the maldistribution of burdens but it in fact predates the current Berlin Republic, and as such is rooted in a historical German ideology and political culture. Crucial to this argument is the recognition that the welfare system was never designed to create economic and social equity along gender lines. We therefore suggest that even if Hirst and Thompson are right in declaring globalization to be a myth, it certainly has provided German politicians with the opportunity to resurrect old gender preferences in the allocation of state resources.

In concluding this introduction we address the question of "why examine Germany?" We have chosen to do so because we believe it generates a broader claim accessible to empirical assessment. For the

---

3. This, of course, does not address the possibility that such issues were purposely suppressed from debate in the political agenda in favor of the axiom of Cold War engagement. The Berufsverbot laws, for example, denied left wing "radicals" positions in the German bureaucracy – a wide categorization that extended to multiple job classifications such as railway workers and school teachers. For details see Gerald Braunthal, *Political Loyalty and Public Service in West Germany: the 1972 Decree Against Radicals and Its Consequences* (Amherst: University of Massachusetts Press, 1990).

last five decades Germany has been considered amongst the most progressive and sophisticated of social welfare systems. Modell Deutschland has enshrined in its constitution the notion of equity and its leaders have consistently professed support of such values. Social welfare programs have been considered a major instrument of achieving those goals.[4] Yet its leaders appear to have been relatively quick, while claiming that globalization generates unprecedented challenges to Germany, to fall back on traditional allocative solutions. Germany's actions raise the question of where economic gender rights will not go unchallenged, if they have so effectively retrenched in one of the advanced industrialized world's most comprehensive systems? There are few obvious candidates.

In sum, it may be that these discriminatory characteristics have always been present and that the pressures wrought by globalization have merely revealed and magnified these tendencies. This may be simply one example of how countries offer different responses to globalization as a systemic pressure. Alternatively, it may be an example of the obverse; the homogenization of different national policies, a characteristic claimed by some proponents of globalization.[5] That is the comparative material for future research. What is sure is that as the coffers of the Berlin Republic shrink, its leaders may increasingly evoke the patriarchal values they were able to submerge during decades of economic growth. This retrenchment is creating a more divided Germany – as reflected in its divisive social policies.

Historic and Institutional Foundations of the German Social Welfare System

One of the institutional cornerstones of Modell Deutschland since the FRG's inception in 1949, has been the objective of creating a

---

4. For example, see Hans Zacher cited in Peter J. Katzenstein, *Policy and Politics in West Germany: The Growth of a Semisovereign State* (Philadelphia: Temple University Press, 1987), p.168.

5. For a discussion of this issue see Suzanne Berger, introduction to Suzanne Berger and Ronald Dore (eds.), *National Diversity and Global Capitalism* (Ithaca: Cornell University Press, 1996), pp. 1-25.

sophisticated and comprehensive social welfare system in the context of a restructured polity, consisting of citizens who profess an
abiding allegiance to democratic values, of which gender equality
is a key aspect.[6] Crucial to the success of this construct is an active
yet limited state. Above all, it requires a state that is aggressively
engaged in setting the social rules and norms governing the institutionalization of social welfare.

Claus Offe has noted that the primary ideological foundation
of the institutions of the German social welfare system since its
inception in the late nineteenth century is trust; specifically, its
stabilizing capacity is predicated on the effectiveness of its institutions in the past.[7] Fundamental to this trust is the receipt of a service or payment to which an individual is entitled for specific
reasons. For example, as originally conceived, since only industrial
workers contributed to the social insurance funds, they were also
the only ones to benefit from them on the basis of their contributions. This notion of restricted entitlement continues today. In
essence, the primary purpose of the social security system is to
maintain the status of those who have already achieved some status within the paid labor force. This approach contrasts, for example, with one designed to create opportunities for those who have
never achieved status within the "public sphere" of paid employment such as an affirmative action program.

When instituted in the 1880s, the purpose of social insurance
was therefore to protect the aristocracy of industrial workers. Over
time, its institutions were slowly expanded to include more of the
population based on the same principle – restitution for those who
are "inside" the system (i.e., employed in the labor force). Not
devised to redress historical inequities, the system therefore has
historically had a minimal effect upon social inequality in Germany. In particular, it does not seek to give a head start to the dis-

6. See the election campaign slogan adopted by the CDU in 1949 (Düssel-
dorfer Leitsätze: Sozialmarktwirtschaft) and subsequent policies implemented by
the Adenauer and Erhard governments. The origins and policies are discussed in
Werner Abelhauser, *Die Langen Fünfziger Jahre* (Düsseldorf: Schwann, 1987).

7. Claus Offe, "Smooth Consolidation in the West German Welfare State:
Structural Change, Fiscal Policies, and Populist Politics," in Frances Fox Piven, ed.,
Labor Parties in Postindustrial Societies (London: Polity Press, 1991), p. 125.

advantaged (e.g., unskilled female labor). Moreover, it is not organized as a universal insurance system, but one of exclusive (yet in most cases, mandatory) membership. This exclusivity permits officials to, when necessary, restrict benefits on a selective basis.[8] While this system of social welfare has been extended, the initial philosophy remains intact, providing a justification for discriminating between claimants: contributions to the state are the basis of entitlement.

The integral role of the modern German state is formally anchored in Germany's constitution (Grundgesetz). Article 20, paragraph one, states that "The Federal Republic of Germany is a democratic and social republic," a proclamation interpreted as meaning that the state has the duty to protect its citizens from material need in case of sickness, accident, or unemployment, as well as to secure its citizens in retirement. The institutional component of this social welfare policy is itself a three-tiered support system, comprising three principles; security, entitlement, and welfare, the state serving a different function in each and ascribing different rights to different groups in society for each. Thus, while the state does have the duty to protect its citizens, that does not guarantee equal access to resources. While the German state does provide an extensive material safety net through varied programs, it does not provide equal access. In fact, social welfare is heavily linked to traditional notions of employment. As one government pamphlet proclaims:

> In the years since the creation of the Federal Republic a whole range of special labor and social legislation has been enacted to provide the citizen with various benefits in the event of sickness, accident, invalidity and unemployment, as well as after retirement. Labor law is a good example of how the social-state principle has been put into effect.[9]

---

8. This is not to imply that there is no social safety net in Germany. During the Weimar Republic the German government introduced the third pillar of the social welfare system, namely the principle of Fürsorge, as discussed below. Yet this safety net remains the most vulnerable of the three pillars of the system.

9. "Social Justice," http://www.bundesregierung.de/ausland/system/sys04.html, 30 June 1997.

First, the security cornerstone consists of "social insurance pro-grams" – health care, retirement pensions, workers compensation, unemployment benefits, and compensation for nursing home/hos-pice care for senior citizens. The entitlement cornerstone includes benefits for those who "serve" the state or have "suffered" for the good of the community. The last cornerstone is welfare, which pro-vides financial and/or material "social assistance." The crucial dis-tinctions are therefore important because both give insight into the discriminatory social ideology at work.

The first pillar, the social insurance institutions, are considered self-financing, private programs because they are financed by con-tributions from the workers themselves. The philosophy behind this formulation is to establish solidarity for "self-help" among pri-vate citizens, getting members of society to aggregate resources in order to share the burdens and risks. Many social welfare benefits (e.g., unemployment, health care, pensions, etc.), are therefore specifically restitutional benefits. The minimal role of the state is to provide whatever subsidies are necessary to cover expenditures not met by contributions but its practical role is more significant, com-manding obligatory membership from its citizens in participant organizations. The state's importance is therefore not in guaran-teeing these benefits but rather its authority in mandating others to do so. This practice discriminates because it validates the con-viction that only those who contribute to the system are entitled to benefits in the form of restitution. This becomes problematic when women are encouraged not to participate in the paid labor force or face extensive obstacles in becoming full-fledged and equal partic-ipants when they do so, thus limiting their eligibility for benefits.

The second pillar consists of entitlement benefits under the rubric of civic maintenance (*öffentliche Versorgung*) and is even more restrictive. Its programs are intended to establish solidarity among the civic community in providing benefits for those who serve the state. This group consists chiefly of World War II veter-ans and their survivors, expellees, and (somewhat perplexingly because of their inclusion with the other "sufferers") civil servants (*Beamten*). These benefits are financed by the taxes of *all* citizens. Again, crucial here is the confirmation of the belief that only those who concretely contribute to the good of the state are entitled to benefits from the state at a collective cost. Since the option of serving in the military is foreclosed to women, and the German civil service is overwhelmingly dominated by males at the upper echelons, the viable options here are limited.

The last cornerstone – welfare institutions – is the most recent and the least restrictive in terms of access. *Fürsorge*, or social assistance, can be best understood as the equivalent of traditional welfare, providing financial and material aid for the needy. The German state, however, has critically not contracted to aid those who "fall through the cracks." Rather, such aid is the beneficence of the state. Financial and material aid is administered by the state as a privilege, not a right. This means that in times of economic adversity this so-called privilege can more easily be curtailed, or even revoked by the state. Furthermore, while social assistance is available to all who can demonstrate need, its benefits can be successfully claimed only when it is proven by a potential claimant that the benefits of the other two institutions are insufficient or when relatives are unable to provide the necessary means. No contributions are required and its programs are financed by federal taxes. Here the role of the state is intended to provide assistance to enable all of its citizens to lead a "dignified" life, not to facilitate equity or equalize citizens. Yet, this most crucial pillar of the social market economy is also the institution most susceptible to curtailments and other reductions and women are also disproportionately in need of this type of social welfare.

In institutional terms, the system of social security thus operates on a private, nonprofit basis with a clear mandate from the government. Its various programs are to be self-financed through contributions. Yet it has always been the case that the government subsidizes the generous benefits of these programs. Sustaining such a system for those that potentially qualify therefore requires maintaining a careful balance between contributions and expenses.

Logically, any change (such as the competitive challenges posed by globalization) that threatens to disturb this fundamental balance on a permanent basis has to be redressed by either expanding revenues through taxes or constraining benefits by awarding fewer benefits to a growing pool of unemployed. The question for government officials is therefore a reasonably stark one; how much should wage earners "sacrifice" to assist the unemployed? Whatever the resulting arrangement, the system always operates on the assumption that only past contributors can legitimately seek restitution when faced with adversity; financial aid recipients are dependent on the largess of the state.[10]

Such an arrangement finds few dissenting voices. German conservatives consider this construct acceptable because it gives workers a "stake in the system." Socialists tend to see it as way of institutionalizing class solidarity. Trade unionists support it because they fear that any reforms will hurt their interests. Finally, given the fact that the system is generally administered outside of the auspices of the central state, political liberals support it precisely because it mitigates against state intervention.[11] Welfare payments and services are developed and dispensed through a decentralized system.[12]

But, according to Offe, all of these justifications share a common attribute – they are based on a very narrow definition of work. Acquiring "full welfare citizenship" requires conforming to a "normal" work process – continuous employment on, minimally, a half-time basis. The social insurance system is thus a "core working class fortress" that does not include "precarious labor" defined as low skilled, low paid, "flexible" labor. Women are particularly vulnerable in this system because many do not fit this definition. Since most employment opportunities for those who do not work in this "nor-

10. This distinction is clearly illustrated when one observes the legal channels available should a German citizen choose to challenge a decision regarding her or his social welfare benefits. In the case of social security benefits (health insurance, retirement benefits, disability or unemployment compensation) or entitlements (e.g., veteran benefits), there is a Sozialgericht (or a type of court system similar to public administration boards in the U.S.). For appeals involving these two areas of the social welfare system the legal process is very explicitly defined. On the other hand, those who wish to challenge a decision regarding financial and/or material aid (welfare) face a labyrinth of bureaucratic routes that must be pursued. Indeed, in the government publication describing this process the authors themselves note that although there are legal channels, for such a course of action a citizen must "have much time, since this process is long, very long, if s/he is to make it through all appeal stages" (*Soziale Marktwirtschaft im Schaubild*, 1994, p. 56).

11. Offe, "Smooth Consolidation in the West German Welfare State," pp. 127-128 and p. 130.

12. For details on the institutional structure of the German welfare system see Peter J. Katzenstein, *Policy and Politics in West Germany*, pp.175-180.

mal" way (as required for social insurance) are "fixed term" or casual labor, they tend to fall between the cracks of the system. Moreover, there is little momentum to change this system from within. Granting full welfare citizenship rights to these disadvantaged workers would be costly to both employers and employees alike since they would have to finance the added costs through their contributions. Indeed, the incentives of the system encourage firms to use temporary or part-time labor, denying access to those seeking to establish the basis for subsequent social welfare restitution.[13]

Measured against its own prescribed goals, the system has been remarkably successful. Workers in Germany enjoy substantial ben-

Figure 9.1

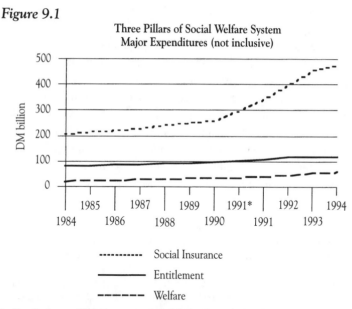

Three Pillars of Social Welfare System
Major Expenditures (not inclusive)

.... Social Insurance

———— Entitlement

— — — Welfare

*   For the former West Germany only; after this, for united Germany.

Social insurance expenditures include unemployment programs and retirement pensions (note: does *not* include health insurance expenditures). Entitlement expenditures include civil service benefits, war victim benefits, child allowances, and childrearing allowances. Welfare expenditures include social assistance and social aid.

Source: Statistiches Bundesamt, "Sozialbudget nach Institutionen," in *Statistisches Jahrbuch* (years 1986-1996).

13. Offe, "Smooth Consolidation in the West German Welfare State," p. 131.

efits and protections, surely one explanation for the long periods of labor stability in the FRG. We suggest, however, that these accomplishments have never been extended beyond the German male; women (overwhelmingly) have been left behind. In the section that follows we examine how institutions reflect prevailing norms.

Implicit Boundaries: Women Marginalized

Women remain marginalized in each of the three pillars of the FRG's social welfare system, at best receiving a modicum of the generous benefits available, even as its budget has grown. Figure 9.1 reflects spending trends for the three pillars of the social welfare system for the past decade. The evidence demonstrates that the category of social welfare where spending increased the most was the social insurance sector. To what degree did women benefit from increased social insurance spending?

Figure 9.2

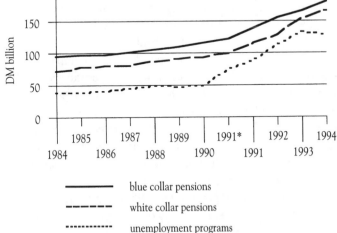

Social Insurance Pillar of Social Welfare System
Major Expenditures by Category (not inclusive)

blue collar pensions
white collar pensions
unemployment programs

* For the former West Germany only; after this, for united Germany.

Source: Statistiches Bundesamt, "Sozialbudget nach Institutionen," in *Statistisches Jahrbuch* (years 1986-1996).

Figure 9.3

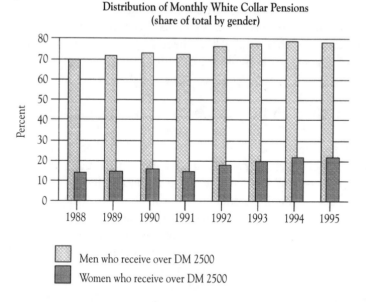

Distribution of Monthly White Collar Pensions
(share of total by gender)

☐ Men who receive over DM 2500

■ Women who receive over DM 2500

Source: Statitisches Bundesamt, "Gesetzliche Rentenversicherung," in *Statistisches Jahrbuch* (1986-1996).

Figure 9.2 illustrates that the two social insurance programs whose budget increased the most during the Bonn Republic (i.e., before 1990) were the federally-subsidized pension plans for both blue- and white-collar workers. Spending for unemployment programs only increased marginally until after unification, when it went through a rapid increase, leveling off after 1993. This trend had a notably adverse effect on women because the majority of them receive the lowest pension payments in both blue- and white-collar pension programs. This differential is greatest in the case of white-collar pensions, illustrated in Figure 9.3. The percentage of white-collar women receiving monthly pensions of more than DM 2,500 barely reached 20 percent by 1995, whereas the share of men receiving that sum was consistently over 70 percent. Proportionate to male retirees, female retirees therefore did not gain from the increasing federal expenditures for pension plans.

The second largest sum of expenditures in the past ten years was for "Civil Maintenance" (entitlement) benefits for "service" to the state. This is one aspect of the social welfare system where women could gain relatively easy access, i.e., by bearing children. The Federal *Erziehungsgesetz* (child rearing legislation), introduced in 1985, includes a provision for *Erziehungsgeld* (or child rearing benefits). According to the legislation, one parent, independent of previous employment status, is entitled to receive financial compensation for up to two years after a child's birth. Eligibility for this benefit, however, requires the relevant parent to stay at home to take care of the child. But this gives little incentive for working men, who generally earn more, to take advantage of this opportunity because the payments are a mere DM 600 per month. Indeed, available data point to the limited effect of this provision – at its inception in 1986, only 1.44 percent of the parents receiving child

Figure 9.4

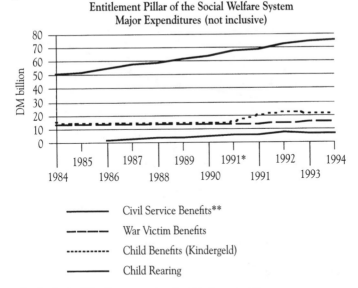

Entitlement Pillar of the Social Welfare System
Major Expenditures (not inclusive)

———— Civil Service Benefits**

– – – – War Victim Benefits

············ Child Benefits (Kindergeld)

———— Child Rearing

* For the former West Germany only; after this, for united Germany.

** Includes pensions, family supplements, and other subsidies for *Beamten* only. Civil servants do *not* make contributions for these benefits.

Source: Statistisches Bundesamt, "Sozialbudget nach Institutionen" and "Kriegsopferversorgung," *Statistisches Jahrbuch* (years 1986-1996).

rearing benefits were male, by 1991 this figure had only climbed to 1.48 percent.[14]

Most German women do not receive this potential benefit because many have rejected a traditional family structure by electing not to have children. As an indicator of the fiscal effects, Figure 9.4 documents that expenditures for *Kindergeld* stagnated throughout the 1980s, rising slightly after unification only to level off again, whereas benefits for *Beamte* (civil servants) rose substantially.

The least expensive pillar of the German social welfare system, Social Assistance, is the one type of state expenditure from which women disproportionately benefit. Figures 9.5 illustrates that women are overrepresented as recipients of welfare aid. In fact the figures show that the gap between men and women has increased

Figure 9.5

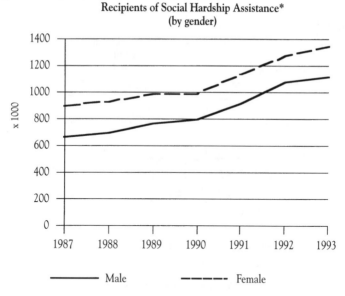

Recipients of Social Hardship Assistance*
(by gender)

———— Male   ------- Female

* For persons living outside of institutions.

Source: Statistisches Bundesamt, "Hilfeempfänger nach Geschlecht und Altersgruppen," in *Statistisches Jahrbuch* (1986-1996).

14. Johannes Frerich and Martin Frey, *Sozialpolitik der Bundesrepublik Deutschland bis zur Erstellung der deutschen Einheit* (Munich: R. Oldenbourg Verlag, 1993), p. 332.

after unification. As Figure 9.1 previously demonstrated, Social Assistance spending remained nearly constant in the 1980s relative to social insurance spending. While Social Maintenance benefits nearly doubled in the years before unification, it has never reached the same levels of spending as that on entitlement benefits. Clearly, although women are in greater need of the benefits from these programs, their collective benefits have not increased at the same rate as those earmarked for men.

Implicit Discrimination: Institutionalized Gender Norms

What explains this apparent paradox; that despite the "pressures wrought by globalization" and the growth of the state's spending, women seem to be relatively worse off in the Berlin Republic in terms of social welfare? In this section we address this puzzle by arguing that the answer lies in Germany's predominant and institutionalized gender norms. These pervasively influence attitudes about employment and thus, given the structure we have already outlined, welfare.

The concept of gender equality occupies a somewhat ambivalent position in German society. Article 3, paragraph two of the Basic Law anchors the ideal of equal gender rights. Yet at the same time the Basic Law also explicitly incorporates many patriarchal laws from Weimar and Nazi Germany, particularly as reflected in the German social welfare system.[15] These are most deeply rooted in the norms and rules governing labor, paid and unpaid (i.e., familial). Indeed, the German model relies on an explicitly gendered division of labor: Men are assumed to be the employed breadwinners while women are to be responsible for the home life. Moreover, the socially implicit understanding of women's role, and thus their welfare citizenship rights, is that of carrying out reproductive labor, i.e., the non-paid labor of childbearing and care taking.

15. See in particular Robert Moeller, *Protecting motherhood: women and the family in the politics of postwar West Germany* (Berkeley: University of California Press, 1993).

Table 9.1 Societal Norms Regarding Women and Their Roles

Situation of Women	In the Work Force	Not in the Work Force
With Children	Working Mothers (1)	Assuming Natural Role as Caretakers (2)
Without Children	Potential Mothers (4)	"Silent Labor Reserve" (3)

In Table 9.1 we illustrate the composition of these gendered norms regarding women's role in productive and reproductive labor.

Box 1 of Table 9.1 reflects the norm of how women in the paid work force are regarded by society: namely, in need of protection because their gender is identified with the ability to bear children. In contrast to this norm, those women with children who work are considered to be neglecting their primary role as childcare providers. Such a gendered norm means that working mothers are not catered to by alternative policies (e.g., day care) that would enable them to have both careers and families. Even women without children still face discriminatory norms in that they are steered (explicitly or implicitly) in the direction of low-paying, unskilled jobs by virtue of the fact that they are considered to be only working "temporarily" (i.e., until they bear children).

Box 2 and box 3 of the matrix describes how women who do not regularly participate in the labor force are viewed: namely, as potential, yet dispensable labor. As box 2 suggests, in times of labor surplus, women with children receive financial incentives to remain at home with their children to perform their "natural" responsibility as childcare providers. As box 3 indicates, even those women without children are regarded as flexible labor available when needed, part of Germany's "structurally unemployed" – those not registered as unemployed (thus not receiving benefits) yet seeking part-time work.

These distinctions are most evident in three basic sets of codified norms: those regarding "family rights," "motherhood protection," and female employment. In terms of norms and laws regarding "family rights," German laws have historically placed a strong emphasis on women's duties as housewives and mothers.[16]

---

16. For a complete account of Germany's "mommy politics" both as a patriarchal and racist policy, see Moeller, ibid., and Myra Marx Ferree, "The rise and

The original Family and Marriage Code of the Bonn Republic enshrined a woman's domestic role in law and even gave husbands some control over their wives' rights to work. In fact, the Code explicitly stated that it was a wife's duty to take care of the household, a task from which she could be freed only in consultation with her husband.[17]

It was not until 1977 that this law was reformed, at which time gender-neutral language was introduced. The household division of labor was not to be gender-specific and partners should agree on the running of the household. Yet according to Eva Kolinsky, German courts continue to interpret the law as it was before 1977, explicitly assigning women to housekeeping responsibilities. Subsequent judgments and legal commentaries, for example, have specified that young children need a full-time person to care for them, and that this person is usually the mother. Furthermore, Kolinsky claims that in divorce cases, the power of courts to grant maintenance payments appears to have been used as an instrument to perpetuate traditional role patterns for women.[18]

Consistent with this historic view, the government itself ensured that the interpretation of the 1977 reforms would not precipitate the demise of social norms. Elaborating on the amended rule that each partner has to take due regard of the family when accepting employment, court officials nonetheless stated:

> The rule does not suggest a schematically equal treatment of man and woman. The wife has ... to take particular regard of the needs of the family, for example when children have to be cared for and brought up.[19]

The second example of codified norms concerns the laws governing "motherhood protection" – the employment of pregnant women and mothers. Germany has very explicit regulations regard-

---

fall of 'mommy politics': feminism and unification in (East) Germany," *Feminist Studies*, vol. 19 (Spring 1993): 89-115.

17. See Paragraph 1356 and 1360a of the 'Family and Marriage Code.'

18. Eva Kolinsky, *Women in West Germany: life, work, and politics* (Oxford: Berg Publishers, 1989), pp. 54-55.

19. *Bundestagsdrucksache* 7/650, p. 98, as cited in Kolinsky, ibid., p. 53.

ing the work force protection it affords pregnant women and mothers of newborns. Article 6 of the constitution states that every mother has a claim to the protection and assistance of the community (not the state). Fulfilling its role of establishing norms and procedures for the private social insurance sector, the German state mandated private health insurance firms to guarantee certain women extensive services. Furthermore, employed mothers are guaranteed up to four months maternity leave. This legislation is clearly nondiscriminatory in nature since it allows female choice, providing guarantees that enable women to pursue both parental and employment roles.

Where the legislation, such as the Act on the Protection of Working Mothers, becomes discriminatory is in the context of actual work regulation. Pregnant women are prohibited from working either the last six weeks of their pregnancy or beginning work again until at least eight weeks after delivery (twelve weeks for multiple births or premature births). Pregnant women and nursing mothers are prohibited from working night shifts and weekends. Moreover, expectant or working mothers are also forbidden to engage in labor considered physically demanding or associated with high risk for illness.[20]

Many hail these laws as "progressive" because they guarantee the labor rights of working mothers.[21] But they are, contends Hevener, simultaneously implicitly biased against women as a codification of "implied incompetence":

> The view of women that such documents [e.g., motherhood protection] project is analogous to that of children. Since women, like children, are considered unable to make intelligent, informed, and rational decisions about their own lives, they are subjected to the paternal power of the State.[22]

20. "Protection For Working Mothers," *Social Security*, http://www.bma.de/soziales/englisch/chaptr05.htm#e11.

21. It is a great irony that while many consider these laws socially progressive, the fact is that these motherhood protection laws stem from legislation passed in 1938.

22. Natalie Kaufman Hevener, *International Law and the Status of Women* (Boulder: Westview Press, 1983), p. 5.

They are not designed to facilitate choice, but rather mandate that all mothers are equally "disabled" during and after pregnancy.[23]

The third type of codified discriminatory norm concerns the employment of women in general. Due chiefly to the efforts of the SPD, the same basic prohibitions or "protections" for working mothers have been universally applied to women. All women, for example, are forbidden to work in any position that requires physically demanding labor. Thus, regardless of whether a woman wants to (or is able to) bear children, she has been subjected to the same restrictions. These type of protections reemphasize the traditional social definition of a woman as wife and mother. Hence:

> [t]he focus of legislative attention is not on her actual activity but rather remains on her domestic role, and it is the perceived characteristics of this role that the law allegedly seeks to protect. Thus, when the sphere of her actual work involvement is viewed as being outside the normal domain of women, her presence may be seen as necessitating protection if her primary role [as mother and caregiver] is to be preserved.[24]

Yet any argument about norms must extend beyond the state. How have different societal actors responded to the issue of discrimination against women? Within the context of the competitiveness debate in Germany (Standortdebatte), labor and management have reached compromises that seem to employ the same pattern of gender norms as the state. These practices are most evident in the efforts to move the German economy from "clean competition" to "lean production"; away from the concept of thwarting low-wage competition toward the notion of "greater flexibility" in labor regulations. This shift confounds critics because it confirms the

23. Kolinsky, *Women in West Germany*, p. 6-7. Here it is notable that in the official document published by the German government to explain its social welfare system, the page describing "motherhood protection laws" is juxtaposed against the laws protecting youth in the labor force, creating the impression that women and children are equally in need of protection. Moreover, these are the only two employment laws also considered "protection" laws [*Schutz*], the rest being defined as "regulations," see, *Soziale Marktwirtschaft im Schaubild*, 1994, pp. 50-51.

24. This discussion of the patriarchal treatment of women as codified in "protective conventions" is taken from Natalie Kaufman Hevener, *International Law*.

belief that the German model can be maintained this way, albeit for an ever smaller and privileged core.

The agreement between Adam Opel AG and its workers of 1994 provides a telling example. In an attempt to lower labor costs, labor and management agreed to allow certain jobs to be contracted out to supplier firms, ensuring that the wages and benefits of these workers would no longer be covered by plant-wide agreements. Since the majority of these jobs fell within the service category (e.g., cleaning, food preparation, etc.), and the majority of these jobs are traditionally filled by women, female employees bore an overwhelming proportion of the burdens for this decision as it shifted from unionized to non-unionized female employment.[25]

An illustration of organized labor's acceptance of these gender norms is a landmark court case which ruled that differing pay rates for men and women at the same job are permissible. In this case, four women filed the suit, with the support of their labor union, claiming that they were not receiving equal pay for equal work. The unfavorable ruling was justified by the court on the grounds that although the job being performed was the same, the men had been hired under a different job description, thus justifying different wage scales. According to the plaintiffs' lawyer, however, the case was lost because the union had incorrectly filed suit; the union should have pursued the issue of gender-specific job descriptions and not accepted the notion that jobs could be defined as being in gender-specific terms, with the slightest distinction being used to justify pay discrimination.[26]

25. Remarks made by David Herman, Managing Director, Adam Opel, at the American Institute for Contemporary Studies Annual Conference, "Competitiveness: Defining the Terms, Shaping the Policies: A German-American Dialogue," Washington, D.C., 15/16 December 1994.

26. This ruling demonstrates that the constitutional norm of equal rights has not been translated into working life and the collective bargaining agreements that govern it. The Grundgesetz itself is contradictory. While Article 3 guarantees equal rights, Article 9 guarantees the autonomy of the two sides of industry and their right to agree amongst themselves the conditions of work and pay. Kolinsky claims that the trade unions and employer associations have interpreted this as the freedom to set women's and men's pay and working conditions at different levels. Kolinsky, *Women in West Germany*, p. 54.

Paradoxically, even the state in the new Berlin Republic has recognized the anachronistic nature of these norms. These restrictive job classifications for women were not extended to women in east Germany where they are free to work evenings, weekends, and in physically-demanding positions. This exception was justified by claiming that the west German code needed to be revised, although no subsequent changes were made.

Norms in Practice: Effective Barriers to Change

Trapped between economic needs and cultural norms, German women find a host of obstacles to their efforts to combine both being parents and having careers. Table 9.2 illustrates how these norms get operationalized into policies and practices in the Federal Republic.

Consistent with the norms identified in Table 9.1, box 1 of Table 9.2 suggests that working mothers face a series of problems relating to insufficient day care and restricted store hours. Mothers outside of the paid labor force face major disincentives to reentry (box 2). "Potential mothers" experience the glass ceiling effect noted in box 4 and the limitations to becoming more viable as a high-skilled employee noted in box 3.

One of the most sensitive issues for working mothers has been the lack of adequate and affordable day care. Dating from the mid-1970s, there has been a debate about revamping day care as part of the FRG's constitutional duty to protect life. The 1990 unification

Table 9.2 Obstacles to Women

Situation of Women	In the Work Force	Not in the Work Force
With Children	Insufficient Day Care; Restricted Store Hours; School Half-Days (1)	Paid Family Leave (biased towards female participation); Lack of "flex-time" or part-time employment (2)
Without Children	"Glass Ceiling"; No Quotas or Affirmative Action Programs (4)	Over-represented number trained in sunset industries; Cutbacks in vocational training to re-enter labor force (3)

treaty laid the basis for a nationwide overhaul of the child care system. According to the treaty, the federal states were mandated to provide day care by 1996 – a provision with which they failed to comply, explaining a shortage of an estimated 600,000 day care places and 40,000 professional day care staff. [27]

Several states sought to postpone implementation of day care provisions until 1999 on financial grounds. The shortage of day care facilities is actually in western Germany. In eastern Germany the decreasing birth rate has actually created a surplus of day care facilities. Thus, it is the wealthier states of western Germany that are not fulfilling their obligations. By 1 August 1996, only one western Land (Rheinland-Pfalz) and four eastern Länder had fulfilled their legal obligation to provide sufficient day care space. [28]

Six further forms of evidence support these general claims of sustained discrimination embedded within state and society. The first concerns governmental measures relating to child care provisions in the 1980s. Although the number and availability of child care opportunities increased in the 1980s, these new facilities were *not* designed to free women for full-time employment, because they only provided morning child care. Moreover, little effort was devoted to creating suitable facilities for children under the age of three. [29] Thus, the primary concern of many German mothers wishing to return to full-time employment (e.g., infant care and day-long childcare) was not alleviated. These government measures only enabled more part-time employment for working mothers.

Second, the 1985 Employment Protection Act, ostensibly designed to provide protective legislation for part-time work, only increased the attractiveness of part-time employment. In a progressive manner, the legislation does give regular, part-time employees

27. *This Week in Germany*, p. 54.

28. Data from the "Deutscher Familienverband," *Internet*, 27 July 1996.

29. Indeed, Germany regards the provision of childcare for three-to-five-year-olds as a public responsibility for educational reasons rather than as support for working mothers. By 1986 governmental Kindergartens provided places for 12.6 percent of two-year olds; 38.7 percent of three-year olds; and 72.3 percent of four-year olds. These schools last only until one o'clock and do not provide lunch. Only 4 percent of school-age children were in after-school care centers. See Christel Lane, "Gender and the labor market in Europe: Britain, Germany and France compared," *The Sociological Review* (1993), p. 298.

(more than fifteen hours per week) the same employment rights and benefits as full-time workers, if only in pro rata terms.[30] Yet these reform measure appear to have merely locked women into dead-end, part-time positions instead of facilitating full-time employment for women, for example, by means of introducing flex-time or job sharing.

A third piece of evidence is the previously discussed Federal *Erziehungsgesetz* of 1985. Although this Family Leave legislation was designed ostensibly to enable either parent to take up to three years of unpaid family leave from their place of employment,[31] the data shows it has been and continues to be women who interrupt their career advancement. Notably, legislation designed to provide incentives for fathers to participate in the official child rearing (a similar provision is included in the Swedish family leave policy) was rejected.

Fourth, the FRG's support for women as wage or salaried labor has not been so generous or aggressively pursued since the mid-1980s due to action designed to protect male employment. For example, European Community directives on equal opportunity legislation were initially strongly opposed in Bonn. Subsequent pressure lead to weak implementation of these measures.[32]

Fifth, the modification of vocational education and training benefits in the 1980s tended to benefit men more than women. Little effort was made to provide incentives in training young women for jobs with a future. In fact, women are disproportionately employed in the "sunset" industries.[33] Additionally, when benefits for vocational education and training were cut in the 1987 reform, women

30. Employees working less than fifteen hours per week are exempt from the mandatory contributions to unemployment, worker's compensation, and pension programs, and are excluded from most collective bargaining agreements and fringe benefits.

31. Although unpaid, health care benefits would continue without contribution from the parent on leave; the three years would also count as years of employment in terms of pension benefits after retirement.

32. Ibid, p. 280.

33. Frerich and Frey, *Sozialpolitik der Bundesrepublik Deutschland*, pp. 178-82; and Friederike Maier, "The labor market for women and employment perspectives in the aftermath of German unification," *Cambridge Journal of Economics*, vol. 17 (1993): 267-280.

were again the primary losers, because retraining programs received a maldistributed proportion of budget cuts. Women were unduly burdened by these cuts because they benefited disproportionately from these programs, a major instrument to avoid careers offering little prospect for advancement. Finally, even though female employment tends to be concentrated in the service sector, women in Germany have not benefited from the shift from manufacturing to service industry as elsewhere because Germany's service sector remains small in comparison to other industrial nations.

The Economic Consequences of Institutionalized Norms

Since German schools are only in session for halfdays and since restrictive store hours in Germany until recently did not allow evening (or even weekend) shopping, it is virtually impossible both to work and be a primary provider of parental responsibilities on a full-time basis without some extensive assistance. The consequence is that part-time work has become the domain of women – nearly 33 percent of all employed women work only part-time. Even more revealing is the fact that nearly 90 percent of all part-time employees are women.[34] Moreover, the demand exceeds the number of available positions, so women have become part of the "silent reserve" of unemployed.

Ultimately, even if women prefer part-time work, the consequences are less than desirable:

> Part-time working has not enhanced anything but the quick-and-ready opportunity to earn some money. On the ambitious level of employing women in line with their qualifications and potential, and rewarding them with job security, promotion chances and substantive opportunities of equal employment, part-time working has been a hindrance rather than an asset in the search for equality. It has consolidated the gender gap in the labor market, and the posi-

34. Kolinsky, *Women in West Germany*, p. 174.

tion of women at the less favored end as far as status, prospects, and pay are concerned.[35]

And among full-time employees, women often fall within "light salary groups" because they are ineligible for many higher paying, physically demanding jobs.

Crucially for our argument, if a woman is proscribed from working in certain jobs and effectively restricted in her hours, then her entitlements are similarly constrained. But even women who choose the "traditional" role that is expected of them still face barriers in terms of qualifying for compensatory social welfare benefits. These norms have two explicitly negative consequences for these women when they reach "retirement age."

The first relates to Germany's social security benefits. Since housewives do not pay into the social security system (e.g., pension programs), they are not entitled to its retirement benefits. Instead, they are expected to rely on a spouse who had a full-time, "normal" work experience. Offe describes the consequences:

> As such, the social security system contains a "hidden curriculum" which declares labor and employment to be much more than a legal and economic category, namely a form of respectable and even dignified existence .... The male breadwinner spends his economically active life in full-time employment ... while his wife does not spend her life in (full-time) employment and hence does not earn any independent social security entitlements. The male breadwinner's wife relies on the legal rights and claims that she derives, directly or indirectly, from her institutional status within the family.[36]

Second, as already noted, those women who remain at home are not considered to be serving the state. They are therefore not eligible for any of the entitlement benefits discussed earlier beyond *Kindergeld*.[37]

Yet even for those women who do manage to work full-time, it is clear that they also face pay discrimination. The difference in monthly earnings in 1980 was about DM 900; by 1993 this wage gap had grown to a disparity of about DM 1,400.

35. Offe, "Smooth Consolidation in the West German Welfare State," p. 178.
36. Offe, "Smooth Consolidation in the West German Welfare State," pp. 126-7.
37. Frerich and Frey, *Sozialpolitik der Bundesrepublik Deutschland*, p. 33.

Chart 1   Average Gross Monthly Income of All Employed
Persons by Gender

	1980	1993
male	DM 2811	DM 4625
female	DM 1930	DM 3221

Source: Deutsches Institut für Wirtschaftsforschung, "Zur Einkommenslage der westdeutschen Arbeitsnehmerinnen," *Wochenbericht* no. 31 (September 21, 1994).

The differential is even greater among white-collar employees:
in 1980 the gap grew from DM 1,400 to DM 2,300 by 1993. Moreover, female white-collar workers in 1993 were still earning less
than their male counterparts were in 1980.

Chart 2   Average Gross Monthly Income of White-Collar
Employees (by gender)

	1980	1993
male	DM 3691	DM 5987
female	DM 2249	DM 3670

Source: Deutsches Institut für Wirtschaftsforschung, "Zur Einkommenslage der westdeutschen Arbeitsnehmerinnen."

The German Economics Institute attributes this difference primarily to the fact that women still very rarely advance to high managerial positions. The results are therefore most influenced by the
fact that women are overly represented in low paid, unskilled jobs.
Figures 9.6 and 9.7 demonstrate more starkly these growing gaps.

The dilemma for women striving for full welfare citizenship is
most problematic for single working mothers. They are a growing
category, the number of female-headed households having nearly
doubled from 1.9 million in 1980 to 3.2 million in 1993 while the
number of male-headed households has remained nearly constant
at 11.3 million. Yet disposable income in households headed by single mothers lags fully two-thirds behind similar households headed
by men. Moreover, female-headed households had less disposable
income in 1993 than male-headed ones had in 1980.

Figure **9.6**

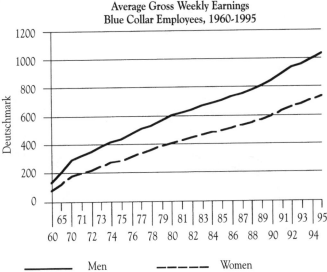

Average Gross Weekly Earnings
Blue Collar Employees, 1960-1995

———— Men   — — — — Women

Source: "Durchschnittliche Bruttowochenverdienste in der Industrie: Arbeiter,"
http://www.bma.de/bmahome/statisti/stb5_3.htm, 30 June 1997.

Chart 3   Average Monthly Disposable Income for
Single-headed Households (by gender)

	1980	1993
male	DM 3553	DM 5535
female	DM 2245	DM 3482

Source: Deutsches Institut für Wirtschaftsforschung, "Zur Einkommenslage der
westdeutschen Arbeitnehmerinnen."

Women as the Long-term Unemployed

It cannot be overemphasized that unification has bought the advantages of democratization and greater prosperity to eastern Germany.
We are not apologists for the GDR's regime. But it is equally as
important to point out, however, that women have maldistributively
borne the economic costs of unification. Support structures for
women in the GDR included institutional features such as nursery

Figure 9.7

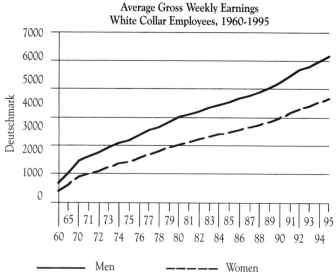

Average Gross Weekly Earnings
White Collar Employees, 1960-1995

Men   - - - - - Women

Source: "Durchschnittliche Bruttowochenverdienste in der Industrie und Handel: Angestellte," http://www.bma.de/bmahome/statisti/stb5_3.htm, 30 June 1997.

schools and Kindergartens for more than 80 percent of the children below school age, and publicly-run service-houses attached to firms, at which, for example, laundry could be dropped in the morning, to be picked up at the end of day. Labor law regulations were equally generous. These included obligatory affirmative action programs, paid reductions in normal working hours for women with more than one child, and provisions which entitled women to a second chance to obtain formal vocational or professional credentials.[38] These provisions were eradicated at unification.

38. There is an extensive literature examining the impact of German unification on east German women; e.g., Hedwig Rudolph, Eileen Appelbaum and Friederike Maier, "After German Unity: A Cloudier Outlook for Women," *Challenge* (November/December 1990): 33-40; Gertrude Schaffner Goldberg, "Women on the Verge: Winners and Losers in German Unification," *Social Policy* (Fall 1991): 35-44; Myra Marx Ferree and Brigitte Young, "Three Steps Back for Women: German Unification, Gender, and University 'Reform,'" *PS: Political Science and Politics*, (June

Data from March 1995 reveal that, of the more than one million unemployed in eastern Germany, fully 62.4 percent were women.[39] Nearly 20 percent of all women were unemployed in March 1995; at the same time only 11 percent of males were unemployed.[40] Efforts to alleviate long term unemployment (defined as one year or longer) among east German women were mixed. Nearly one-half of all German unemployed fall under this category and women are overrepresented, marginally so in the case of west Germany and extensively so in the case of the former GDR (see Table 9.3). While women currently compose 42.8 percent of the German paid labor force, in eastern Germany they constituted 77 percent of long-term unemployed by the mid 1990s.

Table 9.3   Structural Dimensions of German Unemployment (end of September 1994)

Area	Category	Totals	Men	Women
WEST GERMANY	Short-term unemployed	1,655,500	56.6%	43.4%
	Long-term unemployed	798,000	55.2%	44.8%
EAST GERMANY	Short-term unemployed	680,000	38.4%	61.1%
	Long-term unemployed	361,000	23.0%	77.0%

Of these long-term unemployed women, 22 percent were previously employed as part-time workers. As a consequence, their unemployment assistance benefits are proportionately lower than those received by long-term unemployed men (of whom only 0.5 percent were previously part-time employees). Moreover, these women also receive less aid in retraining and qualification advancement programs. Last, but not least, there are a very limited number of qualified part-time jobs.[41]

1993): 199-205; Friederike Maier, "The labor market for women," *Cambridge Journal of Economics*, vol. 17 (1993): 267-280; and Marilyn Rueschemeyer, "Women in the Politics of Eastern Germany," in Marilyn Rueschemeyer et al (eds.), *Women in the Politics of Postcommunist Eastern Europe* (Armonk, N.Y.: M.E. Sharpe, 1994): 87-116.

39. The following account is taken from Friederike Maier, "The labor market for women."

40. "Die Arbeitsmarkt im März 1995 Bundesrepublik Deutschland," *Presse Informationen* no. 24/95, Bundesanstalt für Arbeit, Nurnberg. Note that critics suggest that these official figures grossly underestimate unemployment levels.

41. Bundesanstalt für Arbeit, "Längerfristig Arbeitslose," *Arbeitsmarkt in Zahlen*, September 1994.

While the Kohl government has sought to reduce the number of long-term unemployed, it consciously chose *not* to mandate that long-term unemployed women be given special assistance despite their numbers. In 1989 the federal government established an elaborate program to reduce long-term unemployment by encouraging employers to hire this category of unemployed. The incentives for employers to cooperate are wage subsidies that range up to 80 percent. The program has been described as a success by its creators and in 1995 the Bundestag extended its funding through 1999 (the program totaling DM 3 billion). Yet six years after the program commenced, government officials recognized that women were not benefiting proportionately from its measures. However, they rejected establishing some type of quota system for these women proportionate to their share of unemployment, ostensibly on the basis that it would infringe on the procedures of the liberal market economy and was beyond the authority of government.[42] Instead, "guideposts" were established for employment offices and potential employers.

The number of women able to secure work through the aforesaid employment program did rise from 28 percent in 1989 to 34 percent by the early 1990s in western Germany, and then 50 percent by 1994 in all of Germany. But such success was mitigated by the fact that they remained underrepresented in the successes of the employment program, still accounting for the majority of long term unemployed – over 70 percent in eastern Germany.

What accounts for these gender differences? Decisions regarding the closing of old east German companies appear often not to have been based on the grounds of efficiency, since such inefficient core industries as steel and shipbuilding did not slow down as rapidly as others. Rather, according to Freidericke Maier, the restructuring process in these equally (if not more) inefficient east German sectors was "slowed down by state and trade-union intervention, whereas in female-dominated industries exposure to the market had an immediate effect." Citing a German Institute for Economics study, Maier explains how other cutbacks have disproportionately affected women:

42. Gerhard Groebner, "Mit verstaerkter Kraft: Langzeitarbeitslosen Programm," Bundesarbeitsblatt, no. 4 (1995), p. 12.

The social departments of enterprises were closed down as the firms were now seen as exclusively economic organizations, thus reducing employment opportunities for nurses, teachers, cooks, etc. and destroying the social infrastructure used by the women employed in these firms. Women occupying typical male jobs in the industrial production sphere, such as foremen, were dismissed more often than their male counterparts and women in intermediate managerial positions tended to lose these positions, if not their jobs.[43]

Such decisions have therefore apparently been politicized according to Maier, forcing women to bear a disproportionate share of the burden.

Something Old, Something New? A Gendered, Shrinking Core in the Age of Globalization

Essentially we have suggested that, contrary to public rhetoric, German welfare state expenditures have risen despite the pressures of globalization, but that the distribution of expenditures has narrowed. Did this tendency predate the onset of globalization or are the two somehow related? Is globalization a myth used here to justify processes that predate its onset? The implications of Claus Offe's work supports the notion that these patterns predate the 1980s; that dating from the mid 1970s, successive German governments of the Left and the Right have pursued bipartisan policies that systematically reduced access by tightening eligibility requirements for those seeking social welfare citizenship.[44]

According to Offe, such policies were the product of a conscious strategy shared by Germany's major political parties – designed to protect the organized heart of Germany's work force at the detriment of the weaker members of the labor force who could be easily isolated. He identifies a series of policies implemented after 1975 which created what Germans have come to refer to as the "two-thirds society" (*Zweidrittelgesellschaft*), the larger group enjoying all the benefits associated with the extensive German

43. Maier, "The labor market for women," p. 274.
44. Frerich and Frey, *Sozialpolitik der Bundesrepublik Deutschland*.

welfare system, while one-third remains unprotected by labor regulation and welfare.[45] Evidence of such tendencies is reflected in bipartisan legislation, dating from the Budget Structure Act and the restrictive regulations on employment insurance of 1975, to the Fiscal Consolidation Laws of 1977 and 1978, and ultimately to the Old Age Pension Reform Act of 1989. This bipartisan approach, Offe contends, enabled both sides to narrow the benefits and expand the burdens of groups in society in proportion to their political clout: "Under these tactics of careful, gradual, and largely consensual management of potential conflict, a polarized politicization of social policy issues could not emerge."[46] A process of selective allocation ensued in which the gendered norms concerning women operated with significant distributive effects. Images and symbolic demarcations were projected in which the "deserved" were rewarded while others, consistent with cultural norms, were ignored or berated.[47] For example, the 1975 economic crisis touched off a public campaign of defamation of the unemployed by accusing them of refusing work in order to profit from generous unemployment benefits. This shift in public perception enabled the first major modification in unemployment laws. In particular, officials tightened up the categories of "reasonable employment," which meant that should an unemployed worker refuse such a "reasonable employment," his or her unemployment benefits could be rightfully curtailed.

The distinction between groups became exacerbated with the ensuing growth of German structural unemployment in the 1970s and 1980s, rising quickly and steeply from 273,000 in 1973 to an average of 1.1 million by 1975.[48] While total employment grew by 729,000 between 1977 and 1980 in a period of relative vibrancy, total unemployment only fell by 141,000 despite a 22.7 percent decline in the number of foreign workers in Germany.[49] For the first

45. Offe, "Smooth Consolidation in the West German Welfare State," p. 135.

46. Ibid., pp. 140-141.

47. Offe, "Smooth Consolidation in the West German Welfare State," pp. 128-129.

48. Fritz W. Scharpf, *Crisis and Choice in European Social Democracy* (Ithaca: Cornell University Press, 1991), p. 139.

49. Ibid., pp. 50 and 146.

time, it became apparent that the labor market exhibited deep disparities. Unemployed women became a special problem group as their numbers swelled to constitute more than a half of the unemployed and many settled for part-time employment.[50] By the early 1980s, it was clear that this new problem of long-term unemployment was not a temporary one. As a means of coping with the welfare burdens, Bonn officials slashed programs and benefits.[51]

Consistent with our expectations, women were disproportionately hurt by these policy reforms. The rules, for example, were again tightened up in terms of eligibility; that is, a longer period of employee contributions prior to unemployment was demanded in order to become eligible for unemployment benefits. For women who had taken time off to raise children, this new regulation was particularly problematic: given that they were disproportionately represented among the long-term unemployed, they were often hit hardest by these restrictions. Women were generally most in need of retraining programs. Yet it was precisely these programs, and assistance for unemployed part-time workers, which were first cut in the 1983 budget of the Labor Agency (Bundesanstalt für Arbeit). Ironically, even when the Agency subsequently achieved a budget *surplus* the following year, it did not move to restore these programs to their former funding level, instead choosing to lower the contributions required of already-employed workers.[52]

Employed Germans accepted this arrangement because women were supposed to stay home, and every increase in benefits to the unemployed or under-employed was contingent upon greater contributions by the employed, but not the employers.[53] In this context, unions chose not to defend the interests of the unemployed and unempowered (predominantly women). Despite subsequent growing trade surpluses (averaging DM 100 million between 1984 and 1988) and impressively low levels of inflation, no political leadership in the zero-sum game of the German social welfare system

50. Frerich and Frey, *Sozialpolitik der Bundesrepublik Deutschland*, pp. 176-7.

51. Offe, "Smooth Consolidation in the West German Welfare State," pp. 138-139.

52. Frerich and Frey, *Sozialpolitik der Bundesrepublik Deutschland*, pp. 178-80.

53. Offe, "Smooth Consolidation in the West German Welfare State," pp. 141 and 144.

emerged that was willing to grant full welfare citizenship rights to those not enfranchised by Germany's social security system.

Consistent with our broader argument, Fritz Scharpf suggests that women were predominant among those who disproportionately suffered during this period while middle-aged, male workers remained relative unaffected.[54] This claim corroborates the suggestion that the emerging system represented a retrenchment to the historic norms of German society: it was (and is) acceptable to protect male-workers at the expense of women, since their "natural" (in reality, socially-constructed) role in the division of labor is in the field of reproductive labor. The core group of the social insurance system – skilled male workers – were thus shielded from any cuts in their benefits wrought by the pressures of declining economic growth. Discrimination predated globalization. It was not produced by it. This supports the contention that the conservative focus on recent events is merely a smokescreen – an excuse to accelerate such retrenchment, not the reason for its initiation. Thus, the efforts to turn back the welfare state predates at least the present exigencies brought on by globalization.

Conclusion: Globalization as an Instrument, Globalization as a Cause?

Defenders of the retrenchment of German social welfare programs can still correctly point out that even if it is currently under attack, its system of benefits still far outdistances its European neighbors.[55] Generous family leave legislation, for example, is the envy of any British, French, Italian, or indeed American parent. Only the Swedes can match the relative expanse of German welfare benefits among the countries of Europe, although they too passed laws in the early 1990s designed to cut the range and cost of welfare programs.[56]

54. Ibid., pp. 50-51.

55. For a discussion of this issue and some supporting data comparing social welfare benefits across Europe, see Roger Cohen, "Europe's Recession Prompts New Look at Welfare Costs," *New York Times*, 9 August 1993, p. A1.

56. Sweden, for example, has introduced measures raising the first year of pension eligibility from 65 to 66, and has eliminated sick pay for the first day of work missed. See ibid.

So a limited cut in relatively generous German welfare benefits alone would hardly constitute a major indictment. But, our evidence suggests, no such cut took place. In fact a second, more notable trend than the constriction of these benefits, has taken place in Germany in the 1990s. It is toward introducing increasingly severe constraints on who has access to the pool of welfare resources in the FRG. It is not the amount of benefits but the membership pool itself that is significantly changing.

In reaction to new competitiveness problems, the FRG appears to be pursuing welfare policies that systematically narrow the membership pool by exacerbating a trend initiated before unification. It favors the protected, who have unhindered access to all the resources that Germany offers to those who are temporarily displaced, while correspondingly ignoring those who have not qualified for full welfare rights, or who appear to be undeserving on the basis of societal norms. This distinction largely follows gender lines.

Chancellor Kohl has restated that Germany needs a new "social consensus" for confronting modern social and economic challenges. And he made it clear that "if we are to display solidarity with the weaker members of society, we require an efficient economy."[57] But how are the burden of costs to be distributed? It is the Kohl government that has been a major agent in answering this question – in a maldistributive manner that further divides a labor aristocracy from the rest of the German work force.

The basis for this maldistribution is the distinction between entitlement and privilege in Germany, a distinction that has generated policies for which the institutions of the German social welfare system have proven remarkably malleable. Predicated on an enduring normative structure, the FRG's institutions have proven adept at shifting the costs of retrenchment away from traditionally protected core groups.

The fact that such tendencies have been reinforced by measures supported by the major political parties is indicative of how ingrained such norms are. The 1986 Child Care reforms, the 1988 legislation concerning retraining and vocational education, the

---

57. Part of his statement issued with the announcement of the "Program for increased growth and employment," Press Release, 30 April 1996.

dissolution of the GDR's extensive daycare system after unification, or, more recently, the preferential employment of men over
women in the traditionally female-dominated service sector are
decisions made or reinforced by the state. The willingness of trade
unions to adopt measures that do not necessarily protect the
employment rights of women represents a complementary response
by society. That the state has sustained such gendered norms by
societal actors is reflected in its ambivalent behavior regarding
help-wanted advertisements. The Second Equal Rights Act went
into effect in September 1994 with a provision forbidding employers to write job ads in such a way that it is directed solely toward
men or toward women. Yet a subsequent study confirms that an
overwhelming number of firms continue to do so (41 percent of a
survey of 13,000 job advertisements). For upper management positions, discriminatory advertising was even more common, and had
a stronger adverse trend: only 29.3 percent of such ads used neu-
tral language in 1995, down from 53.4 percent in a similar sample
the year before.[58]

We recognize that, in aggregate terms, the German welfare
system remains among the most progressively organized and coherent in Europe. It retains clear rules of governance that protect
employees, and co-opts large sections of the labor force. But there
lies an alternative reality that contradicts elements of this progressive image. For Germany to be progressive, someone must pay the
bill. And, like much of German history, the living wage of the dominant political and economic actors are now subsidized by those
groups marginal to the central economic and political processes.
The core of Germany's impressive Modell remains gender-biased.
Men, particularly white men, have been the last ones forced to pay
the bill in Germany for the cost of unification and globalization –
at least in the realm of social welfare and employment.

While the German state may be fragmented, it retains a hier-
archical and discriminatory streak; one fostered by political parties
who often appeal to cynical electoral need, but whose consensual
normative proclivities also condone structural discrimination and

58. "Promoting Upward Mobility for Women in the Corporate World: A Matter of Language," *This Week in Germany*, 22 September 1995.

whose institutional structures implement appropriately consistent policies. This approach is a manifestation of a common enough theme in contemporary politics – the revolt of the white male in the face of rising costs and shrinking pies. In Germany, however, this discriminatory edge is submerged under the guise of an apparent social consensus. This consensus, nevertheless, is a view shared only among the politically and economically enfranchised, as the deaf talk to the deaf – and the mute pay the price.

Chapter 10

GRACE? UNDER PRESSURE?

The Goldhagen Controversy after Two Years

*Jeremiah M. Riemer**

O ver two years have gone by since journalists and scholars on
both sides of the Atlantic started wondering out loud how
they should react to the overnight success of Daniel Goldhagen's
Hitler's Willing Executioners. Nearly as much time has elapsed since
Goldhagen went on tour to discuss and debate his book's provoca-
tive thesis in auditoriums from Hamburg to Munich, in front of
eager crowds often impatient with the professorial panelists standing between them and the author whose book these postwar Germans had unexpectedly pushed to the top of Germany's bestseller
list. And it has been more than a year since Jürgen Habermas
lauded Goldhagen at an award ceremony in the outgoing capital of
the "old Federal Republic," where Goldhagen praised the "model"

*   A shorter version of this article by myself and Andrei Markovits originally
appeared under the title "The Goldhagen Controversy" in *Tikkun*, Vol. 13, No. 3
(May/June 1998), pp. 48-49. This essay reflects the state of the debate in the summer of 1998. Thanks to Thane Rosenbaum, Jo Ellen Green Kaiser, Michael Lerner,
Daniel Goldhagen, and Andrei Markovits for comments, criticism, and editing.

character of the Bonn democracy for a political culture he expected to see carried over into the "Berlin Republic" of a united Germany.[1]

These have been the public highlights of the Goldhagen controversy, which began with a podium discussion at the Holocaust Museum in April 1996, reached its climax with the book tour accompanying the German edition that fall, but then seemed to quiet down after Goldhagen received the Democracy Prize last spring. To this day, the centerpiece of both scholarly and journalistic discussion remains the series of essays (mostly critical, occasionally sympathetic, generally moderate in tone) sponsored by *Die Zeit* before and shortly after Goldhagen's book came out in German translation.[2] (*Die Zeit* devoted an extraordinary amount of space to the controversy against the wishes of its elder stateswoman on the editorial board, Countess Marion Dönhoff. She feared that so much attention to Goldhagen might provoke a new outbreak of anti-Semitism.[3] If it anything, though, Goldhagen's book tour seemed to elicit the very opposite reaction.) Since the summer of 1997, an addendum to the controversy took shape as several of Goldhagen's detractors lined up behind two late reviews of his book. Unlike the series in *Die Zeit*, the sole criterion linking these belated responses to Goldhagen was disparagement of his scholarship. With little to distinguish them except their anti-Goldhagen animus, these two pieces ended up packaged between the covers of a single volume misleadingly entitled *A Nation on Trial*.[4] To readers unfamiliar with these controversies, two features must seem puzzling:

1. See Jürgen Habermas, "On the Public Use of History: Why a Democracy Prize for Daniel Goldhagen," trans. Max Pensky, Chapter 29 in Robert Shandley, ed. and Jeremiah M. Riemer, trans. *Unwilling Germans? The Goldhagen Debate* (Minneapolis and London: University of Minnesota Press, 1998), pp. 263-73; and Daniel Jonah Goldhagen, "Modell Bundesrepublik: National History, Democracy, and Internationalization in Germany," Chapter 30 in the same work, pp. 275-85. Both talks were originally reprinted in *Blätter für deutsche und internationale Politik* (April 1997).

2. Most of these may be found in Shandley, *Unwilling Germans?* and Julius H. Schoeps, ed., *Ein Volk von Mördern: Die Dokumentation zur Goldhagen-Kontroverse um die Rolle der Deutschen im Holocaust* (Hamburg: Hoffmann und Campe, 1996).

3. See Marion Gräfin Dönhoff, "Why Daniel Jonah Goldhagen's Book is Misleading" Chapter 23 in Shandley, *Unwilling Germans?* (Chapter Twenty-Three), pp. 203-206, esp. p. 206.

4. Norman Finkelstein and Ruth Bettina Birn, *A Nation on Trial: The Goldhagen Thesis and Historical Truth*. (New York: Owl Books, 1998). Birn's original article

First, apart from the predictable reactions by conservative German papers, the Goldhagen controversy has mostly been a fight among the "good guys" of German historical studies. Goldhagen's typical detractor has not been a Holocaust denier or someone incapable of acknowledging Germany's anti-Semitic tradition, though such deniers have eagerly picked up on the relentless and often vicious attacks on Goldhagen by the "good guys." Some of his most vociferous opponents in Germany were leading left-liberal protagonists on the winning side of (West) Germany's last major controversy about the Holocaust, the "historian's dispute" (Historikerstreit) of

---

"Revising the Holocaust," *The Historical Journal*, vol. 40. no. 1, (1997), seemed to make many historians believe that a colleague with knowledge of the relevant archives (mostly at the Zentrale Stelle der Landesjustizverwaltungen zur Aufklärung nationalsozialistischer Verbrechen in Ludwigsburg) had finally proved Goldhagen wrong. Little attention was paid to Goldhagen's rebuttal, "The Fictions of Ruth Bettina Birn," *German Politics and Society*, vol. 15, no. 3, (1997). But after reviewing both articles, I came to the following conclusion in an exchange with other scholars of German history on the Internet:

Nothing in Birn's essay persuaded me that the documents prove Goldhagen wrong. I found no archival "smoking gun." While the article piqued my curiosity about what those papers in the Ludwigsburg Zentralstelle (ZStL) actually say, and how I might be able to test both Goldhagen's and Birn's interpretations against them, Birn offered nothing more conclusive than footnotes at the bottom of the page and interpretive assertions in the body of the article. By my count, there are just two actual quotes from ZStL documents that allow any reader to see who is being more forthright about this evidence. In one case, where the issue is whether a Police Battalion medical orderly expresses shame about killing Jewish patients in a hospital or merely about "this way of acting" ("diese Handlungsweise"), it appears that Goldhagen has given us the fuller citation [see Birn, "Revising the Holocaust," p. 199 & fn. 6; Goldhagen, "The Fictions of Ruth Bettina Birn," p. 135 and p. 161, fn. 17). In the other case, where the issue is whether one word ("Nuessknacken)" in a song about teaching Jews a lesson refers metaphorically to the cracking of skulls, Goldhagen concedes that he may have misread this one word in the poem, but rejects Birn's claim that his is a "blatantly false rendering of original text" and points out how Birn neglects to mention the contexts (Christmas and one other "social gathering of the killers") in which this poem celebrating the humiliation of Jews was recited (see Birn, "Revising the Holocaust," p. 211, and fn. 41; Goldhagen, "The Fictions of Ruth Bettina Birn," p. 163, fn. 27). In both cases, incidentally, the more complete record of information is to be found not only in Goldhagen's GPS response to Birn, but also in *Hitler's Willing Executioners.*

the Eighties. Why have historians like Hans Mommsen, Hans-Ulrich Wehler, Eric Hobsbawm, Raul Hilberg, and Fritz Stern deemed it important to berate Goldhagen's scholarship? One of the sources of this animosity probably derives from the fact that the "good guys" wrote nothing about the actual perpetrators in their analysis of the Holocaust. (Among Goldhagen's detractors, only Christopher Browning wrote extensively about the killers "in the field." Hilberg and Mommsen confined their interest largely to the so-called *Schreibtischtäter* – perpetrators working from their office desks.) They did not deny it, like neo-Nazis; they did not relativize it, like the right; but they were masters of "structuralizing" the Shoah, talking about the social, economic and/or social psychological conditions that would produce a Shoah rather than focussing on the actual motives of the participants.

Equally confounding is another puzzle: what is so radical about a scholar claiming to show that anti-Semitism was the driving force behind the Holocaust? Did Goldhagen really need to emphasize the originality of what many observers (and certainly most victims of the Holocaust) would regard as obvious? And, even if his critics believe it is an overstatement to call Goldhagen's scholarship pathbreaking, why can't his critics at least recognize his thesis – that a widely shared "eliminationist antisemitism" in pre-War Germany motivated the "ordinary" perpetrators of the Shoah – as a foundation for further insight and research?

Many ridiculous things have been said in public about *Hitler's Willing Executioners*, both as a work of scholarship and public phenomenon. At a symposium sponsored by The Johns Hopkins University in Washington last year, emeritus NYU Professor Herbert Strauss stated that he regarded this "folkloristic Jewish book" as an example of the kind of "critical race theory" one finds at Harvard nowadays.[5] Imputing a kind of reverse racism to Goldhagen is also something two of his most prominent critics, Omer Bartov and Christopher Browning, have done. The charge has frequently been made that this is a book calculated to appeal to Jewish, and espe-

5. *Rethinking Responses to the Holocaust: German and American Commentaries on Daniel Goldhagen's "Hitler's Willing Executioners"* (Washington, D.C.: American Institute for Contemporary German Studies at the Johns Hopkins University, AICGS Seminar Papers No. 20, May 1997), p. 30.

cially American Jewish, audiences. In its highly inaccurate reporting on a dispute between Goldhagen and the Holocaust researcher Ruth Bettina Birn (who later joined the anti-Zionist polemicist Norman Finkelstein as coauthor of *A Nation on Trial*), Germany's conservative newspaper of record, the *Frankfurter Allgemeine Zeitung (FAZ)*, misconstrued the views of an Israeli historian (Gulie Neeman Arad) who (in the inaccurate *FAZ* version) "analyzed the Goldhagen controversy in the cultural context of the United States and saw therein the expression of a deep-seated insecurity among American Orthodox Jews."[6] (Anyone halfway familiar with the sociology of American Jews would know that the Orthodox are, if anything, extremely confident about the rightness and future prospects of their strictly observant life.) In fact, the real view put forward by Arad and some other critics – slightly less ill-informed, though no more plausible – is essentially that Goldhagen appeals to a secular American Jewish craving for a surrogate religion. And in an interview with the weekly magazine *Der Spiegel*, Birn stated that Goldhagen's book "marks the Holocaust, to put it balefully, as a devotional icon for the rich posthumous donor in America, for all those who are meant to feel disconcerted but not experience self-doubt."[7]

From the "critical" discussion surrounding Goldhagen's book, one might gain the impression that its chief appeal is to a community of faith (or to a secular ethnic group experiencing a crisis of faith and religious identity). But *Hitler's Willing Executioners* is a work of scholarship, not of theology. Goldhagen does not share the view of his admirer Elie Wiesel that the Shoah is a phenomenon *beyond* belief. But the book is very much *about* what the ordinary perpetrators of the Holocaust believed. According to Goldhagen, they believed that it was "just" to kill Jews, because most Germans at that time could be persuaded that Jews were innately harmful to the German nation. That these ordinary killers had views (indeed, a world view) about the murders they were asked to commit is, for Goldhagen, both a working assumption and a datum supported by the available nonexculpatory evidence. If the Holocaust repre-

---

6. *Frankfurter Allgemeine Zeitung*, 4 November 1997, p. 41.
7. Interview with *Der Spiegel*, 10 November 1997, p. 267.

sented radical evil, it was neither "banal" nor ineffable, but explicable in human terms.

Goldhagen and his chief interpretive rival, Christopher Browning, agree that no German was ever seriously punished for refusing to participate in the genocide. Where Browning and Goldhagen part company is over how to interpret the essentially voluntary character of the killings. Browning insists on locating the men's motives within a social psychology that is simultaneously situational and universal. The environment of the Nazi dictatorship and killing fields turned these men into killers, but the factors pushing them to genocide (peer pressure, authoritarian upbringing, fatigue, alcoholism, stress) belong to the emotional repertoire of many cultures. Browning concludes his book with the rhetorical question: "If the men of Reserve Police Battalion 101 could become killers under such circumstances, what group of men cannot?"[8]

Against Browning and most other students of the Holocaust, Goldhagen argues persuasively that the perpetrators did not have to overcome "our" kind of moral scruples in order to kill; they had to act upon *their* beliefs that this was the right thing to do. The Nazi regime's role was to mobilize this preexisting sentiment, not to force the members of its national community to overcome some more charitable moral code. Goldhagen also insists that conformity and authoritarianism will not do as explanations. The history of Weimar Germany provides too many examples of Germans who were willing to resist what they regarded as unjust authority. Even the Nazi dictatorship was vulnerable to public pressure and protest (it curtailed its euthanasia program, and it preferred to arrive at a modus vivendi with the two Christian churches rather than paganize German society immediately), of which there was precious little when it came to measures against the Jews. Since Goldhagen argues that a virtually unchallenged image of Jews as "metaphysical" enemies of Germany could be readily mobilized against unarmed men, women, and children, group psychology has no place in his explanation. If there was conformity, then only in the sense of going along with what a *majority* already believed.

8. Christopher Browning, *Ordinary Men: Reserve Police Battalion 101 and the Final Solution in Poland* (New York: Harper Collins, 1992), p. 189.

At another level, though, the thesis of *Hitler's Willing Executioners* is about conformity. Goldhagen often writes as though the Germans who voluntarily killed Jews had little choice about the *views* they entertained regarding their victims. However, it is important to be aware of the difference between Goldhagen's view of what compelled the perpetrators and the Browning version. For Browning, conformity sets in at the very brink of the killing trenches. It is conformity at the point of murder, in the forests, fields, and camps of Poland and Ukraine. To Goldhagen, the onset of conformity is prior to the killing, because it occurs at the level of political socialization. More than anything else, *Hitler's Willing Executioners* is a book about political culture, about what members of communities are educated to believe.

This interpretive difference over the meaning of conformity brings out an underlying problem that was hidden by the victory of the "good guys" in the Historikerstreit of the 1980s. Beginning with the Bitburg controversy (and spilling over into the Historikerstreit), Habermas and his supporters were keen on resisting a conservative backlash symbolized by Chancellor Kohl's remark that his generation of Germans was blessed by "the grace of late birth." In objecting to this statement, the "good guys" of the Historikerstreit were refuting the notion that postwar Germans no longer had any past to confront – or that, if Germany did have a shameful past, it could be "relativized" by comparing it with those "Asian" totalitarian states where it was said, incorrectly, that genocide "originated" and that had outlasted Nazism to become a democratic Germany's postwar rivals. It was important for the liberal historians to beat back this apologist conservative offensive. But in defeating "the grace of a late birth" and the abuse of comparison for the sake of letting German history off the hook, the liberal historians may have overlooked an opposing and equally disturbing view implicit in their own comparative perspective on the Holocaust. This view, congruent with Browning's interpretation, might be labeled: "There but for the grace of God go I the genocidal killer."

One of the strengths of the Goldhagen interpretation is that it more honestly confronts the conservative accusation that a liberal democracy cannot function if it is overburdened by incessant confrontation with its past. Nobody except a right-wing apologist or lackadaisical libertarian would want to argue that liberal democracies like the United States and the Federal Republic of Germany should be complacent about hate groups or even ordinary racism. To the extent that past crimes against humanity (whether American slavery or Nazi genocide) overshadow current efforts to break free from racist legacies, it remains important to refute the pedagogically reactionary argument that educating a nation's citizens about its past cripples their ability to stand tall in the future. But how much do the grandchildren of the Nazi generation (or the great-great-grandchildren of slaveholders) really need to indulge in *self*-examination when they are ready to acknowledge what their ancestors did? The answer depends entirely on what is meant by "the grace of late birth." For Chancellor Kohl, the fortune of being born too late for Hitler means divine historical release from a state that had *coerced* its citizens into violating respect for all life. But there is another interpretation: why shouldn't Germans today feel grateful that they have been brought up in a political and social system that quite self-consciously and comprehensively *educated* them (for the first time in German history) to democratic values? It is this second sense of "grace" to which Goldhagen subscribes.

Oddly, Goldhagen has received a lot of criticism in Germany (mostly from the left) for shifting the focus of political psychology in modern Germany from coercion to education, from the intractable "authoritarian personality" to the willing exemplar of the regnant political culture. Many German leftists have mocked (his always carefully worded) contention that postwar (Western) Germany became a different country because of "reeducation" and "generational replacement." Parodying this truth has typically taken the form of two false accusations against Goldhagen: 1) for buying into the myth of 1945 as Germany's "zero hour" (*"Stunde null"*), when Germany supposedly shed its entire political heritage overnight for Western values, and 2) for overstating the influence of the Western occupying powers on political reeducation in the Federal Republic. Goldhagen has never subscribed to either one of these legends. But – most notably in his acceptance speech for the Democracy Prize – he *has* paid tribute to postwar Germany's effort at democratic *self*-reeducation. Whatever one may think of Goldhagen's characterization of the Federal Republic as a model of democratic transition worth emulating, there can be little doubt that no country has done more to transform itself via political education. Every major institution in German society – its federal and state governments, political parties, churches, schools, trade unions, and business associations, not to mention a vast network of tax-supported foundations – is in the business of political education. (In how many other countries can employees take paid "educational leaves" to attend a retreat where one of the religious or political foundations teaches a seminar on social ethics or workplace codetermination?) Whatever continuities there may be in the administrative and economic structures of the Germany as a modern industrial state (and here, too, the postwar period witnessed major shifts), Goldhagen is certainly right to emphasize the profound change that took place in political culture and mental outlooks there.

Goldhagen's stress on education as the crucial variable and his appeal to a changed political culture in the Federal Republic jointly constitute a thread linking the argument of *Hitler's Willing Executioners* to the public reception of the book. The congruence between his scholarship and public presentation has been widely misunderstood by Goldhagen's critics. In order to account for why the author of a book deemed hostile to an older generation of Germans was supposedly able to charm their grandchildren into guilt-tripping themselves during Goldhagen's remarkable book tour, Fritz Stern resorted to a Jekyll-and-Hyde caricature of Goldhagen in the pages of *Foreign Affairs*.[9] But Goldhagen – portrayed as a Grand Inquisitor one day and as a Pied Piper the next (*Die Welt* headlined one of its feature stories "The Avenger Has Charm") – has followed a single strategy of persuasion since the publication of *Hitler's Willing Execu-*

---

9. See Fritz Stern, "The Goldhagen Controversy – One Nation, One People, One Theory?" in *Foreign Affairs*, vol. 75 (November/December 1996), pp. 128-138, esp. pp. 137-138 and fn. 4, where Stern reports hearing second-hand about how Goldhagen's "charm, telegenic presence, and conciliatory manner enthralled his audiences and bested his critics" and concludes: "German commentators remain puzzled, as I am, by the discrepancy between the public acclaim and the scholarly criticism, coming especially from the liberal side, and by the discrepancy between the writer's arrogance and the speaker's appealing modesty." Goldhagen answered Stern in "Germans versus the Critics" in *Foreign Affairs*, vol. 76 (January/February 1997), pp. 163-166.

tioners. The therapeutic effect his tour appeared to have had on many Germans is consistent with the book's view that political socialization is the key to a culture's changing ethical receptivity.

What of the charge that Goldhagen is using or abusing the memory and reality of the Holocaust for a political agenda? If anything, this accusation is better redirected at many of the critics who hurl it. Norman Finkelstein, the coauthor of *A Nation on Trial*, sees Goldhagen's insistence on the very specific German context of the Shoah as the latest example of liberal American Jewry's abandonment of universalist commitments, which started during the Six Day War when progressive intellectuals like Michael Walzer became preoccupied with Israel's survival. According to Finkelstein, this Jewish renunciation of universalism requires a Manichaean "us-versus-them" outlook on the world, for which Judeocentric interpretations of the Holocaust serve as a perfect instrument.[10] If this is what Goldhagen is up to, it is hard to understand a number of things about the way he has used his new-found prominence in the public arena. Why has his only intervention in the Berlin Holocaust memorial debate been in favor of commemorating the persecution of homosexuals and Roma and Sinti gypsies alongside Jews?[11] Why does he report that he earns the biggest applause from American Jewish audiences whenever he tells them how profoundly postwar Germany has changed and that the only people who should be deemed guilty are those who were alive at the time and who themselves committed crimes?

Indeed, one of the reasons why many opinion-leaders on both the left and right in Germany are so dissatisfied with Goldhagen is that he has scrupulously refused to buy into the various ways that both ends of the ideological spectrum there have instrumentalized the Holocaust. The German left has used the Holocaust in order to draw a line from capitalism to fascism, occasionally even to make it sound as though you'll find a Nazi if you scratch a Christian Democrat. The German right used the Holocaust to beat up on the left in various ways – for not mentioning Communism when-

10. See Finkelstein's essay in *A Nation on Trial*, pp. 92-93, esp. fn. 84.
11. See Daniel Jonah Goldhagen, "There Is No Hierarchy Among Victims," *The New York Times*, 18 January 1997.

ever fascism is invoked, or sometimes just for mentioning the Holocaust at all. Goldhagen will have none of these squabbles and simply gives credit where it is due: he gives credit to the Social Democrats for being that rare political party which never put a hiring freeze on Jewish politicians, but he gives no credit to any social or political force in Imperial or Weimar Germany for fostering a positive image of Jews to counter the dominant anti-Semitic one. He acknowledges the "generation of 68" for ending complacency about the German past, but he parts company with New Left scholars who attempt to explain anti-Semitism as an epiphenomenon of capitalism. While agreeing with conservatives about the primacy of political culture, ideas, and beliefs, Goldhagen does not subscribe to the conservative notion that Hitler was an accident of German history. Conservative, liberal, and leftist historiography all have their ideologically charged versions of what the Nazi regime's *"Zivilisationsbruch"* ("rupture in civilization") has meant for their respective political agendas; Goldhagen's independent-minded interpretation radically departs from all of these in one respect or another.

In responding to his latest critics, Goldhagen has occasionally characterized their attacks on him as part of a new *Vermeidungsdiskurs*.[12] This is true, but it is important to see exactly what is new about this latter-day "discourse of avoidance." For we are not dealing with Holocaust "deniers" or "relativizers" here – or even with people who would deny that anti-Semitism was a necessary condition for the Shoah. Their avoidance, rather, has been a refusal to get past a stridency they detect in *Hitler's Willing Executioners* and pay close attention to what Goldhagen is actually saying. It is, above all, a refusal to concede that Goldhagen argues carefully and contextually (even when, like most scholars, he makes mistakes) and to characterize his argument accurately and fairly.

Close attention to Goldhagen's argument would force his critics to do two things the book prompts them to do but which they have mostly resisted so far: rethink Holocaust research methodology and the meaning of the Shoah's "singularity." Among his German reviewers, only two historians – Ingrid Gilcher-Holtey and Wolf-

---

12. Daniel J. Goldhagen, "Ein neuer Vermeidungsdiskurs. Antwort auf die im Spiegel veröffentlichen Anwürfe," *Frankfurter Rundschau*, 18 August 1997, p. 7.

gang Wippermann – have taken Goldhagen's "methodological challenge" seriously.[13] Gilcher-Holtey has drawn attention to the originality of Goldhagen's focus on the mental outlook (or world view) of the perpetrators while also pointing out what "Goldhagen's study does not show" – namely, "how it became possible to transfer the ideology of antisemitism into a mentality-shaping behavior."[14] (To bridge the gap between ideology and active mental outlook, she says, "would have required a longitudinal analysis of the mentality-shaping effect of antisemitism during the 19th and 20th centuries. Such a study remains to be desired; it would simultaneously clarify the causes underlying the weakness of that countermodel of German history … that lost out under National Socialism – the countermodel of a civil society based on human rights."[15] Wippermann, who "believe[s] that Goldhagen's book should be praised, in spite of all the technical defects," has pointed out the perils of drawing inferences about entire populations based on a "methodological procedure … Goldhagen has taken over from public opinion and electoral survey research."[16] Yet in order to highlight (as Wippermann does) the pros and cons of the way Goldhagen draws broad conclusions from highly contextual settings, one first has to concede that Goldhagen undertakes (and links) both levels of analysis, the detailed case study and the unavoidable abstraction.

Among Goldhagen's detractors, Ruth Bettina Birn has excelled all others in denying that Goldhagen does what all good scholars do – shuttle back and forth between the general and the concrete. She accomplishes this feat by twisting carefully worded statements he has made about specific situations into wildly distorted collective generalizations he has never asserted.[17] A good critic might

13. Ingrid Gilcher-Holtey, "The Mentality of the Perpetrators," Chapter 12 in Shandley, *Unwilling Germans?* pp. 105-107.

14. Ibid, p. 107.

15. Idem.

16. Wolfgang Wippermann, "The Jewish Hanging Judge? Goldhagen and the 'Self-Confident Nation'," Chapter 27 in Shandley, *Unwilling Germans?* pp. 229-253. Wippermann raises the issue of how appropriate survey research techniques are on p. 230.

17. Goldhagen's rebuttal "The Fictions of Ruth Bettina Birn" does a good job of demonstrating how she systematically takes specific, contextual statements scattered throughout *Hitler's Willing Executioners* and then misrepresents these as gross

well argue that Goldhagen has raised the methodological stakes too high by requiring a kind of inferential quantum leap between the contextual and the general.[18] But in order to join a real debate (methodological or other) between Goldhagen and his critics (something that, so far, has not really happened), the latter would have to acknowledge that the former argues carefully (something they apparently cannot bring themselves to do). It is a shame for everyone concerned that Goldhagen's detractors have missed constructive opportunities to clarify, fill out, and correct his picture of German society and European anti-Semitism simply by refusing to pay attention to a legitimate type of scholarly scrutiny that happens to yield unorthodox conclusions.[19]

---

generalizations neither ventured by Goldhagen nor consistent with his explicit explanatory framework.

18. I would not argue this myself, but in an early comment on the book I did wonder why Goldhagen's critics were not subjecting *both* Goldhagen's "highly leveraged explanation" and Browning's extremely problematic method to equal scrutiny. See Jeremiah M. Riemer, "Burdens of Proof," Chapter 20 in Shandley, *Unwilling Germans?* pp. 175-182 (a shorter version of which appeared in *die tageszeitung* on 29 August 1996). Although historians sometimes characterize Goldhagen's book (almost begrudgingly) as an interesting case study embedded in a cumbersome work of social science with an untenable thesis, I have yet to hear an historian warmly endorse the highly speculative conclusion to Browning's *Ordinary Men* as glowingly as *his* case studies are praised. Nor have I seen anyone really debate the serious differences between Goldhagen's and Browning's readings of the evidence without introducing extraneous new issues like what to make of a battalion of killers from Luxemburg.

19. Some aspects of Goldhagen's sketchy history of German anti-Semitism – such as his reading of its place in party politics – do need to be corrected. Describing the Reichstag election results of 1893 as a victory for an anti-Semitic majority only makes sense if parties that tolerated or promoted anti-Semitic candidates in local chapters, such as the National Liberals and Catholic Center, are treated the same way as the Conservative party, which had adopted an anti-Semitic program nationwide. See Goldhagen, *Hitler's Willing Executioners* (New York: Knopf, 1996), pp. 75-76. However, Goldhagen's general point – that no major political or social institution in Imperial or Weimar Germany countered the dominant anti-Semitic view with a strong positive image of Jews as fellow citizens with rights to be defended unconditionally – stands. (Seeing anti-Semitism as a needless distraction from class struggle, which was the fundamental position of the prewar German Left, does not meet this test.) This point also seems to have been forgotten by the many historians who think they have discredited Goldhagen by pointing to the high levels of anti-Semitism in Second Republic France. What France from Dreyfus to Vichy would seem to show,

Closer attention to what Goldhagen actually says would also reveal that he challenges the prevailing (and one-dimensional) understanding of the Holocaust's "singularity" in original and important ways. Here, too, Goldhagen probes more deeply into the unexamined consensus of the Historikerstreit's "good guys" with greater savvy as a comparativist than his critics have been willing or able to see. For there are more and different dimensions to the comparative study of genocide than conventionally assumed. Sometimes comparison is warranted, while at other times it is beside the point. The complexity of the Holocaust does not necessarily dictate the kind of investigation into comparative anti-Semitism that Goldhagen's critics have assumed it must.[20] The unexamined habits of historians have laid down well-worn research grooves concealing these important points of contention. So did the ease with which the "good guys" won the Historikerstreit. By defeating the "relativizer" Ernst Nolte's ridiculous attempt to play up the bogus question of where modern genocide "originated" geopolitically in the "epoch" of modern totalitarianism, historians like Jürgen Kocka won too effortless a victory. The liberal historians believed they had disposed of the "singularity" issue once and for all by placing Germany squarely within a comparative framework that included other Western industrial countries but excluded those agrarian or industrializing civilizations where other genocides have taken place. To be sure, this methodological focus on a different set of nations with which Germany might compare itself provided insurance against certain types of "relativization" – versus the crude anti-Communist and "Germany as victim" varieties, as well as against Nolte's more sophisticated sort of Cold War neo-Heideggerianism. But the same insistence on comparing Germany with France or the U.K. for all purposes also made relevant variations other than whole country comparisons along lines of socioeconomic development nearly impossible.

This *particular version* of the Sonderweg approach, reinvigorated by knocking over straw man Nolte, has virtually ruled out

---

instead, is that one half of the French political community (clerical and reactionary) was anti-Semitic while the other half (secular and republican) rallied to a defense of human rights that included Jews.

20. See Goldhagen, *Hitler's Willing Executioners*, Chapter 16, and especially p. 419.

the possibility of raising a question Goldhagen posed in a *New York Times* op-ed article a few weeks before the publication of *Hitler's Willing Executioners*:

> Few people believe that the Serbs who butchered and brutalized Muslims in Bosnia were forced to do so. Few believe that the Hutus who slaughtered in Rwanda, the Turks who killed Armenians and the Khmer Rouge who decimated the Cambodian people thought that they were doing wrong.
>
> Only when discussing the Holocaust do people routinely say that the killers were unwilling. This is odd, since so much evidence demonstrates that the German killers were like those who committed other mass slaughters.[21]

In effect, Goldhagen is pointing out that the Nazi Holocaust was "singular" in some respects but comparable to other genocides along other dimensions. Its singularity as a mass genocide (highlighted by the way one murderous regime treated different vanquished and victimized groups) rested on a compulsion to eliminate a "metaphysical" enemy with whom the killers had no objective conflict over economics, territory, or state-building. But on another dimension – that of *motivation* – there is no reason to assume that anything about early twentieth century German society (its level of industrial development, culture, or "modernity") ought to rule out asking the same questions one asks about people in other countries where genocide was perpetrated. By making "singularity" an empirical question about the range of variation in murderous behavior, rather than an a priori developmental question about the "country club" to which historians think pre-War Germany properly belonged, Goldhagen has thrown the much-discussed problem of Germany's "*Zivilisationsbruch*" in an entirely new light.

An earlier, perhaps more optimistic version of this essay concluded that "anybody working on the Holocaust from now on simply *has* to deal with Goldhagen's thesis and work." For "no matter how his work is criticized, even vilified – it cannot be ignored." Would that this were so.

21. Daniel J. Goldhagen, "The People's Holocaust" in *The New York Times*, 17 March 1996. Two years later, Goldhagen forcefully restated this position in "The Paradigm Challenged," *Tikkun*, May/June 1998.

LIST OF CONTRIBUTORS

Christopher S. Allen is an Associate Professor in the Department of Political Science at the University of Georgia.

Patricia Davis is an Assistant Professor in the Department of Government at the University of Notre Dame.

Karen Donfried is a Specialist in European Affairs in the Foreign Affairs, Defense, and Trade Division of the Congressional Research Service.

Thomas Ertman is an Associate Professor in the Department of Government at Harvard University.

Philip S. Gorski is an Assistant Professor in the Department of Sociology at the University of Wisconsin-Madison.

Carolyn Höfig received her doctorate from the Department of History of the University of California, Santa Cruz.

Michael G. Huelshoff is an Associate Professor in the Department of Political Science at the University of New Orleans.

Carl Lankowski is the Research Director at the American Institute for Contemporary German Studies in Washington, D.C.

Beth Simone Noveck is Director of International Programs of the Yale Law School Information Society Project and practices information technologies and media law at Duane, Morris and Heckscher LLP.

Simon Reich is a Professor in the Graduate School of Public and International Affairs and the Department of Political Science, University of Pittsburgh.

Jeremiah M. Riemer is currently a freelance translator in Washington, and has taught at the School of Advanced International Studies at Johns Hopkins University, Boston University, and Oberlin College.

Stephen J. Silvia is an Associate Professor at the School of International Service, American University, Washington, D.C.

INDEX